Chemistry 2

Brian Ratcliff

Helen Eccles

Series editor: Brian Ratcliff

CAMBRIDGE
UNIVERSITY PRESS

PUBLISHED BY THE PRESS SYNDICATE OF THE UNIVERSITY OF CAMBRIDGE
The Pitt Building, Trumpington Street, Cambridge, United Kingdom

CAMBRIDGE UNIVERSITY PRESS
The Edinburgh Building, Cambridge CB2 2RU, UK
40 West 20th Street, New York, NY 10011-4211, USA
10 Stamford Road, Oakleigh, VIC 3166, Australia
Ruiz de Alarcón 13, 28014 Madrid, Spain
Dock House, The Waterfront, Cape Town 8001, South Africa

http://www.cambridge.org

First published 2001

Printed in the United Kingdom at the University Press, Cambridge

Typeface   Swift   *System*   QuarkXPress®

A catalogue record for this book is available from the British Library

ISBN 0 521 79882 5 paperback

Produced by Gecko Ltd, Bicester, Oxon

Front cover photograph: Soapsuds testing, Images Colour Library

Contents

Introduction

Cambridge Advanced Sciences

The *Cambridge Advanced Sciences* series has been developed to meet the demands of all the new AS and A level science examinations. In particular, it has been endorsed by OCR as providing complete coverage of their specifications. The AS material is presented as a single text for each of biology, chemistry and physics. Material for the A2 year comprises six books in each subject: one of core material and one for each option. Some material has been drawn from the existing *Cambridge Modular Sciences* books; however, many parts are entirely new.

During the development of this series, the opportunity has been taken to improve the design, and a complete and thorough new writing and editing process has been applied. Much more material is now presented in colour. Although the existing *Cambridge Modular Sciences* texts do cover most of the new specifications, the *Cambridge Advanced Sciences* books cover every OCR learning objective in detail. They are the key to success in the new AS and A level examinations.

OCR is one of the three unitary awarding bodies offering the full range of academic and vocational qualifications in the UK. For full details of the new specifications, please contact OCR:

OCR, 1 Hills Rd, Cambridge CB1 2EU
Tel: 01223 553311

The presentation of units

You will find that the books in this series use a bracketed convention in the presentation of units within tables and on graph axes. For example, ionisation energies of $1000 \, kJ \, mol^{-1}$ and $2000 \, kJ \, mol^{-1}$ will be represented in this way:

Measurement	Ionisation energy (kJ mol^{-1})
1	1000
2	2000

OCR examination papers use the solidus as a convention, thus:

Measurement	Ionisation energy / kJ mol^{-1}
1	1000
2	2000

Any numbers appearing in brackets with the units, for example $(10^{-5} \, mol \, dm^{-3} \, s^{-1})$, should be treated in exactly the same way as when preceded by the solidus, $/10^{-5} \, mol \, dm^{-3} \, s^{-1}$.

Chemistry 2 – the A2 chemistry text

Chemistry 2 is all that is needed to cover the whole of the A2 chemistry material. It is divided into three parts which correspond to the modules Chains, Rings and Spectroscopy, Trends and Patterns, and Unifying Concepts. It is designed to be accessible to students with a double-award science GCSE background. This book combines entirely new text and illustrations with revised and updated material from *Foundation Chemistry*, *Chains and Rings*, *Trends and Patterns*, and *How far? How fast?*, formerly available in the *Cambridge Modular Sciences* series.

Part 1, Chains, Rings and Spectroscopy, begins with a review of the organic chemistry met in *Chemistry 1* and goes on to explore new families of organic compounds. There are then chapters on stereoisomerism, polymers, and spectroscopy, with an emphasis on industrial applications. These chapters make use of material from *Chains and Rings*. Chapter 8, 'Spectroscopy' contains a completely new section describing the functioning and applications of modern analytical techniques such as nuclear magnetic resonance spectroscopy.

Part 2, Trends and Patterns, has been almost entirely rewritten. Chapter 9 examines trends in lattice enthalpy, chapter 10 looks at the elements and compounds of Period 3 of the Periodic Table, and chapter 11 introduces the chemistry of the transition elements. These can be studied further in an A2 option module of their own.

In Part 3, Unifying Concepts, material on rates of reaction (chapter 12) and equilibrium constants (chapter 13) is extended and applied, using examples and self assessment questions. The book ends with chapter 14, 'Acids, bases and buffers' which makes use of both new material, and chapter 5 of *How far? How fast?*

Acknowledgements

6, Courtesy of Aventis Pasteur; 7, Courtesy of Chiroscience; 12*t*, *cb*, 15, 17, 18*l*, 25, 30, 31, 32, 39, 40, 41, 56, 86*bl*, *br*, 91, 92*t*, *ct*, *cb*, 98, 130, 140, Andrew Lambert; 12*ct*, Dan Sams/A–Z Botanical Collection Ltd; 12*b*, Tick Ahearn; 13, Images Colour Library; 16, B Kuiter/Foto Natura Stock/Frank Lane Picture Agency; 18*r*, 22*t*, 26, 28, 29, 48, 51, Michael Brooke; 22*bl*, Alan Gould/A–Z Botanical Collection Ltd; 22*br*, 34, 83, Garden Matters/Wildlife Matters; 33, Courtesy of Lever Brothers Ltd; 37*t*, Rafi Ben-Shahar/ www.osf.uk.com; 37*b*, A. Barrington Brown/ Science Photo Library; 38, Roger G. Howard Photography; 57*t*, Dave Joiner/Popperfoto; 85*br*, Collections/Shout Picture Library; 59, 60*br*, Courtesy of ICI; 60*t*, Britstock-IFA/Amadeus; 60*bl*, James Holmes/Zedcor/Science Photo Library; 62*l*, Courtesy of James Evans; 62*r*, RCSB Protein Data Bank; 66, Cape Grim B.A.P.S./Simon Fraser/Science Photo Library; 68, Courtesy of Bruker-Franzen Analytik GmbH; 69, Gray Mortimore/Allsport; 82, 92*b*, Robert Harding Picture Library; 86*t*, Boeing/TRH Pictures; 105*t*, Jack Finch/Science Photo Library; 105*b*, George Porter; 114, Elenac/BASF; 121, Mark Deeble & Victoria Stone/www.osf.uk.com; 122, courtesy of Baxter Hemoglobin Therapeutics, USA; 128, David Frazier/Science Photo Library; 145, La Belle Aurore

Part 1: Chains, Rings and Spectroscopy

CHAPTER 1

Chains and rings revisited

By the end of this chapter you should be able to:

1 interpret and use the following terms: *nomenclature*, *molecular formula*, *general formula*, *structural formula*, *displayed formula*, *skeletal formula*, *homologous series*, *functional group*;

2 describe and explain *structural isomerism* in compounds with the same molecular formula but different structural formulae;

3 describe and explain *cis–trans isomerism* in alkenes, in terms of restricted rotation about a double bond;

4 determine the possible structural and/or *cis–trans* isomers of an organic molecule of given molecular formula;

5 describe and explain *optical isomerism* arising from molecules with a *chiral centre*;

6 recall, from *Chemistry 1*, the chemical reactions of *alkanes*, *alkenes*, *alcohols* and *halogenoalkanes*;

7 show knowledge and understanding of the following reaction mechanisms: *free radical substitution*, *electrophilic addition*, *nucleophilic substitution*.

(Nomenclature should follow IUPAC rules for naming of organic compounds. For example, 3-methylpentane for $CH_3CH_2CH(CH_3)CH_2CH_3$.)

The module *Chains, Rings and Spectroscopy* continues the study of organic chemistry that you began in the *Chains and Rings* module in *Chemistry 1* (chapters 7–12). You should have a sound knowledge and understanding of the organic chemistry from *Chemistry 1* before you study the new material introduced in this module. This chapter provides an opportunity for you to review and extend appropriate material from *Chemistry 1*.

Organic chemistry can be studied in a particularly structured and systematic manner because each different group of atoms that becomes attached to carbon has its own characteristic set of reactions. Chemists refer to these different groups of atoms as **functional groups**. In *Chemistry 1*, you studied the reactions of the alkene functional group (>C=C<). The functional groups that you will study here are shown in *table 1.1*.

Table 1.1 provides you with the classes and structures of these functional groups. An example is also provided of a simple molecule containing each functional group. Each functional group gives rise to a **homologous series**. For example, the alcohol functional group gives rise to the homologous series of alcohols. The first four of these are methanol (CH_3OH), ethanol (CH_3CH_2OH), propan-1-ol ($CH_3CH_2CH_2OH$) and butan-1-ol ($CH_3CH_2CH_2CH_2OH$). The members of a homologous series all have similar chemical properties.

Organic compounds are also classified as either aliphatic or aromatic. **Aromatic** compounds contain one or more arene rings; all other organic compounds are **aliphatic**.

Chemists use different types of formulae to represent organic molecules.

■ A **general formula** may be written for each

Class of functional group	Structure of functional group	Names of example(s)	Structural formula(e) of example(s)
alkenes	$\diagdown C = C \diagup$	ethene	$CH_2{=}CH_2$
arenes	(benzene ring)	benzene	(benzene ring)
halogenoalkanes	$-X$, where X = F, Cl, Br, I	chloromethane	CH_3Cl
alcohols and phenols	$-OH$	methanol, phenol	CH_3OH, C_6H_5OH
aldehydes	$-C\overset{O}{\underset{H}{\diagdown}}$	ethanal	CH_3CHO
ketones	$-C - C\overset{O}{\diagdown C-}$	propanone	CH_3COCH_3
carboxylic acids	$-C\overset{O}{\underset{OH}{\diagslash}}$	ethanoic acid	CH_3COOH
esters	$-C\overset{O}{\underset{O-C-}{\diagdown}}$	ethyl ethanoate	$CH_3COOC_2H_5$
amines	$-NH_2$	methylamine	CH_3NH_2
amides	$-C\overset{O}{\underset{NH_2}{\diagslash}}$	ethanamide	CH_3CONH_2
nitriles	$-C{\equiv}N$	ethanenitrile	CH_3CN

● **Table 1.1** Functional groups.

homologous series. For example, the general formula of the aliphatic alcohols is $C_nH_{2n+1}OH$ (where n is the number of carbon atoms present).

■ **Empirical formulae** (simplest formulae) are determined by experiments, but they give no indication of structure.

■ The **molecular formula** of a compound is useful when, for example, you need to calculate its molecular mass.

■ **Structural formulae** are particularly useful when writing equations involving aliphatic compounds.

■ **Skeletal formulae** are the clearest and easiest way to represent cyclic compounds in equations.

■ **Displayed formulae** (sometimes called full structural formulae) are useful in checking that you have included the correct number of atoms and bonds. You will often be called upon to provide displayed formulae in your examination answers. However, remember that they do give a completely false impression of the shapes of the molecules concerned.

■ Shapes are best represented using **three-dimensional formulae**.

SAQ 1.1

a Draw the following types of formulae of 2-methylbutan-2-ol.
(i) displayed (ii) structural (iii) skeletal.

b Represent 2-bromobutane using
(i) three-dimensional (ii) molecular formulae.

Various computer-produced images of molecular models will be used where appropriate throughout this book.

The colours used in these are shown in *table 1.2*. Another type that will be used is a space-filling

Colour	Element
white	hydrogen
dark grey	carbon
red	oxygen
blue	nitrogen
yellow-green	fluorine
green	chlorine
orange-brown	bromine
brown	iodine
violet	phosphorus
pale yellow	sulphur

● **Table 1.2** The colours used for elements in molecular models.

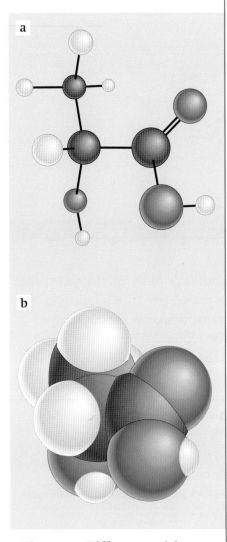

● **Figure 1.1** Different model types for lactic acid (2-hydroxypropanoic acid):
a ball-and-stick model;
b space-filling model.

model. In space-filling models, atoms are shown including the space occupied by their electron orbitals. As their orbitals overlap significantly, a very different image to the ball-and-stick image results. *Figure 1.1* shows these two types of model for lactic acid.

Naming organic compounds

The names used in this section are known as **systematic** names. Such names precisely describe the structure of a molecule and enable chemists to communicate clearly. International rules of **nomenclature** have been agreed for the systematic naming of organic compounds.

The basic rules for naming hydrocarbons are as follows.

1   The number of carbon atoms in the longest chain provides the stem of the name. Simple alkanes consist entirely of unbranched chains of carbon atoms. They are named by adding -ane to this stem, as shown in *table 1.3*.

2   Branched-chain alkanes are named in the same way. The name given to the longest continuous carbon chain is then prefixed by the names of the shorter side-chains. The same stems are used with the suffix -yl. Hence CH_3- is methyl (often called a methyl group). In general, such groups are called alkyl groups. The position of an alkyl group is indicated by a number. The carbon atoms in the longest carbon chain are numbered from one end of the chain. Numbering starts from the end which produces the lowest possible numbers for the side chains. For example, this molecule is 2-methylpentane, not 4-methylpentane.

$$CH_3 - CH - CH_2 - CH_2 - CH_3$$
$$|$$
$$CH_3$$

Molecular formula	Number of carbon atoms in longest chain	Stem	Name
CH_4	1	meth-	methane
C_2H_6	2	eth-	ethane
C_3H_8	3	prop-	propane
C_4H_{10}	4	but-	butane
C_5H_{12}	5	pent-	pentane
C_6H_{14}	6	hex-	hexane
C_7H_{16}	7	hept-	heptane
C_8H_{18}	8	oct-	octane
C_9H_{20}	9	non-	nonane
$C_{10}H_{22}$	10	dec-	decane
$C_{20}H_{42}$	20	eicos-	eicosane

● **Table 1.3** Naming simple alkanes.

3 Each side-chain must be included in the name. If there are several identical side-chains, the name is prefixed by di-, tri- etc. For example, 2,2,3-trimethyl- indicates that there are three methyl groups, two on the second and one on the third carbon atom of the longest chain. Note that numbers are separated by commas whilst a number and a letter are separated by a hyphen.

4 Where different alkyl groups are present, they are placed in alphabetical order, as in 3-ethyl-2-methylpentane.

5 Compounds containing a ring of carbon atoms are prefixed by cyclo-. Cyclohexane is represented by:

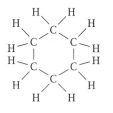

displayed formula   skeletal formula

6 Hydrocarbons containing one double bond are called **alkenes**. The same stems are used, but they are followed by -ene. The position of an alkene double bond is indicated by the lower number of the two carbon atoms involved. This number is placed between the stem and -ene. Hence $CH_3CH=CHCH_3$ is but-2-ene.

7 The simplest arene is benzene. When one alkyl group is attached to a benzene ring, a number is not needed because all the carbon atoms are equivalent. Two or more groups will require a number. For example:

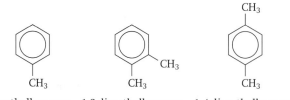

methylbenzene   1,2-dimethylbenzene   1,4-dimethylbenzene

8 Halogeno or nitro compounds are named in the same way as alkyl-substituted alkanes or arenes:

$CH_3CH_2CHBrCH_3$

2-bromobutane   1,3-dinitrobenzene

9 Aliphatic alcohols and ketones are named in a similar way to alkenes:

$CH_3CH_2CH_2OH$ $CH_3CH_2COCH_2CH_3$

propan-1-ol   pentan-3-one

10 Aliphatic aldehyde and carboxylic acid groups are at the end of a carbon chain, so they do not need a number. There is only one possible butanoic acid, $CH_3CH_2CH_2COOH$, or butanal, $CH_3CH_2CH_2CHO$. The names of ketones, aldehydes, carboxylic acids and nitriles include the carbon atom in the functional group in the stem. Hence CH_3COOH is ethanoic acid and CH_3CN is ethanenitrile.

11 Amines are named using the alkyl- or aryl-prefix followed by -amine. Hence $CH_3CH_2NH_2$ is ethylamine.

SAQ 1.2

a Give systematic names to the following compounds:

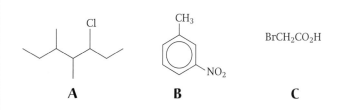

A   B   C

b Draw structural formulae for the following compounds:
D 2-aminoethanoic acid
E 2-hydroxybenzoic acid
F 2,4,6-tribromophenol

Isomerism

Structural isomers have the same molecular formula but different structural formulae. For example, 1-bromopropane and 2-bromopropane are structural isomers. They both have the molecular formula C_3H_7Br. Their skeletal formulae are as follows

1-bromopropane   2-bromopropane

SAQ 1.3

Draw six structural isomers containing a carboxyl group, $-C\overset{O}{\underset{O-}{\diagdown}}$, of compounds with the molecular formula $C_4H_8O_2$.

Cis–trans **isomerism** arises in alkenes because rotation about a double bond cannot occur unless a π bond (pi bond) is broken. As well as the double bond, the molecule must have two identical groups, one on each of the two carbon atoms involved in the double bond.

SAQ 1.4

Draw and label the *cis–trans* isomers of butenedioic acid, HOOCCH=CHCOOH.

Isomers which contain the same atoms with the same order of bonds but with different spatial arrangements of atoms are called **stereoisomers**. *Cis-trans* isomerism is one type of stereoisomerism. Another type is optical isomerism. You will find out more about optical isomerism and stereoisomerism in chapter 6. We shall take a brief look at optical isomerism in the next section.

Optical isomerism

The simplest form of optical isomerism occurs when a carbon atom is joined to four different groups. The groups can be arranged in two different ways and the two isomers so formed are mirror images of each other, which cannot be superimposed. Try making models of the amino acid alanine.

$$H-\overset{\overset{\displaystyle CH_3}{|}}{\underset{\underset{\displaystyle NH_2}{|}}{C}}-CO_2H$$

If you have made two models that are mirror images of each other, you will find that you are unable to superimpose them so that they match. Molecular models of the two optical isomers (**enantiomers**) of alanine are shown in *figure 1.2*.

Molecules that are mirror images, and so cannot be superimposed, are known as

chiral molecules. The name comes from the Greek for hand. Place your hands together with the palms in contact. Hands are mirror images of each other. Place one hand on top of the other with both palms uppermost. Your thumbs are now on opposite sides. Like chiral molecules, hands cannot be superimposed. Optical isomerism is often referred to as **chirality**. The carbon atom which carries four different groups is a **chiral centre**.

Many of the molecules found in living organisms contain chiral centres. Usually only one of the isomers is biochemically active. This is not surprising when you consider the shape selectivity of, for example, enzymes. Medicines that have chiral molecules may need to be administered as a pure isomer. Synthetic organic reactions usually result in a mixture containing equal amounts of both isomers (a racemic mixture). Purification of such mixtures can be done by crystallisation with a chiral acid or base. However, new separation techniques such as chiral high-performance liquid

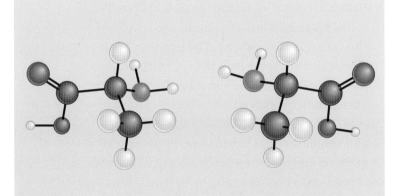

● **Figure 1.2** Ball-and-stick models of alanine enantiomers.

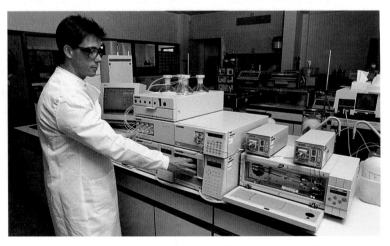

● **Figure 1.3** High-performance liquid chromatography equipment.

chromatography are enabling much better separations (*figure 1.3*). To avoid expensive separation techniques, a few 'leading technology companies' are now using synthetic routes which produce only the required isomer (*figure 1.4*).

SAQ 1.5

a Draw the optical isomers of bromochlorofluoromethane.

b Copy the following formulae and mark the chiral centres with an asterisk:

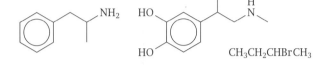

$CH_3CH_2CHBrCH_3$

Summaries of reactions from the *Chains and Rings* module

Alkanes

Apart from combustion and substitution by halogens, alkanes are relatively unreactive, due to strong covalent bonds and lack of polarity.

$$CO_2 + H_2O \xleftarrow[+O_2]{combustion} \underset{ethane}{C_2H_6} \xrightarrow[\substack{UV\ light \\ +\ Cl_2}]{substitution} C_2H_5Cl + HCl$$

In general, hydrocarbons burn. Many are important sources of energy.

Substitution by a halogen on an alkane involves a free-radical mechanism. Three stages are involved, as follows.

■ **Initiation** to form Cl· free radicals. Ultraviolet light provides sufficient energy to break the covalent bonds in chlorine, $Cl_2(g)$. Homolytic fission occurs and two chlorine free radicals are formed.

$Cl–Cl(g) \rightarrow Cl·(g) + Cl·(g)$

■ **Propagation** involving a chain reaction to form C_2H_5Cl.

$Cl·(g) + H–CH_2CH_3(g) \rightarrow Cl–H(g) + ·CH_2CH_3(g)$
$Cl–Cl(g) + ·CH_2CH_3(g) \rightarrow Cl·(g) + Cl–CH_2CH_3(g)$

■ **Termination** involves free-radical combination reactions. These reactions will predominate when concentrations of reactants decline. Examples of possible termination steps include the following.

$Cl·(g) + Cl·(g) \rightarrow Cl–Cl(g)$
$·CH_2CH_3(g) + ·CH_2CH_3(g) \rightarrow CH_3CH_2CH_2CH_3(g)$

SAQ 1.6

a Explain what is meant by homolytic fission.

b With reference to the mechanism for the reaction between ethane and chlorine, explain what is meant by the term **chain reaction**.

c Explain why the chlorine free radicals, Cl·(g), do not catalyse the chain reaction.

● **Figure 1.4** Work experience at Celltech Chiroscience, a company that specialises in making a single optical isomer of a medicine.

Alkenes

The C=C double bond undergoes a variety of addition reactions (*figure 1.5*).

SAQ 1.7

Limonene occurs naturally in oranges and lemons. Look at the structure of limonene.

How many moles of bromine, Br_2, will add to one mole of limonene?

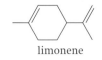

limonene

SAQ 1.8

a Explain what is meant by the term **electrophile**.

b The decolourisation of bromine water is frequently used as a test for an alkene functional group. When ethene is bubbled through bromine water, 2-bromoethanol is formed alongside 1,2-bromoethane. Suggest a reason for the formation of 2-bromoethanol.

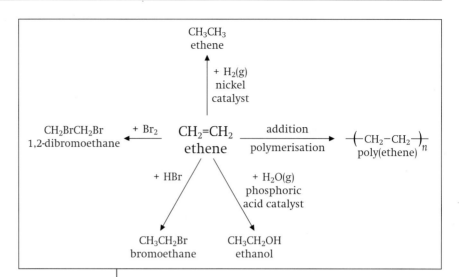

● **Figure 1.5** Summary of the addition reactions of alkenes.

The mechanism for the electrophilic addition of bromine is as follows. Not all addition reactions to alkenes involve electrophiles.

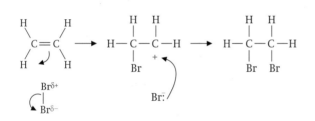

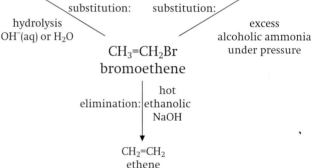

● **Figure 1.7** Summary of reactions of bromoethane.

Halogenoalkanes

Halogenoalkanes undergo both substitution and elimination reactions, as shown in *figure 1.7* for bromoethane.

The hydrolysis of halogenoalkanes involves a nucleophilic substitution and may be represented as in *figure 1.8* for bromomethane, CH_3Br.

Alcohols

Alcohols undergo a wide variety of reaction types, which are illustrated in *figure 1.6* for ethanol.

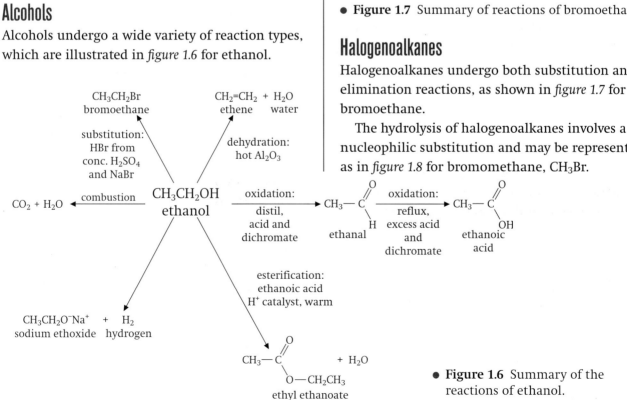

● **Figure 1.6** Summary of the reactions of ethanol.

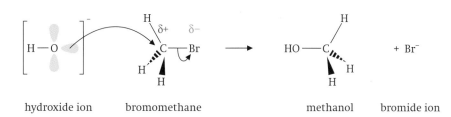

hydroxide ion   bromomethane   methanol   bromide ion

● **Figure 1.8** Nucleophilic substitution of CH_3Br.

SAQ 1.9

a Explain what is meant by the term **nucleophile**.

b Ammonia reacts with bromomethane to form methylamine.
  (i) Draw a three-dimensional formula for methylamine.
  (ii) Suggest, using curly arrows, how bonds are formed and broken when ammonia reacts with bromomethane to form methylamine.

SUMMARY

◆ All organic compounds contain carbon and hydrogen. Most organic compounds also contain other elements, such as oxygen, nitrogen and chlorine.

◆ Functional groups, which have their own characteristic reactions, are attached to the hydrocarbon framework of an organic molecule. Alkenes, arenes, halogen atoms, alcohols, aldehydes and ketones, carboxylic acids, esters, amines, amides and nitriles are examples of functional groups.

◆ Chemists use a wide variety of formulae to represent organic molecules. These include general, empirical, molecular, structural, skeletal, displayed and three-dimensional formulae.

◆ Various types of molecular models (ball-and-stick, space-filling) are used to visualise organic molecules.

◆ Organic molecules are named in a systematic way, related to their structures.

◆ Organic molecules with the same molecular formula but with different structures are called isomers. Three common types of isomerism are structural, cis–trans (or geometrical) and optical. Structural isomers have different structural formulae, cis–trans isomers have different displayed formulae and optical isomers have different three-dimensional formulae. Optical isomers are molecules that are mirror images of each other. They contain one or more chiral centres.

◆ The study of organic reactions is traditionally organised by functional group. Each functional group has its own characteristic reactions.

◆ Alkanes are relatively unreactive due to strong covalent bonds and low polarity. They burn in air to produce carbon dioxide and water. In ultraviolet light, they undergo free-radical substitution reactions with halogens, forming halogenoalkanes.

◆ Alkenes typically undergo addition reactions with hydrogen, bromine, hydrogen bromide and steam. They will undergo addition polymerisation. The reaction of bromine with ethene involves an electrophilic addition mechanism.

◆ Alcohols burn in air producing carbon dioxide and water. They may be dehydrated to alkenes over hot aluminium oxide. Substitution by HBr produces a bromoalkane. Alcohols produce hydrogen gas and sodium alkoxides with sodium metal. Esters are formed on refluxing with a carboxylic acid and a strong acid catalyst. Primary alcohols are oxidised to aldehydes and then to carboxylic acids with acidifed dichromate(VI).

◆ Halogenoalkanes undergo nucleophilic substitution reactions with aqueous alkali to form alcohols. With alcoholic ammonia under pressure they form amines. Elimination of a hydrogen halide occurs on refluxing with ethanolic alkali.

◆ Reaction mechanisms may involve electrophiles, nucleophiles or free radicals. Each of these reagents is capable of forming a new covalent bond to the atom attacked. Electrophiles attack atoms with a high electron density, nucleophiles attack atoms with a low electron density. Free radicals are highly reactive, attacking any atom with which they are capable of forming a bond.

◆ Covalent bonds may be broken homolytically to form two free radicals, each with an unpaired electron. Polar bonds will frequently break heterolytically to form one cation and one anion.

◆ Curly arrows show the movement of electrons in a reaction mechanism. A full-headed curly arrow is used for two electrons.

◆ Electrophiles must be capable of accepting a pair of electrons; nucleophiles must have a lone-pair of electrons available for bond formation.

CHAPTER 2

Arenes

By the end of this chapter you should be able to:

1 Show understanding of the concept of *delocalisation* of electrons as used in a model of benzene;

2 describe the *electrophilic substitution* of arenes with concentrated nitric acid in the presence of concentrated sulphuric acid, a halogen in the presence of a halogen carrier, and a halogenoalkane such as chloromethane in the presence of a halogen carrier (Friedel–Crafts reaction);

3 describe the mechanism of *electrophilic substitution* in arenes, using the mononitration of benzene as an example;

4 understand that reactions of arenes, such as those in point 2 above, are used by industry during the synthesis of commercially important materials, for example explosives, pharmaceuticals and dyes (from nitration), and polymers such as polystyrene (from alkylation);

5 explain the relative resistance to bromination of benzene, compared with cyclohexene, in terms of *delocalisation* of the benzene ring;

6 describe the reactions of phenol with bases and with sodium to form salts and with bromine to form 2,4,6-tribromophenol;

7 explain the relative ease of bromination of phenol, compared with benzene, in terms of activation of the benzene ring;

8 state the uses of phenols in antiseptics and disinfectants.

The simplest arene is benzene. Benzene is added to unleaded petrol and is used to make many other chemicals, as shown in the pie chart (*figure 2.1*): 65% of benzene is used to make alkylbenzenes. These include ethylbenzene (used to make phenylethene, the monomer for poly(phenylethene), more commonly known as polystyrene); dodecylbenzene (which is used to make detergents) and 1-methylethylbenzene (cumene), used to make phenol and propanone. Benzene is the feedstock for the manufacture of compounds as varied as medicines, dyes and explosives (*figure 2.2*). Cyclohexane, which is a starting material for making nylon, is also made from benzene. You will not use benzene in a school laboratory as it is believed to cause leukaemia.

Benzene is a planar hexagonal molecule. This structure has considerable chemical stability. Kekulé was first to suggest that benzene was a

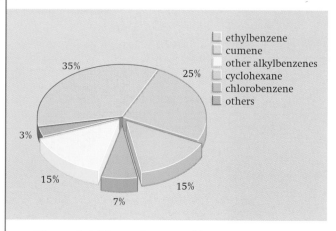

● **Figure 2.1** The main uses of benzene.

cyclic molecule but he also thought benzene had alternating single and double carbon–carbon bonds. Such a structure would have two different lengths for the carbon–carbon bonds. The single and double bonds may be placed in two alternative positions:

or

(It may help you to see these as alternative positions if you imagine that you are standing on the carbon atom at 12 o'clock: one structure will have the double bond on your left, the other has the double bond on the right.)

The Kekulé structure for benzene would be expected to show the typical addition reactions of an alkene. However, benzene undergoes addition reactions far less easily than a typical alkene. For example, an alkene such as cyclohexene will rapidly decolourise aqueous bromine in the dark. Bromine must be dissolved in boiling benzene and exposed to ultra-violet light before addition occurs (see page 15).

Also, the carbon–carbon bond lengths in benzene molecules are all identical, with lengths intermediate between those of single and double bonds (*table 2.1*).

The current model of the bonding in benzene accounts for

Bond	Bond length (nm)
C–C	0.154
C=C	0.134
benzene C–C	0.139

● **Table 2.1** Carbon–carbon bond lengths.

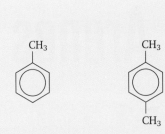

methylbenzene (toluene) and 1,4-dimethylbenzene (xylene) – additives which improve the performance of petrol

vanillin – present in oil of vanilla extracted from the pod of the vanilla orchid, and familiar as vanilla flavouring

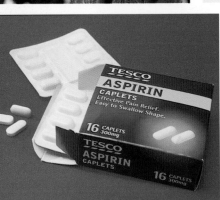

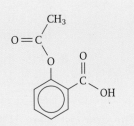

aspirin – used as an analgesic (pain killer)

a diazo dye – used as colouring in paints and on fabrics

● **Figure 2.2** Some compounds manufactured from benzene.

these observations. Each carbon atom contributes one electron to a π bond. However, the π bonds formed do not lie between pairs of carbon atoms as in an alkene: the π bonds spread over all six carbon atoms. The electrons occupy three delocalised π orbitals. They are said to be **delocalised** as they are not localised between adjacent pairs of carbon atoms but are spread over all six. (An alkene π bond *is* localised between a pair of carbon atoms.) The π molecular orbitals are formed by overlap of carbon p atomic orbitals. To achieve maximum overlap, the benzene molecule must be planar. One of the delocalised π molecular orbitals is shown below:

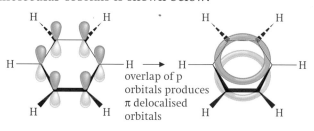

overlap of p orbitals produces π delocalised orbitals

This model produces six C–C bonds of the same length, as observed. The planar shape is clearly seen in a space-filling molecular model of benzene:

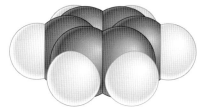

The reluctance of benzene to undergo addition reactions is due to the increased energetic stability that the delocalised system gives it (see page 16).

Substitution reactions

Breaking the delocalised π electron system on benzene requires a considerable input of energy. Arenes such as benzene exhibit many reactions in which the delocalised system is retained. The majority of these are substitution reactions. Groups which may directly replace a hydrogen atom on a benzene ring include halogen atoms, nitro (–NO_2) groups and alkyl groups.

The formation of nitroarenes

The explosive trinitrotoluene (TNT) is made by substituting nitro groups, –NO_2, for hydrogen

atoms on the benzene ring of methylbenzene (toluene). It is explosive because the nitro groups bring six oxygen atoms into close proximity to the carbon atoms of the benzene ring. When detonated (*figure 2.3*), the compression pushes these atoms closer together, causing rapid formation of carbon dioxide and water vapour, and leaving the nitrogen atoms to join together as nitrogen molecules. The explosion is caused by the very large and rapid increase in volume as the solid TNT is converted to gases. (There is not sufficient oxygen to convert all the carbon to carbon dioxide, so carbon is also formed and is seen as black smoke.)

In addition to its use in explosives, the nitro group is a versatile and useful group in the preparation of drugs and dyestuffs.

Until the hazardous nature of benzene was fully appreciated and its use in schools and colleges was banned, the preparation of nitrobenzene was a routine practical in A level chemistry. You may have the chance to nitrate a substituted benzene such as the much less harmful methyl benzoate. Both benzene and methyl benzoate require the use of **nitrating mixture**. This is a mixture of concentrated nitric acid and concentrated sulphuric acid. For benzene, the reaction mixture is heated gently under reflux at a temperature of about 50–55 °C. Careful temperature control is needed to minimise the formation of dinitrobenzene. The reaction equation is:

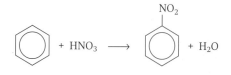

● **Figure 2.3** The use of trinitrotoluene (TNT) as an explosive in quarrying.

This is a substitution in which a hydrogen atom has been replaced by the nitro group, $-NO_2$.

The **mechanism of nitration** involves an electrophilic substitution. The function of the sulphuric acid in the nitrating mixture is to generate the attacking species from the nitric acid. (An attacking species may be a reactive molecule, a free radical or an ion.) The benzene ring has a high electron charge density associated with the delocalised π electrons. Hence an attacking reagent that is attracted by this negative charge is needed – an electrophile. An electrophile must be capable of forming a new covalent bond to carbon if it is to react successfully.

The electrophile produced in the nitrating mixture is the nitryl cation, NO_2^+:

$$HNO_3 + H_2SO_4 \rightarrow H_2NO_3^+ + HSO_4^-$$
$$H_2NO_3^+ \rightarrow NO_2^+ + H_2O$$

There are two stages in the mechanism of electrophilic substitution by the NO_2^+ ion. Figure 2.4 shows this mechanism using curly arrows.

1 Electrophilic attack by the nitronium ion takes place as the positively charged ion is attracted by the delocalised π electrons on benzene. A new covalent bond forms to one of the carbon atoms in the benzene ring. This carbon atom is now saturated, so the delocalised π electrons, together with the positive charge from the NO_2^+, are shared by the remaining five carbon atoms.

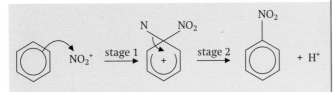

● **Figure 2.4** Electrophilic substitution on benzene.
Stage 1. Notice that the curly arrow starts at the delocalised π electrons and finishes on the nitrogen atom in NO_2^+. Two electrons are lost from the delocalised π electrons to produce a new covalent bond to the nitrogen atom in NO_2^+.
The intermediate is a cation with a single positive charge and a 'horseshoe' representing delocalisation of four electrons over five carbon atoms.
Stage 2. The second curly arrow moves two electrons from the C–H bond to restore the full delocalised system of six π electrons. Nitrobenzene and H^+ are formed. The circle in the benzene ring of the product shows that the full delocalised π electron system has been restored.

2 Loss of a proton (H^+) produces nitrobenzene and restores the full delocalised π electron system. Thus in electrophilic substitution, the chemical stability of the benzene ring is retained.

SAQ 2.1
a Draw and name three isomers which might be produced following electrophilic substitution of NO_2^+ for one hydrogen atom in methylbenzene.
b TNT has the systematic name 1-methyl-2,4,6-trinitrobenzene. Draw the structural formula of TNT.

The formation of halogenoarenes

Benzene also undergoes an electrophilic substitution reaction with chlorine or bromine. For example, if chlorine is bubbled through benzene in the presence of a halogen carrier, chlorobenzene is formed at room temperature:

The halogen carrier is usually introduced as metallic iron. This reacts with the chlorine to produce anhydrous iron(III) chloride. Iron(III) chloride is a covalent chloride and is soluble in the benzene.

The effect of the iron(III) chloride is to polarise the chlorine molecule so that it behaves as an electrophile:

$$\overset{\delta+}{Cl} \text{---} \overset{\delta-}{Cl} \text{---} FeCl_3$$

The dotted lines show bonds breaking between chlorine atoms and forming between a chlorine atom and the iron(III) chloride. Anhydrous aluminium chloride may also be used as a halogen carrier.

SAQ 2.2
Suggest the stages involved in the mechanism for substitution by chlorine on benzene.

The formation of alkylarenes

Alkylarenes are made using the Friedel–Crafts-type reaction. This makes use of a halogen carrier and a halogenoalkane. With chloromethane, for example, benzene forms methylbenzene:

SAQ 2.3

a Suggest a suitable halogen carrier to use in the reaction of benzene with chloromethane.

b Suggest suitable reactants which might lead to the formation of the following compound in the presence of a halogen carrier.

c Write a balanced equation using your suggested reactants.

Ethylbenzene is an important alkylbenzene that is used to make phenylethene (styrene). Ethylbenzene can be made from benzene and chloroethane using a Friedel–Crafts catalyst. However, industrially ethylbenzene is made more cheaply from benzene and ethene, as follows.

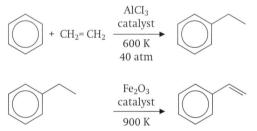

Phenylethene is the monomer for the production of the poly(phenylethene). This polymer is the familiar plastic (polystyrene) foam that is widely used in an expanded form for packaging and insulation. Polystyrene is also used for industrial mouldings, telephones, the casing of portable stereos and CD players and toys (*figure 2.5*).

Addition of halogens to benzene

The Kekulé structure of benzene with three alternating carbon–carbon double bonds would suggest that benzene might readily undergo an

● **Figure 2.5** Some uses of polystyrene.

addition reaction with a halogen such as chlorine or bromine. We have already seen that chlorine and bromine, in the presence of a halogen carrier, produce substituted products. For example, bromine in the presence of anhydrous iron(III) bromide produces bromobenzene.

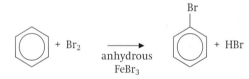

Addition of bromine to benzene is much more difficult to achieve. This is somewhat surprising if we represent benzene by the Kekulé structure.

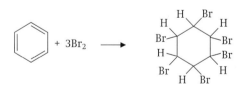

Our knowledge of the addition of bromine to an alkene such as cyclohexene would suggest that this reaction would require mild reaction conditions. Cyclohexene produces 1,2-dibromocyclohexane on shaking cyclohexene with bromine water. Indeed, this reaction is used as a quick test to show the presence of an alkene.

The relative resistance of benzene to bromination as compared to cyclohexene may be explained in terms of delocalisation of the π electrons in the benzene ring.

Benzene requires more vigorous reaction conditions for the addition of a halogen such as chlorine or bromine because of the chemical stability of the delocalised π electron system. Extra energy is required to overcome this stability. We shall examine this in more detail for the chlorination of benzene.

Benzene has been used to manufacture the chlorinated insecticide Lindane.

Use of chlorinated hydrocarbon insecticides has now virtually ceased. This follows the discovery of a link between their use and a decline in the population of peregrine falcons (figure 2.6).

SAQ 2.4

a What does the use of ultraviolet light suggest about the nature of the attacking species in the addition of chlorine to benzene?

b How does your suggestion compare to the attacking species in the addition of chlorine to an alkene?

A comparison of the enthalpy changes for the reactions of chlorine with benzene or cyclohexene provides a measure of the extra energetic

● **Figure 2.6** Peregrine falcon populations have increased significantly since chlorinated hydrocarbon insecticides have been replaced by new, safer alternatives.

stability of benzene. The equations and enthalpy changes are as follows:

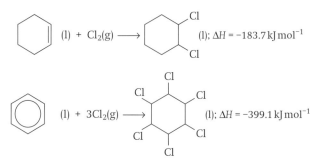

If benzene had the Kekulé (or cyclohexatriene) structure with alternating single and double bonds, it would be reasonable to suppose that the enthalpy change on reacting benzene with three moles of chlorine would be three times that of the addition of one mole of chlorine to a mole of cyclohexene:

$$\text{(l)} + 3Cl_2(g) \longrightarrow C_6H_6Cl_6(l); \Delta H = -551.1\,\text{kJ}\,\text{mol}^{-1}$$

However, this is $152\,\text{kJ}\,\text{mol}^{-1}$ more exothermic than the experimentally derived value. The extra energy is needed to overcome the delocalisation of the π electron bonds. This energy is sometimes referred to as the **stabilisation** (or delocalisation) energy of benzene.

Phenols and their properties

Phenols, like alcohols, occur widely in nature. In phenols, the −OH group is joined to a benzene ring. Two very different examples are vanillin and estradiol.

■ Vanillin is found in the seed pods of the vanilla orchid. It is widely used as a flavouring in foods like chocolate or ice cream. The structure of vanillin is:

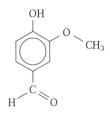

■ Estradiol is an important female sex hormone. It maintains female sexual characteristics and stimulates RNA synthesis (and hence promotes growth). Estradiol contains a secondary alcohol as well as a phenol. The structure of estradiol is:

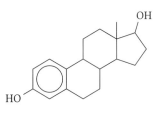

SAQ 2.5

a Copy the structures of vanillin and estradiol.
b Label the phenolic –OH group on each.
c Identify and label any other functional groups present.

Solubility in water

Phenol is sparingly soluble in water. The –OH group forms hydrogen bonds to water, whilst the benzene ring reduces the solubility because it forms only weak van der Waals' bonds to other molecules. Two liquid layers are formed if a sufficient amount of phenol crystals is added to water (*figure 2.7*). The excess phenol absorbs water (again, by forming hydrogen bonds) and produces a lower liquid layer. This lower layer is a solution of water in phenol, the upper layer being a solution of phenol in water.

The acidity of alcohols

Phenol ionises slightly in water. The O-H bond in phenol breaks to form a hydrogen ion and a negative phenoxide ion. This bond breaking occurs more readily in a phenol molecule than in a water molecule, because the phenoxide ion is stabilised by a partial delocalisation over the benzene ring of the negative charge on the oxygen atom. Phenol is therefore more acidic than water.

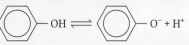

Ethanol ionises even less than water. The positive inductive effect in ethanol increases the electron charge density on the oxygen atom. This increases the ability of the ethoxide ion to attract hydrogen ions, so ethanol is less acidic than water.

The order of acid strength decreases as:

phenol (most acidic) > water > ethanol

All three are very weak acids in comparison to other weak acids that you may meet. Acids (or bases) which are fully ionised in solution are known as strong acids (or strong bases). Chapter 14 has more on acids and bases.

Reactions in which the O-H bond is broken

The reaction with bases

As phenol is a weak acid, it neutralises strong bases. For example, with sodium hydroxide the products are sodium phenoxide and water:

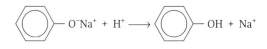

Sodium phenoxide is an ionic compound. Phenol dissolves completely in aqueous sodium hydroxide, but it is only sparingly soluble in water.

Addition of a strong acid to a solution of sodium phenoxide produces the reverse of the reaction with sodium hydroxide. Initially, a milky emulsion of phenol in water forms. This is followed by phenol separating out as a dense, oily liquid layer. We can represent the equation as:

Reaction with sodium

Phenol reacts vigorously with sodium:

Sodium phenoxide is formed and hydrogen is liberated. The greater reactivity (in comparison with ethanol) is again due to the weak acidity of phenol.

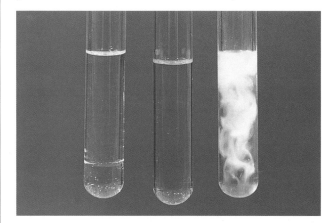

● **Figure 2.7** The left-hand tube shows phenol in water: the phenol does not mix, and settles out at the bottom of the tube. The central tube contains phenol dissolved in alkali. The right-hand tube shows the formation of a milky emulsion when the alkaline phenol is acidified.

Reactions involving the benzene ring

Phenol undergoes electrophilic substitution reactions far more readily than benzene. The hydroxyl group, –OH, raises the electron charge density of the benzene π orbitals, considerably enhancing the reactivity of phenol towards electrophiles. The carbon–oxygen bond in phenol has about 16% double-bond character. This is caused by a partial delocalisation into the benzene ring of lone-pair electrons on the oxygen. The increased electron charge density is greatest at the 2, 4 and 6 positions on the ring.

Substitution with bromine

Aqueous phenol decolourises bromine water to form a white precipitate of 2,4,6-tribromophenol (*figure 2.8*):

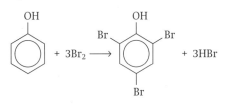

Similar reactions occur with chlorine and iodine. Contrast these very mild conditions with the need to use pure bromine and pure benzene, together with an iron(III) bromide catalyst, to produce the mono-substituted bromobenzene.

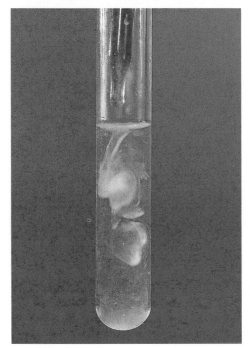

● **Figure 2.8** The reaction that occurs when bromine water is added to aqueous phenol.

The presence in phenol of the –OH group increases the susceptibility of the benzene ring to electrophilic attack. The oxygen in the –OH group has two lone pairs of electrons. These can overlap with the delocalised π electrons, partially extending delocalisation to the oxygen atom. Overall, the π electron charge density is increased (especially at the 2, 4 and 6 positions). Chemists say the –OH group **activates** the benzene ring.

SAQ 2.6

How does bromine in aqueous solution become sufficiently polar to achieve electrophilic substitution on phenol?

Phenol is used to manufacture a wide range of useful chemical products (*figure 2.9*). A dilute aqueous solution of phenol was first used in 1865 as an antiseptic by Lister. Phenol was soon widely used in hospitals and greatly reduced the number of infections, particularly during surgery. Phenol as the solid or in concentrated form is harmful by skin absorption and can cause burns. Safer compounds such chlorophenols have now largely replaced phenol in antiseptics and disinfectants.

● **Figure 2.9** Compact discs, araldite and TCP are all manufactured using phenol as a raw material.

SUMMARY

- Arenes have considerable energetic stability because of the delocalised π electrons. Arenes require much more vigorous reaction conditions to undergo addition reactions because of this extra stability.

- Arene chemistry is dominated by substitution reactions that enable arenes to retain the delocalised π electrons. Hydrogen atoms on the benzene ring may be replaced by a variety of other atoms or groups including halogen atoms, nitro (–NO$_2$) groups and alkyl groups.

- The variety of substitution reactions on benzene provides access to many useful compounds including medicines, dyes, explosives and polymers.

- When the –OH group is joined directly to a benzene ring, the resulting alcohol is called a phenol.

- Phenols are acidic (relative to aliphatic alcohols) and form phenoxides on reaction with sodium hydroxide. The acidity of phenol is due to stabilisation of the negative charge in the phenoxide ion into the π electron system on the benzene ring.

- The reaction of sodium with phenol produces sodium phenoxide and hydrogen.

- The –OH group enhances the reactivity of the benzene ring towards electrophiles. Bromine water is decolourised by phenol, producing a white precipitate of 2,4,6-tribromophenol.

Questions

1   Wood contains an arene-based polymer known as lignin. Approximately a quarter of the dry weight of wood is lignin. The lignin polymer is built from more than one monomer molecule, with 4-hydroxycinnamyl alcohol being the most frequent. The structure of 4-hydroxycinnamyl alcohol is shown below.

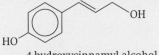
4-hydroxycinnamyl alcohol

   a   Describe what you might observe when 4-hydroxycinnamyl alcohol is treated with the following reagents. In each case, suggest a structure for the organic product(s).
   - (i) Aqueous sodium hydroxide, NaOH(aq).
   - (ii) Hot, acidified aqueous potassium dichromate(VI).
   - (iii) Aqueous bromine, Br$_2$(aq).

Recent research has shown that, in the kitchen, use of a wooden chopping board may be more hygienic than one made from poly(propene).

   b   With reference to the structure of 4-hydroxycinnamyl alcohol, comment on this research finding.

2   a   Using a suitable diagram, describe and explain the bonding in methylbenzene.
   b   Aerosols to ease the pain of wasp stings may contain the local anaesthetic, benzocaine. The structure of benzocaine is shown below.

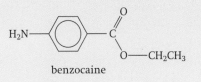
benzocaine

In the production of benzocaine, ethyl 4-nitrobenzoate is converted to benzocaine. Ethyl 4-nitrobenzoate is itself made from 4-nitrobenzoic acid. The structure of 4-nitrobenzoic acid is shown below.

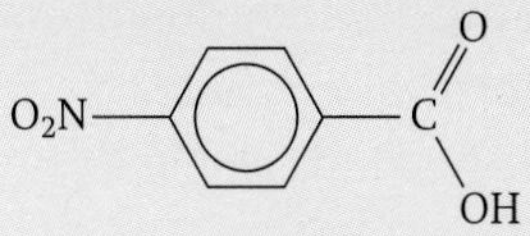

4-nitrobenzoic acid

c (i) State the reagents and conditions for the introduction of a nitro group, NO_2^-, into the benzene ring.

(ii) Write a balanced equation for the formation of 4-nitrobenzoic acid from benzoic acid.

(iii) Describe the mechanism of this reaction, using 4-nitrobenzoic acid to illustrate this mechanism.

CHAPTER 3

Carbonyl compounds

By the end of this chapter you should be able to:

1 describe the reduction of *carbonyl compounds* using NaBH$_4$ to form alcohols;

2 describe the mechanism for *nucleophilic addition* reactions of hydrogen cyanide (in the presence of potassium cyanide) with aldehydes and ketones;

3 describe the use of 2,4-dinitrophenylhydrazine to detect the presence of a carbonyl group in an organic compound and to identify a carbonyl compound from the melting point of the derivative;

4 describe the use of Tollens' reagent (ammoniacal silver nitrate) to detect the presence of an aldehyde group and to distinguish between aldehydes and ketones, as explained in terms of the oxidation of aldehydes to carboxylic acids with reduction of silver ions to silver.

You first encountered carbonyl compounds in the *Chains and Rings* module, in the form of aldehydes and ketones. Aldehydes are formed in the first stage of oxidation of primary alcohols whilst ketones are the only product formed on oxidation of secondary alcohols. (See *Chemistry 1*, chapter 11.)

Both aldehydes and ketones contain the carbonyl group, C=O. In aldehydes, the carbon atom of this group is joined to at least one hydrogen atom. The aldehyde group is often written as −CHO. (This must not be confused with the hydroxyl functional group in alcohols, which is written as ⩾COH.) In ketones, the carbonyl group is joined to two other carbon atoms, so the simplest ketone, propanone, must contain three carbon atoms. *Table 3.1* shows the first few members of the

homologous series of aldehydes and ketones. Common names of these compounds are shown in brackets. Note that aldehydes are named by taking the alkane stem and replacing the '-e' with '-al'; with ketones the '-e' is replaced by '-one'.

Aliphatic aldehydes and ketones occur widely. The simple sugars, such as glucose and fructose, are present in aqueous solutions as equilibrium mixtures of chain and ring forms (*figure 3.1*). The chain form of glucose has an aldehyde group at one end, whilst the chain form of fructose contains a ketone group. Aldehydes and ketones frequently contribute to the distinctive odours of foods and plants, though odour depends more on the overall shape of a molecule rather than on the functional groups present. Heptan-2-one is responsible for the odour of blue cheese (*figure 3.2*).

Another example of a naturally occurring ketone is carvone. This is a chiral molecule and exists as two optical isomers (page 6) with very different odours.

Aldehydes		Ketones	
Name	**Structural formula**	**Name**	**Structural formula**
methanal (formaldehyde)	HCHO		
ethanal (acetaldehyde)	CH$_3$CHO		
propanal	CH$_3$CH$_2$CHO	propanone (acetone)	(CH$_3$)$_2$CO
butanal	CH$_3$CH$_2$CH$_2$CHO	butanone	CH$_3$COCH$_2$CH$_3$

● **Table 3.1** The homologous series of aldehydes and ketones.

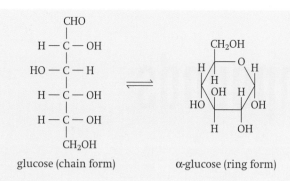
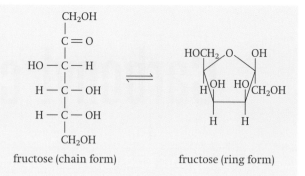

glucose (chain form)   α-glucose (ring form)   fructose (chain form)   fructose (ring form)

● **Figure 3.1** Chain and ring forms of sugars.

One optical isomer is responsible for the odour of spearmint, whilst the other is the principal odour in caraway seed (*figure 3.3*).

SAQ 3.1

Copy the structures for carvone and the chain forms of glucose and fructose. Label the aldehyde and ketone groups present. Mark the chiral carbon atom in carvone with an asterisk.

● **Figure 3.2** The ketone, heptan-2-one, is responsible for the odour of blue cheese.

The simplest aromatic aldehyde is benzaldehyde, C_6H_5CHO, and the simplest aromatic ketone is phenylethanone, $C_6H_5COCH_3$:

benzaldehyde   phenylethanone

The aromatic carbonyl compounds have very distinctive, almond-like odours. Benzaldehyde is used to make almond essence, the flavouring used in Bakewell tarts and puddings. Benzaldehyde also contributes to the flavours of many fruits such as almonds, cherries, apricots, plums and peaches (*figure 3.4*). Such fruits contain amygdalin, $C_{20}H_{27}O_{11}N$. This molecule is hydrolysed by enzymes, forming benzaldehyde, glucose and hydrogen cyanide, HCN:

$$C_{20}H_{27}O_{11}N + 2H_2O \rightarrow C_6H_5CHO + 2C_6H_{12}O_6 + HCN$$

Hydrogen cyanide is a toxic, colourless gas which also has an aroma of almonds. It contributes to the flavour of the fruits. Fortunately it is not a danger as it is only present at a very low concentration!

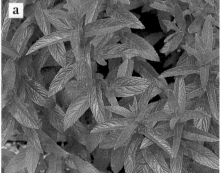

carvone

● **Figure 3.3** The very different flavours of spearmint, **a**, and caraway, **b**, are produced by the enantiomers of the ketone, carvone, **c**.

● **Figure 3.4** Benzaldehyde contributes to the flavours of many fruits.

SAQ 3.2

Amygdalin is an example of a glycoside. Many different glycosides occur naturally in plants. They are built up from glucose and either an alcohol or phenol. The structure of amygdalin is shown in *figure 3.5*.

a Identify the parts of the amygdalin molecule which give rise to
  (i) hydrogen cyanide
  (ii) benzaldehyde
  (iii) glucose.
b Explain what is meant by the term **hydrolysis**.

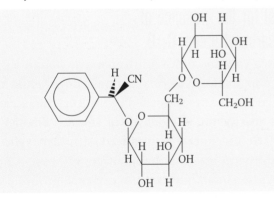

● **Figure 3.5** The structure of amygdalin.

Physical properties

The carbonyl group is significantly polar:

$$\overset{\delta+}{\diagdown}\underset{\diagup}{C}=\overset{\delta-}{O}$$

The polarity is sufficient to enable the lower members of the homologous series of aldehydes and ketones to be completely miscible with water.

Water will form hydrogen bonds to the carbonyl group:

$$\overset{\delta+}{\diagdown}\underset{\diagup}{C}=\overset{\delta-}{O}$$
$$H$$
$$O-H$$

SAQ 3.3

Explain the following in terms of intermolecular forces:

'Aldehydes and ketones containing more than four carbon atoms become increasingly immiscible with water.'

Redox reactions

Reduction

Aldehydes are obtained by mild oxidation of primary alcohols, and ketones are formed when secondary alcohols are oxidised (see *Chemistry 1*, chapter 11). Aldehydes or ketones may be reduced to their respective alcohols. Sodium tetrahydridoborate, $NaBH_4$, is a suitable reducing agent. The aldehyde or ketone is warmed with the reducing agent using water or ethanol as a solvent. It is usual to represent $NaBH_4$ by [H] in the equation for the reduction. (Compare this to the use of [O] in the equations for the oxidation of alcohols with acidified dichromate(VI).) Here are two examples.

Ethanal is reduced to ethanol:

$$CH_3CHO + 2[H] \rightarrow CH_3CH_2OH$$

Propanone is reduced to propan-2-ol:

$$CH_3COCH_3 + 2[H] \rightarrow CH_3CH(OH)CH_3$$

The reactions may also be regarded as addition of hydrogen to the carbonyl double bond. Remember that, under different conditions, hydrogen may also add to the carbon–carbon double bond in alkenes.

SAQ 3.4

Draw the structural formulae for the products obtained when the following are treated with $NaBH_4$:
a butanone
b butanal.

Oxidation

Under mild conditions, aldehydes are oxidised further to carboxylic acids. The aldehyde is usually refluxed with acidified potassium dichromate(VI). Ketones are not oxidised under these conditions. We have already studied the oxidation of primary alcohols to aldehydes and aldehydes to carboxylic acids in *Chemistry 1*, chapter 11, and you may find it helpful to revise that section now.

SAQ 3.5

Draw the skeletal formula for the product formed when butanal is refluxed with acidified potassium dichromate(VI).

Addition of hydrogen cyanide

Both aldehydes and ketones will react with hydrogen cyanide. The product is a hydroxynitrile. For example, propanal will form 2-hydroxybutanenitrile:

$$CH_3CH_2\diagdown C=O + HCN \longrightarrow CH_3CH_2-\underset{\underset{H}{|}}{\overset{\overset{OH}{|}}{C}}-C\equiv N$$

Notice that this reaction introduces an extra carbon atom into the molecule. Hence the stem name changes from propane to butane.

Unlike addition to alkenes, which involves an electrophilic mechanism (*Chemistry 1*, chapter 10), the polarity of the carbonyl compounds allows **nucleophilic addition** to occur. The reaction is catalysed by the presence of a base. Hydrogen cyanide is a very weak acid and the presence of a base increases the concentration of cyanide ions. The cyanide ion is a stronger nucleophile than hydrogen cyanide. The lone-pair of electrons on the carbon atom in the cyanide ion attacks the positively charged carbon atom of the carbonyl group:

The intermediate ion rapidly reacts with a proton (either from an HCN molecule or from a water

molecule in the solvent) to form the hydroxynitrile:

The reaction has considerable synthetic importance due to the formation of a new carbon–carbon bond. The nitrile group is readily converted to a carboxylic acid by hydrolysis:

Hydrolysis is achieved by refluxing with aqueous acid or aqueous alkali.

Alternatively, reduction of the nitrile group produces an amine:

Reduction is carried out using sodium and ethanol.

Characteristic tests

A test for the presence of the carbonyl group, C=O

When a solution of 2,4-dinitrophenylhydrazine is added to an aldehyde or a ketone, a deep yellow or orange precipitate is formed (*figure 3.6*). The test is quite specific for an aldehyde or ketone carbonyl bond. No precipitate is produced with carboxylic acids or with esters, although each of these classes of compounds contain carbonyl groups. The reaction involves an addition across the double bond followed by elimination of a water molecule. The yellow precipitate is a 2,4-dinitrophenylhydrazone.

We use 2,4-dinitrophenylhydrazine rather than phenylhydrazine because it gives better precipitates. These precipitates are easily recrystallised. Recrystallisation, followed by the determination of the melting point of the 2,4-dinitrophenylhydrazone product and determination of the boiling point of the aldehyde or ketone, can help to identify an unknown carbonyl compound.

Distinguishing between aldehydes and ketones

Aldehydes produce carboxylic acids when treated with mild oxidising agents. Ketones are not oxidised by these reagents. Suitable mild oxidising agents, together with the observations seen when they are used to oxidise an aldehyde, are shown in *table 3.2*. The observations are illustrated in *figure 3.7*.

Some uses of propanone are shown in *figure 3.8* and *3.9*.

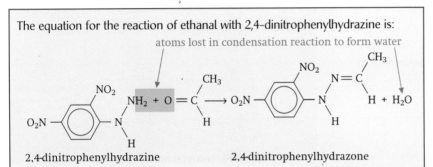

The equation for the reaction of ethanal with 2,4-dinitrophenylhydrazine is:

atoms lost in condensation reaction to form water

2,4-dinitrophenylhydrazine   2,4-dinitrophenylhydrazone

As water is eliminated in the formation of the carbon–nitrogen double bond in the hydrazone, the reaction is a **condensation reaction**. In general, a condensation reaction is one in which two molecules join together to form a larger molecule, with elimination of a small molecule (which is often water, but may be methanol, hydrogen chloride, ammonia, etc.).

● **Figure 3.6** Propanone reacts with 2,4-dinitrophenylhydrazine to form a 2,4-dinitrophenyl-hydrazone.

a   b

● **Figure 3.7** 'Before' and 'after' situations for the oxidation of ethanal by **a** acidified potassium dichromate(VI) and **b** Tollens' reagent.

Oxidising agent	Conditions	Observation on oxidation of an aldehyde	Explanation of observation
acidified potassium dichromate(VI)	boil gently (reflux)	the orange solution turns green	the orange dichromate(VI) ion, $Cr_2O_7^{2-}$, is reduced to green chromium(III) ion, Cr^{3+}
Tollens' reagent (an aqueous solution of silver nitrate in excess ammonia)	warm	a silver mirror forms on the sides of the test tube from the colourless solution	the silver(I) ion is reduced to silver metal

● **Table 3.2** The effects of oxidising agents on aldehydes.

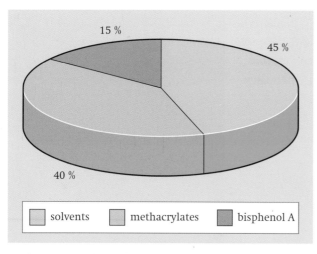

● **Figure 3.8** The major uses of propanone.

● **Figure 3.9** Methacrylate polymerises to a bright, transparent product that is used extensively in vehicle light clusters.

SUMMARY

◆ Aldehydes and ketones contain the carbonyl group, C=O. In aldehydes the carbonyl group is joined to just one other carbon atom; in ketones the carbonyl group is joined to two other carbon atoms.

◆ The systematic names of aldehydes are derived from the name of the alkane with the '-e' repaced by '-al'. Similarly ketones are named with the '-e' replaced by '-one'.

◆ As the carbonyl group is very polar, aldehydes and ketones are water soluble.

◆ Carbonyl compounds are readily reduced by NaBH$_4$. Reduction of an aldehyde produces a primary alcohol; reduction of a ketone produces a secondary alcohol.

◆ Aldehydes are readily oxidised under mild conditions to carboxylic acids. Ketones are not oxidised under mild conditions.

◆ The polar nature of the carbonyl group in aldehydes and ketones enables them to undergo nucleophilic addition of hydrogen cyanide to form hydroxynitriles.

◆ The mechanism of nucleophilic addition involves attack on the carbon atom of a cyanide ion by a lone-pair of electrons. A covalent bond forms to the positively charged carbon atom of the C=O bond. The π bond breaks and produces a negative charge on the oxygen of the C=O, which removes a hydrogen ion from a hydrogen cyanide molecule, forming the hydroxynitrile and another cyanide ion. The reaction is catalysed by sodium cyanide.

◆ The reagent 2,4-dinitrophenylhydrazine produces a yellow precipitate with aldehydes and ketones. A condensation reaction is involved (water is eliminated).

◆ As aldehydes are readily oxidised, they may be distinguished from ketones on warming with suitable oxidising reagents: acidified potassium dichromate(VI) turns from orange to green; Tollens' reagent produces a silver mirror.

◆ Propanone is an important solvent.

Questions

1 Cinnamaldehyde is present in the spice cinnamon. It is used as a flavouring in biscuits, cakes and mulled wine. Cinnamon is also known for its ability to release gases produced by bacteria from the intestine or the stomach, either as a burp or flatulence. The structure of cinnamaldehyde is shown below.

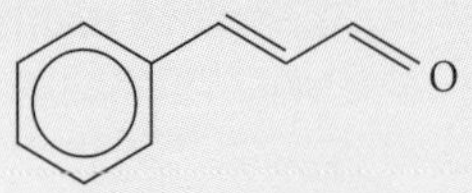

cinnamaldehye

a (i) A sample of cinnamaldehyde was refluxed with dilute sulphuric acid and potassium dichromate(VI). Draw a skeletal formula to show the structure of the product.

(ii) Give the name or formula of the reagent which will reduce cinnamaldehyde to cinnamyl alcohol.

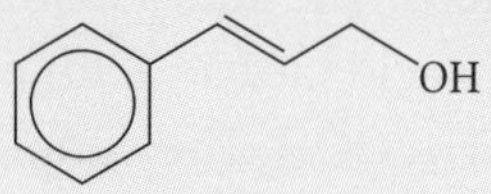

cinnamyl alcohol

(iii) Give the systematic name of cinnamyl alcohol.

b (i) Descibe a chemical test to show the presence of the carbonyl, >C=O, bond in cinnamaldehyde. Give the observations expected.

(ii) Describe a chemical test to show that cinnamaldehyde is an aldehyde and not a ketone. Give the observations expected.

2 Describe the mechanism of the nucleophilic addition of hydrogen cyanide, HCN, to propanone, CH_3COCH_3. Explain in your answer why the reaction is catalysed by cyanide ions, CN^-.

CHAPTER 4

Carboxylic acids and esters

By the end of this chapter you should be able to:

1 describe carboxylic acids as *proton donors*;

2 describe the reactions of carboxylic acids, typified by ethanoic acid, with aqueous alkalis to form carboxylates (salts) and with alcohols, in the presence of an acid catalyst, to form *esters*;

3 state the uses of esters in perfumes and flavourings;

4 describe the *acid and base hydrolysis of esters* to form carboxylic acids and carboxylates, respectively.

● **Figure 4.1** Lemonade often contains benzoic acid as a preservative. Citric acid is present naturally in lemons.

SAQ 4.1

Classify the following compounds as carboxylic acids or esters:

a $CH_3CH_2CH_2COOCH_3$

b $CH_2ClCOOH$

c $HCOOCH_2CH_2CH_3$.

The carboxylic acid functional group is −COOH. This consists of a hydroxyl group joined to a carbonyl group. Simple carboxylic acids are present in many foods. The sharp acidic taste of vinegar is caused by the ethanoic acid (acetic acid) present. Ethanoic acid has the formula CH_3COOH. The simplest aromatic carboxylic acid, benzoic acid, is used as a flavouring and a preservative in sparkling drinks such as lemonade. The acidity of lemons is caused by citric acid (*figure 4.1*). The structures of benzoic acid and citric acid are:

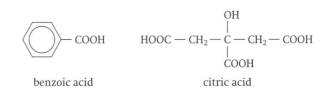

benzoic acid　　　　　　　citric acid

Esters are derivatives of carboxylic acids and are present in many foods. In esters, the hydrogen in the carboxylic acid group is replaced by an alkyl or an aryl group. Aliphatic esters have distinctive, fruity flavours. They are one of the principal flavouring components in most fruits (*figure 4.2*): ethyl 2-methylbutanoate is one component of the flavour of ripe apples; 3-methylbutyl ethanoate contributes to the flavour of ripe pears.

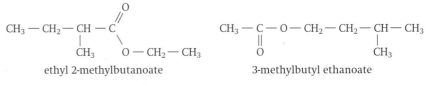

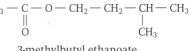

ethyl 2-methylbutanoate　　　　　　3-methylbutyl ethanoate

● **Figure 4.2** Esters are principal flavour components in ripe fruits.

Carboxylic acids

The structure of the carboxylic acid group is.

Carboxylic acids are named by taking the name of the alkane and replacing the final 'e' with '-oic acid'. The first four members of the homologous series of aliphatic carboxylic acids are shown in *table 4.1*. Note that the carbon atom of the carboxylic acid is counted as a carbon atom from the parent alkane. The general formula for the aliphatic carboxylic acids is $C_nH_{2n+1}COOH$.

Sources of carboxylic acids

Natural sources

Both petroleum fractions and natural oils provide sources of carboxylic acids. The naphtha crude oil fraction is an important starting material for making other chemicals; it is called a **feedstock**. Large quantities of ethanoic acid are made by the catalytic oxidation of naphtha.

Structural formula	Systematic name	Common name
HCOOH	methanoic acid	formic acid
CH₃COOH	ethanoic acid	acetic acid
CH₃CH₂COOH	propanoic acid	propionic acid
CH₃CH₂CH₂COOH	butanoic acid	butyric acid

● **Table 4.1** The first four members of the homologous series of carboxylic acids.

The irritation caused by a stinging nettle is caused by methanoic acid. Butanoic acid gives a very unpleasant odour to rancid butter.

Vegetable oils (*figure 4.3*) and animal fats are esters of carboxylic acids and the alcohol propane-1,2,3-triol (also known as glycerol). Hydrolysis of these oils or fats provides an important source of carboxylic acids with longer chains of carbon atoms. Some examples are shown in *table 4.2*.

In general, carboxylic acids that are obtained from oils or fats are called **fatty acids**. They usually contain an even number of carbon atoms and form unbranched chains. Fatty acids with one carbon–carbon double bond are said to be **mono-unsaturated**. They are polyunsaturated if they contain more than one carbon–carbon double bond. Each double bond will give rise to geometric isomers.

Synthetic sources

In the laboratory, there are a variety of synthetic routes to carboxylic acids. These methods include the oxidation of primary alcohols or aldehydes (*Chemistry 1*, chapter 11) and the hydrolysis of nitriles (page 24).

● **Figure 4.3** Oleic acid can be obtained from olive oil, which contains an ester of oleic acid.

Common name	Systematic name	Skeletal formula	Principal source
lauric acid	dodecanoic acid	⋀⋀⋀⋀⋀COOH	coconut oil
myristic acid	tetradecanoic acid	⋀⋀⋀⋀⋀⋀COOH	nutmeg seed oil
stearic acid	octadecanoic acid	⋀⋀⋀⋀⋀⋀⋀COOH	animal fats
oleic acid	octadeca-*cis*-9-enoic acid	⋀⋀⋀⋀═⋀⋀⋀COOH	olive oil

● **Table 4.2** Some natural carboxylic acids.

SAQ 4.2

a Draw the skeletal formula of hexadecanoic acid (palmitic acid).

b Draw the skeletal formula of the *trans* isomer of oleic acid.

c Name the following fatty acid:

⋀⋀═⋀═⋀⋀⋀COOH

d Draw the displayed formula of and name the carboxylic acid formed on oxidation of 2-methylpropan-1-ol.

e Draw the displayed formula of and name the carboxylic acid formed on hydrolysis of propanenitrile.

The reactions of carboxylic acids

You first met the hydroxyl group in *Chemistry 1*, chapter 11, and the carbonyl group in chapter 3 of this book. In carboxylic acids these two groups combine to form the carboxylic acid functional group, –COOH. The combination of these two groups modifies the properties of each of them.

Behaviour as acids

The proximity of the polar carbonyl group enables the hydroxyl group to ionise partly in water. Hence carboxylic acids are weak acids – unlike alcohols, which do not ionise to any significant degree in water.

The ionisation of the carboxyl group is due to delocalisation of the negative charge over the carbon and oxygen atoms. This delocalisation increases the energetic stability of the anion, producing an equilibrium in aqueous solution:

$$R - C {\overset{O}{\underset{O-H}{\diagdown}}} \text{(aq)} \rightleftharpoons R - C {\overset{O}{\underset{O}{\diagdown}}}^{\ominus} \text{(aq)} + H^+\text{(aq)}$$

Carboxylic acids form salts when reacted with metals (such as magnesium or zinc), alkalis, carbonates and basic metal oxides. In addition to producing a salt in the reaction with a carboxylic acid:

■ metals produce hydrogen;
■ alkalis and basic metal oxides produce water;
■ carbonates produce carbon dioxide and water.

For example, if you neutralise ethanoic acid with sodium hydroxide, sodium ethanoate and water are formed:

$$CH_3COOH\text{(aq)} + NaOH\text{(aq)} \rightarrow CH_3COONa\text{(aq)} + H_2O\text{(l)}$$

SAQ 4.3

Write balanced equations for the reactions of:

a zinc with propanoic acid;

b sodium carbonate with methanoic acid;

c magnesium oxide with ethanoic acid;

d benzoic acid with sodium hydroxide.

You can titrate ethanoic acid, or wine that has been oxidised to vinegar, against sodium hydroxide to determine the concentration of acid present (*figure 4.4*). Vinegar is between 6% and 10% ethanoic acid. As ethanoic acid is a weak acid, an indicator for the titration of a strong base against a weak acid is required (such as phenolphthalein).

● **Figure 4.4** The concentration of ethanoic acid in vinegar may be found by titration.

Esters

The ester functional group is:

$$-C\overset{\displaystyle O}{\underset{\displaystyle O-C}{\big\langle}}$$

Esters are formed by the reaction of an alcohol with a carboxylic acid.

The name of an ester comes partly from the parent alcohol and partly from the parent acid. The alcohol part of the name is placed first and is separated by a space before the acid part of the name. An example is ethyl propanoate:

$$CH_3CH_2-O\overset{\displaystyle O}{\underset{\underbrace{}}{C-CH_2CH_3}}$$

ethyl   propanoate

A range of isomers may be formulated by moving carbon atoms from one side of the ester group to the other. Ethyl propanoate has methyl butanoate, propyl ethanoate and butyl methanoate as isomers (all of which are esters).

SAQ 4.4

a Draw skeletal formulae for isomers of ethyl propanoate that are esters and don't have branched carbon chains, and name them.

b Further isomers with the same molecular formula as ethyl propanoate are possible. Draw the skeletal formulae of as many of these as you can and name them.

Formation of esters

The formation of an ester from a carboxylic acid is known as **esterification**. You can prepare ethyl ethanoate by warming a mixture of ethanol and glacial ethanoic acid in the presence of concentrated sulphuric acid as a catalyst. (Glacial ethanoic acid is pure ethanoic acid, free of water. It is called glacial because it freezes in the bottle at 16.7 °C (*figure 4.5*).) The equation for the formation of ethyl ethanoate is:

$$H_3C-C\overset{\displaystyle O}{\underset{\displaystyle O-H}{\big\langle}}+CH_3CH_2OH \rightleftharpoons H_3C-C\overset{\displaystyle O}{\underset{\displaystyle O-CH_2CH_3}{\big\langle}}+H_2O$$

ethyl ethanoate

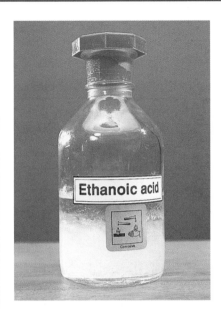

● **Figure 4.5** Glacial ethanoic acid freezes at 16.7 °C.

You can make esters of aliphatic alcohols in this way.

SAQ 4.5

a (i) Draw the structural formula of 1-methylethyl propanoate.

   (ii) Name the carboxylic acid and the alcohol which would form 1-methylethyl propanoate.

  (iii) Write a balanced equation for the formation of 1-methylethyl propanoate using structural formulae.

b (i) Name the ester formed on reaction of methanoic acid with butan-1-ol.

  (ii) Write a balanced equation for the reaction of methanoic acid with butan-1-ol using structural formulae.

The hydrolysis of esters

Esters may be hydrolysed by refluxing with either an acid or an alkali. Refluxing with an acid simply reverses the preparation of the ester from an alcohol and a carboxylic acid. The acid catalyses the reaction. The reaction is an equilibrium; hence there are always molecules of both reactants and products present after the reaction. The equation for the acid hydrolysis of ethyl ethanoate is:

$$H_3C-C\overset{\displaystyle O}{\underset{\displaystyle O-CH_2CH_3}{\big\langle}}+H_2O \underset{}{\overset{H^+(aq)}{\rightleftharpoons}} H_3C-C\overset{\displaystyle O}{\underset{\displaystyle O-H}{\big\langle}}+CH_3CH_2OH$$

When an ester is refluxed with an alkali such as aqueous sodium hydroxide, it is fully hydrolysed to the alcohol and the sodium salt of the acid. The equation for the base hydrolysis of ethyl ethanoate is:

$$H_3C - C \overset{O}{\underset{O-CH_2CH_3}{\big\langle}} \quad + OH^- \longrightarrow H_3C - C \overset{O}{\underset{O^-}{\big\langle}} \quad + CH_3CH_2OH$$

When the ester is a benzoate, base hydrolysis with aqueous sodium hydroxide produces an aqueous solution of sodium benzoate. Subsequent acidification produces a white precipitate of benzoic acid, as benzoic acid is only sparingly soluble in water (*figure 4.6*).

SAQ 4.6

a Write a balanced equation for the base hydrolysis of methyl benzoate. Name the products.

b Write a balanced equation for the acid hydrolysis of methyl propanoate. Name the products.

Fats as natural esters

Vegetable oils and animal fats provide an important store of energy for plants and animals. Oils and fats are esters of propane-1,2,3-triol. This alcohol has three hydroxyl groups, each of which can form an ester when reacted with a carboxylic acid. When only *one* of the alcohol groups has been esterified, the product is called a **monoglyceride**. In **diglycerides**, any *two* of the alcohol groups have been esterified. **Triglycerides** have had all *three*

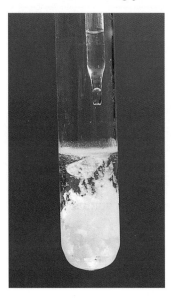

● **Figure 4.6** Benzoic acid precipitates when sodium benzoate is acidified.

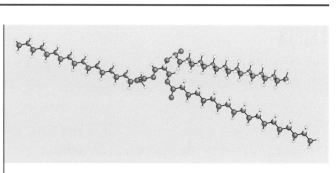

● **Figure 4.7** A triglyceride.

alcohol groups esterified. You can use different carboxylic acids to esterify each of the hydroxyl groups. *Table 4.2* (page 30) shows a few of the carboxylic acids which form these esters. *Figure 4.7* shows a molecular model of a triglyceride.

We shall look more closely at the structure of one triglyceride containing the fatty acid octadecanoic acid (stearic acid). The structures of propane-1,2,3-triol and octadecanoic acid are:

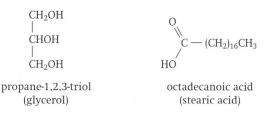

propane-1,2,3-triol   octadecanoic acid
(glycerol)   (stearic acid)

The triglyceride formed from three moles of octadecanoic acid and one mole of propane-1,2,3-triol is:

$$H_3C(H_2C)_{16} - \overset{O}{\overset{\|}{C}} - O - CH \begin{array}{l} H_2C - O - \overset{O}{\overset{\|}{C}} - (CH_2)_{16}CH_3 \\ \\ H_2C - O - \overset{O}{\overset{\|}{C}} - (CH_2)_{16}CH_3 \end{array}$$

SAQ 4.7

a What is the other product when octadecanoic acid and propane-1,2,3-triol form a triglyceride?

b What type of reaction has taken place?

c How many moles of this second product are formed per mole of propane-1,2,3-triol?

d Write a balanced equation for the reaction using structural formulae.

Fats and oils can be hydrolysed (like other esters) by heating with an acid or a base. When they are refluxed with sodium hydroxide, they are converted into propane-1,2,3-triol and the sodium salts of the fatty acids present. These sodium salts of fatty acids are soaps, so this hydrolysis is known as a **saponification**, meaning 'the forming of soap' (from *sapo*, the Latin word for soap). The reaction forms the basis of our modern soap-making industry. Soap making has been known to humans for many thousands of years. Soap is described in the Bible (Jeremiah 2:22). In the first century AD, the Roman historian Pliny described a method of soap manufacture that used goats' fat and beech-wood ashes.

The equation for the saponification of the triglyceride prepared from propane-1,2,3-triol and octadecanoic acid is given in *figure 4.8a*. After the saponification process, the soap is present in solution. It is precipitated as a solid by adding an excess of sodium chloride to the reaction mixture – a process known as **salting out**. Modern soaps (*figure 4.8b*) are made from blends of oils to produce particular combinations of properties.

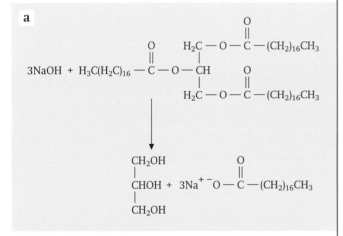

● **Figure 4.8**
a The saponification reaction produces soap.
b A noodling machine, part of the soap-making process.

The uses of esters

Significant quantities of esters are used as solvents in the chemical industry and as adhesives. Nail varnish (or its remover) and whiteboard marker pens may contain ethyl ethanoate as a solvent.

The flavours and fragrances of different esters are widely used to produce food flavourings and perfumes. The natural flavours of fruits are the result of subtle blends of hundreds of organic compounds. Many of these compounds are esters of aliphatic alcohols and simple carboxylic acids. In this context, we have already mentioned ethyl 2-methylbutanoate and 3-methylbutyl ethanoate. *Table 4.3* shows a number of esters with their approximate associated flavours and their molecular models.

The fragrance of a flower or plant is produced by volatile organic compounds. These may be extracted as the 'essential oil' of the flower or plant. These essential oils are the basis of the perfume industry; they contain a variety of compounds such as esters, aldehydes, terpenes and phenols. (The distinguishing feature of terpenes is that they are built up from a common five-carbon-atom unit based on 2-methylbuta-1,3-diene (isoprene).) Oil of jasmine (*figure 4.9*), traditionally obtained from the plant jasmine, is now produced by chemical synthesis and is thus

Flavour	Esters	Molecular model
apple	ethyl 2-methylbutanoate	
pear	3-methylbutyl ethanoate	
banana	1-methylbutyl ethanoate	
pineapple	butyl butanoate	

● **Table 4.3** Some esters and their associated flavours.

cheaply and readily available. Oil of jasmine is phenylmethyl ethanoate:

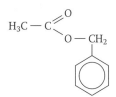

The perfume industry now relies heavily on chemical synthesis to provide the basic fragrances for many expensive perfumes.

● **Figure 4.9** Oil of jasmine is a natural oil used in perfumes. It used to be obtained from the jasmine plant, but now it is manufactured using phenylmethanol and ethanoic acid.

SUMMARY

◆ The carboxylic acid functional group is –COOH. Carboxylic acids are found naturally in many foods. The systematic name for a carboxylic acid derives from the name of the alkane, with the '-e' replaced by '-oic acid'.

◆ Carboxylic acids may be made by oxidation of primary alcohols or by hydrolysing a nitrile. Industrially, they are obtained from fats or by the oxidation of a petroleum feedstock. Carboxylic acids may be reduced to primary alcohols (via aldehydes) using $NaBH_4$.

◆ The close proximity of the carbonyl group to the hydroxyl group is responsible for the acidic behaviour of carboxylic acids. They readily form salts with alkalis, bases or carbonates.

◆ Esters are formed when carboxylic acids react with alcohols. A water molecule is released in the reaction. The ester functional group is

$$
\begin{matrix} & O \\ & \| \\ -&C-O-C \end{matrix}
$$

◆ Esters of aliphatic alcohols have fruity odours and are principal components of the flavours of many fruits. Fats and oils are esters of propane-1,2,3-triol (glycerol) and long-chain carboxylic acids.

◆ Esters are hydrolysed to form alcohols and carboxylic acids by warming the ester with an acid catalyst. Warming an ester with an alkali produces an alcohol and a carboxylic acid salt. Alkaline hydrolysis of a fat or oil produces propane-1,2,3-triol and the salt of a fatty acid. These salts are soaps, so the hydrolysis of a fat or oil is often called saponification.

◆ Esters are used as flavours and fragrances. Apart from its use in vinegar, ethanoic acid is an important feedstock for the chemical industry.

Question

1 An ester found in ripe apples which contributes to the flavour of the apples is ethyl 2-methylbutanoate.

a Draw the structural formula of ethyl 2-methylbutanoate.

b (i) Draw the structural formulae of the alcohol and carboxylic acid that you would use to make ethyl 2-methylbutanoate.

(ii) Write a balanced equation for the formation of ethyl 2-methyl-butanoate.

c A student carried out the following experiment using samples of the alcohol and acid identified in b (i).

- A 9.2 g sample of alcohol (M_r: 46) and 20.4 g of carboxylic acid (M_r: 102) were mixed in a flask.
- 2.0 g of concentrated sulphuric acid was added.
- The mixture was refluxed for several hours and then fractionally distilled.
- 7.4 g of crude ester were obtained.
- The ester was washed using aqueous sodium carbonate. The washing was repeated with fresh aqueous sodium carbonate until no more gas was produced.
- The ester was then washed with distilled water and dried over anhydrous calcium chloride.
- 15.6 g of pure ester were obtained.

(i) What is meant by the term **refluxed**?

(ii) Write a balanced equation for the reaction of the carboxylic acid with aqueous sodium carbonate.

(iii) How many moles of each reactant were used by the student to make the ester?

(iv) Calculate the percentage yield of the pure ester that the student obtained in this experiment.

CHAPTER 5

Nitrogen compounds

By the end of this chapter you should be able to:

1. describe the formation of phenylamine by reduction of nitrobenzene using tin and concentrated hydrochloric acid;

2. explain the basicity of primary amines and the relative basicities of ethylamine and phenylamine in terms of the *inductive effect* and the influence of the delocalised electrons in the benzene ring;

3. describe the reactions of *primary amines* with acids to form salts;

4. describe the synthesis of an *azo dye* by reaction of phenylamine with nitrous acid with the formation of a *diazonium salt*, followed by coupling with phenols under alkaline conditions;

5. describe the use of reactions that produce diazonium salts in the formation of dyestuffs;

6. state the general formula for an α-amino acid as $RCH(NH_2)COOH$;

7. describe the acid–base properties of α-amino acids and the formation of *zwitterions*;

8. explain the formation of a *peptide linkage* between α-amino acids leading to the idea that polypeptides and proteins are *condensation polymers*;

9. describe the acid hydrolysis of proteins and peptides to form α-amino acids.

Nitrogen may be present in an organic molecule in a number of functional groups.

The amine functional group, $-NH_2$, occurs in a wide variety of compounds. These range from simple amines to medicines, dyes and giant biological macromolecules. The smell given off by rotting animal flesh is largely caused by amines such as putrescine, $NH_2(CH_2)_4NH_2$, and cadaverine, $NH_2(CH_2)_5NH_2$. Urea, present in urine, has the structure:

Amphetamine is a medicine used as a stimulant that mimics the effect of noradrenaline. Noradrenaline is a neurotransmitter that prepares animals for a rapid response when, for example, they are suddenly frightened (*figure 5.1*). Noradrenaline and amphetamine increase the heart rate, dilate the air passages in the lungs and increase sweating. They have similar structures:

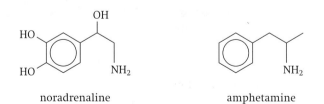

noradrenaline   amphetamine

The double helix present in DNA is held together by hydrogen bonds between pairs of bases (*figure 5.2*). Amine functional groups are involved in some of these hydrogen bonds. The hydrogen bonds between the cytosine and guanine bases are shown in *figure 5.2b*.

- **Figure 5.1** When springbok are frightened they will take flight, frequently leaping high into the air (an activity known as 'pronking'). The rapid response is triggered by a release of noradrenaline.

Amino acids also contain the amine group. For example:

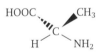

SAQ 5.1

Copy the diagram of hydrogen bonds between the cytosine and guanine bases (*figure 5.2b*). Draw circles round the amine functional groups and label them.

- The amide functional group, –CONH–, is present in proteins and polyamides. Some synthetic polymers, such as nylon, are polyamides. The repeat units of a protein and a polyamide are:

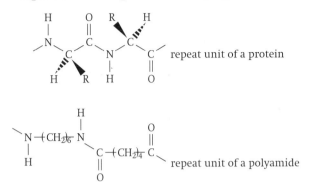

SAQ 5.2

Copy the repeat units of a protein and a polyamide. Draw circles round the amide functional groups and label them.

- The nitrile functional group, –CN, is used to introduce an additional carbon atom during organic synthesis (see page 52). However, it is also present in the synthetic polymer used to make acrylic fibre. Poly(ethenenitrile) (also called polyacrylonitrile) is made by polymerising ethenenitrile:

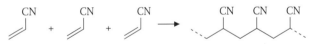

This polymer is used to make acrylic fibre, which is widely used for clothing and furnishing fabrics. It is an interesting thought that when we wear acrylic garments (*figure 5.3*), we cover ourselves in

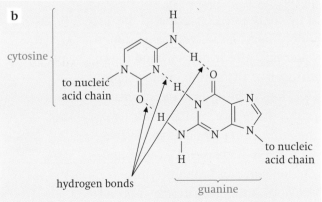

- **Figure 5.2 a** Watson and Crick with their first model of DNA. **b** Hydrogen bonds between a base pair in DNA.

● **Figure 5.3** Acrylics are used in clothing and furnishing materials.

cyanide (nitrile) groups. Sodium cyanide and hydrogen cyanide are highly toxic but, fortunately, the cyanide groups in acrylic fabric are firmly bonded in the polymer, and represent no danger. However, a hazard can arise if the material is burned and the fumes are inhaled. As a result, modern acrylic fibre is modified by the inclusion of some chloroethene. The chlorine atoms provide a substantially increased resistance to combustion.

Primary amines

The primary amines which we shall study in detail are ethylamine and phenylamine. Models of their structures are shown in *figure 5.4*. Primary aliphatic amines are generally water-soluble. The hydrogen atoms in the amine group, $-NH_2$, form hydrogen bonds to the oxygen atoms in the water molecules. A hydrogen atom in water may also hydrogen-bond to the nitrogen of the amino group (*figure 5.5*). The solubility in water of the primary aliphatic amines reduces as the number of carbon atoms in the alkyl group increases. Alkyl groups are non-polar and can only form weak, instantaneous dipole−induced bonds to other molecules. The breaking of these bonds provides insufficient energy to disrupt the

much stronger hydrogen bonding between water molecules. (Phenylamine also has a low solubility in water, for the same reason.)

The preparation of amines

Here are two methods for preparing ethylamine.

■ Heating bromoethane with an excess of a hot, ethanolic solution of ammonia produces ethylamine:

$$CH_3CH_2Br + NH_3 \rightarrow CH_3CH_2NH_2 + HBr$$

You first met this reaction in *Chemistry 1*, chapter 12. The excess ammonia reacts with the HBr forming ammonium bromide, NH_4Br:

$$NH_3 + HBr \rightarrow NH_4Br$$

■ Reducing ethanenitrile with hydrogen produces ethylamine:

$$CH_3CN + 4[H] \rightarrow CH_3CH_2NH_2$$

Sodium and ethanol may be used for this reduction. We also discussed the reduction of a nitrile to an amine in chapter 3 (page 24).

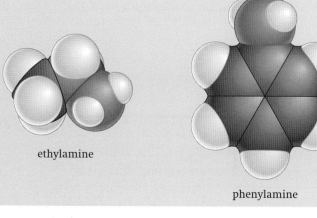

ethylamine

phenylamine

● **Figure 5.4** Amines.

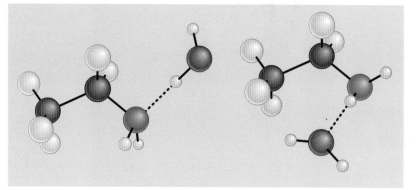

● **Figure 5.5** The formation of hydrogen bonds between water and ethylamine.

Phenylamine is prepared by reducing nitrobenzene:

The reduction is carried out using tin and concentrated hydrochloric acid. The product is separated from the reaction mixture by steam distillation, which involves distilling the mixture whilst passing steam through the mixture (*figure 5.6*). Arenes are readily nitrated, so the reduction of nitroarenes provides a standard route to aromatic amines.

SAQ 5.3

Give the name and structural formula of the organic product from the reactions of:

a propanenitrile with hydrogen (from sodium) and ethanol

b 4-nitrophenol with tin and hydrochloric acid.

Amines as bases

Amines are related to ammonia, which is a weak base. Weak bases will accept a proton from water

to form an alkaline solution. The equation for the reaction of ammonia with water is:

$$H - \overset{..}{\underset{H}{N}} - H + H_2O \longrightarrow \left[H - \overset{H}{\underset{H}{\overset{\uparrow}{\underset{..}{N}}}} - H \right]^+ + OH^-$$

Ammonia has a lone-pair of electrons on the nitrogen atom. This lone-pair accepts a proton from a water molecule to form the ammonium ion. A mixture of ammonia and ammonium ions is present in an aqueous solution of ammonia. If we represent a general amine by the formula RNH_2, the general equation for the reaction with water is:

$$RNH_2(aq) + H_2O(l) \rightleftharpoons RNH_3^+(aq) + OH^-(aq)$$

For example, ethylamine accepts a proton to form the ethylammonium ion:

$$H_3C - CH_2 - \overset{..}{\underset{H}{N}} - H + H_2O \longrightarrow \left[H_3C - CH_2 - \overset{H}{\underset{H}{\overset{\uparrow}{\underset{..}{N}}}} - H \right]^+ + OH^-$$

The base strengths of ethylamine and phenylamine relative to ammonia are shown in *table 5.1*. The order of base strength is due to the **inductive effects** of the ethyl and phenyl groups.

■ Alkyl groups have a positive inductive effect. This means that they have a tendency to push electrons towards a neighbouring atom. In ethylamine, the effect of this is to increase slightly the electron charge density on the nitrogen atom. This increased charge density on the nitrogen atom enhances its ability to donate its lone-pair of electrons to a proton, so ethylamine is a stronger base than ammonia.

■ The phenyl group has a negative inductive effect. The electron charge density on the nitrogen atom in phenylamine is decreased. Consequently, the ability of phenylamine to

● **Figure 5.6** This student is carrying out a steam distillation.

Amine	Order of base strength
phenylamine	
ammonia	increasing strength
ethylamine	

● **Table 5.1** Relative base strengths of amines and ammonia.

accept a proton is decreased, so it is a weaker base than ammonia. This effect is further enhanced in phenylamine because the lone-pair of electrons on the nitrogen atom becomes partially delocalised over the benzene ring.

Making salts with amines

Bases are neutralised by acids to form salts. For example, ammonia with hydrochloric acid produces ammonium chloride:

$$NH_3(aq) + HCl(aq) \rightarrow NH_4^+(aq) + Cl^-(aq)$$

Amines also produce salts. Ethylamine with hydrochloric acid forms ethylammonium chloride:

$$C_2H_5NH_2(aq) + HCl(aq) \rightarrow C_2H_5NH_3^+(aq) + Cl^-(aq)$$

Phenylamine forms phenylammonium chloride:

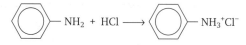

Phenylamine is only sparingly soluble in water, but it dissolves readily in hydrochloric acid because a salt is formed. Addition of alkali to this salt solution causes phenylamine to be released. Initially, a milky emulsion forms, which usually breaks down into oily drops (*figure 5.7*). (Compare this to the behaviour of a solution of phenol in aqueous alkali on treatment with hydrochloric acid (page 17).)

SAQ 5.4

Write balanced equations for the reactions of:
a nitric acid with butylamine;
b hydrochloric acid with 4-aminophenol;
c sodium hydroxide with 4-aminophenol.

Reactions specific to phenylamine

Diazonium salt formation and coupling reactions

When a reaction mixture of phenylamine and nitrous acid is kept below 10°C, a diazonium salt is formed (the diazonium ion is $-N_2^+$). This reaction is known as a **diazotisation** reaction:

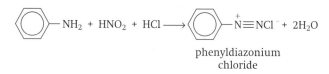

phenyldiazonium
chloride

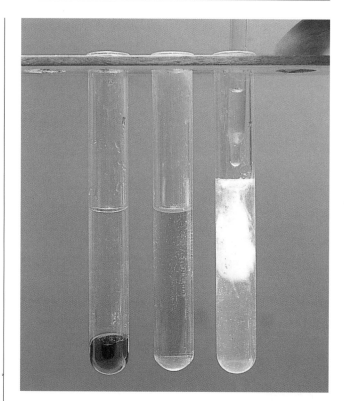

● **Figure 5.7** The left-hand tube contains brown phenylamine, which does not mix with water. The central tube contains a solution of phenylamine in acid. A white emulsion forms when alkali is added to this solution.

(The nitrous acid needed for these reactions is unstable and is produced by reacting sodium nitrite with dilute hydrochloric acid.)

The **diazonium** ion, $-N_2^+$, is rather unstable and decomposes readily to nitrogen. However, delocalisation of the diazonium ion π-bond electrons over a benzene ring stabilises phenyldiazonium sufficiently for it to form at low temperatures.

The phenyldiazonium ion behaves as an electrophile, and will attack another arene molecule such as phenol. Electrophilic substitution takes place at the 4 position, producing 4-hydroxyphenylazobenzene (*figure 5.8*). The reaction is known as a **coupling** reaction:

The compound formed is an energetically stable, yellow azo dye (the azo group is $-N=N-$). The stability is due to extensive delocalisation of the electrons via the nitrogen–nitrogen double bond. You will find out more about the colour of dyes if you study the *Methods of Analysis and Detection* module.

● **Figure 5.9** Methyl orange is used as an indicator.

● **Figure 5.8** A diazonium dye is formed when phenyldiazonium chloride is added to an alkaline solution of phenol.

The dye 4-hydroxyphenylazobenzene is just one of the wide range of dyes that can be made from aromatic amines and other arenes. These are known as diazonium dyes. They are very stable, so they do not fade. Another example is the indicator methyl orange (*figure 5.9*) which has the structure:

$$Na^+ \ ^-O_3S - \underset{}{\bigcirc} - N = N - \underset{}{\bigcirc} - N \underset{CH_3}{\overset{CH_3}{<}}$$

SAQ 5.5

Draw the displayed formula for the azo dye produced on reacting 4-aminophenol with nitrous acid (in dilute hydrochloric acid) below 10°C and coupling the resulting diazonium salt with phenol. Write balanced equations for the reactions involved.

Amino acids

There are about twenty naturally occurring amino acids. Their general structure is:

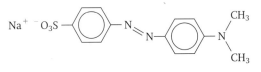

They are all α-**amino acids**, which have the amino group and the carboxylic acid group attached to the same carbon atom. In the simplest amino acid, glycine, the 'R' is a hydrogen atom. In the next simplest amino acid, alanine, the 'R' is a methyl group, CH_3.

Amino acids are **bifunctional**, that is they have two functional groups present in the molecule: the carboxylic acid group, $-COOH$, and the amino group, $-NH_2$. As one of these groups is acidic and the other group is basic, they can interact with one another. The $-COOH$ group donates a proton to the $-NH_2$ group. This forms an 'internal' salt known as a **zwitterion**:

$$\underset{COOH}{\overset{NH_2}{R-C-H}} \longrightarrow \underset{\underset{a\ zwitterion}{COO^-}}{\overset{\overset{+}{NH_3}}{R-C-H}}$$

The zwitterion has a significant effect on the properties of amino acids. It is the predominant form of the amino acid in the solid phase or in aqueous solution. The ionic charges increase the attractive forces between the amino acids in the solid, and so raise the melting point significantly above that of related compounds with similar numbers of atoms and electrons. The amino acid glycine, NH_2CH_2COOH, decomposes at 262°C without melting, whereas propanoic acid, CH_3CH_2COOH, melts at −21°C.

Amino acids form salts when reacted with acids or bases. On addition of a dilute solution of a strong acid (for example, aqueous hydrochloric acid), the zwitterion will accept a proton. The product now carries a net positive charge and may be crystallised as the chloride salt:

$$\overset{+}{N}H_3 \qquad\qquad \overset{+}{N}H_3$$
$$| \qquad\qquad\qquad\quad |$$
$$R - C - H + H^+ \longrightarrow R - C - H$$
$$| \qquad\qquad\qquad\quad |$$
$$COO^- \qquad\qquad COOH$$

Addition of dilute aqueous sodium hydroxide removes the proton from the $-NH_3^+$ group in the zwitterion. This leaves a negatively charged ion:

$$\overset{+}{N}H_3 \qquad\qquad NH_2$$
$$| \qquad\qquad\qquad\quad |$$
$$R - C - H + OH^- \longrightarrow R - C - H + H_2O$$
$$| \qquad\qquad\qquad\quad |$$
$$COO^- \qquad\qquad COO^-$$

Hence at high pH, amino acids are negatively charged in aqueous solution. At low pH, they are positively charged.

SAQ 5.6

a Draw the structural formulae for the ions present when glycine, NH_2CH_2COOH, is dissolved in:
  (i) aqueous hydrochloric acid;
  (ii) aqueous sodium hydroxide.
b Write balanced equations for the reaction of aqueous glycine with:
  (i) aqueous hydrochloric acid;
  (ii) aqueous sodium hydroxide.

Optical isomerism in amino acids

With the exception of glycine, amino acids have four different groups round the α carbon atom, and optical isomers are possible (see chapter 6 for more on this subject). The mirror images of the optical isomers of alanine may be drawn using three-dimensional formulae:

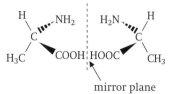

mirror plane

When you need to represent a pair of optical isomers, draw one isomer using the three-

dimensional representation. Next, imagine reflecting this isomer in a mirror plane, and draw the other isomer.

SAQ 5.7

a Leucine has the structure:

$$H$$
$$|$$
$$H_2N - C - COOH$$
$$|$$
$$CH_2$$
$$|$$
$$CH(CH_3)_2$$

Draw three-dimensional formulae to show the optical isomers of leucine.
b Isoleucine has more than one chiral centre. It has the structure:

$$H$$
$$|$$
$$H_2N - C - COOH$$
$$|$$
$$CHCH_2CH_3$$
$$|$$
$$CH_3$$

Copy this structure and mark the chiral centres with asterisks.

Proteins and polypeptides

Proteins and polypeptides are important molecules in living organisms. Muscle and hair are composed of fibres containing long protein molecules. Enzymes are soluble proteins that catalyse many biochemical reactions. Proteins, like nylon, are also examples of polyamides.

Polypeptides are formed when amino acids undergo condensation polymerisation. Two amino acids join together via a peptide link to form a dipeptide and a water molecule – the peptide link is simply the name we use for the amide link in polypeptides and proteins:

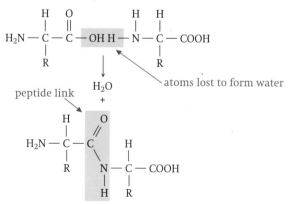

atoms lost to form water

peptide link

Three amino acids produce a tripeptide and two water molecules. Polypeptides and proteins contain a large number of amino acid units. (Proteins generally have much larger relative molecular masses then polypeptides.) In nature, proteins often consist of two or more polypeptides held together by intermolecular forces (such as hydrogen bonds). The sequence of amino acids in a protein is known as the **primary structure** of that protein.

Hydrolysis of a protein involves breaking the peptide links by reaction with water. So hydrolysis is the reverse of the condensation polymerisation of amino acids to form a protein. In living organisms, condensation polymerisation of amino acids

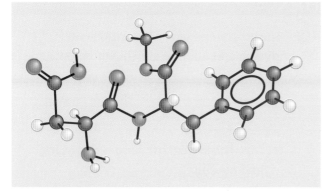

● **Figure 5.10** Aspartame.

and hydrolysis of proteins are both catalysed by enzymes. In the laboratory, acids or alkalis are used to catalyse the hydrolysis of proteins. Since each peptide link is broken, this is simply an extended example of the hydrolysis of an amide. Polyamides and polyesters are also hydrolysed to their monomers by refluxing with an acid catalyst.

SAQ 5.8

Aspartame is the methyl ester of the dipeptide formed between aspartic acid and phenylalanine (*figure 5.10*). Its skeletal formula is:

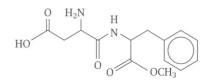

It is used as a sweetener in many 'diet' soft drinks. Aspartame has two links that may be hydrolysed.

a Copy the skeletal formula of aspartame. Mark the bonds that may be broken by hydrolysis, and label them with the names of the types of linkages present.

b Write a balanced equation for the acid hydrolysis of aspartame and name all the products.

SUMMARY

◆ Nitrogen appears in organic compounds in the following functional groups: amine, $-NH_2$; amide, $\overset{O}{\underset{-C-NH-}{\|}}$ nitrile, $-CN$; and azo, $-N=N-$. Such groups are common amongst the biochemical molecules found in living things.

◆ Ethylamine is prepared either by treating bromoethane with an excess of hot, ethanolic ammonia or by reducing ethanenitrile. Phenylamine is prepared by reducing nitrobenzene using tin and hydrochloric acid.

◆ Like ammonia, amines behave as bases, readily accepting protons to form salts. Ethylamine is a stronger base than ammonia because the alkyl group has a positive inductive effect; phenylamine is a weaker

base than ammonia because the phenyl group has a negative inductive effect. Phenylamine is also a weaker base due to the partial delocalisation of a pair of electrons from nitrogen over the benzene ring.

◆ Phenylamine reacts with nitrous acid on warming to give nitrogen and phenol. Below 10°C, the products are phenyldiazonium chloride and water; this reaction is called diazotisation.

◆ Diazonium salts react with other aromatic compounds (such as phenol) to form dyes; this is known as a coupling reaction. Diazonium dyes are commercially useful. Some indicators are diazonium dyes. The colour of diazonium dyes arises from the extensively delocalised π-electron system.

◆ There are about twenty naturally occurring amino acids with the general formula $RCH(NH_2)COOH$. 'R' may be H, CH_3 or another organic group. The amino group interacts with the acid group to form an internal salt or zwitterion. Amino acids react with both acids and bases to form salts.

◆ With the exception of glycine, amino acids possess a chiral carbon atom (a chiral atom has four different groups attached) and so optical isomers are possible.

◆ Polypeptides form when amino acids undergo condensation polymerisation. Two amino acids join together by a peptide (or amide) link to form a dipeptide and water. Repetition of this process leads to polypeptides and proteins.

◆ Proteins or polypeptides are hydrolysed by refluxing in a strong acid, such as HCl(aq), to form α-amino acids.

Questions

1 The last step in the synthesis of benzocaine involves the following conversion.

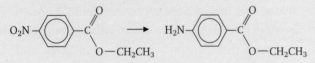

a   (i) State the reactants and conditions required to carry out this conversion.
    (ii) Give the systematic name of benzocaine.

b A student treated a sample of benzocaine with dilute hydrochloric acid at a temperature of 5°C. She then added aqueous sodium nitrite whilst maintaining a temperature of 5°C. After the mixture had stood for 10 minutes, she added the mixture dropwise to a solution of phenol in aqueous sodium hydroxide. A deep yellow-orange precipitate was formed.
Explain the chemical changes, with the aid of equations, which take place during the following steps.
    (i) When benzocaine is treated with dilute hydrochloric acid at a temperature of 5°C.
    (ii) When the mixture is added to aqueous sodium nitrite whilst maintaining the temperature at 5°C.
    (iii) When the mixture from **b** (ii) was added to a solution of phenol in aqueous sodium hydroxide.

2 The structures of the α-amino acids glycine and alanine are shown below.

$$H_2N-\underset{\underset{\displaystyle H}{|}}{\overset{\overset{\displaystyle H}{|}}{C}}-COOH \qquad H_2N-\underset{\underset{\displaystyle H}{|}}{\overset{\overset{\displaystyle CH_3}{|}}{C}}-COOH$$

a Give the systematic names of glycine and alanine.

b Describe and explain, with the aid of equations, the effect of adding the following to an aqueous solution of glycine.
    (i) dilute hydrochloric acid
    (ii) dilute sodium hydroxide.

c Draw a structural formula for alanine to show what is meant by the word **zwitterion**.

d α-amino acids, such as glycine and alanine, polymerise to form peptides and proteins.
    (i) Illustrate this polymerisation by writing a balanced equation to show the dipeptide formed between two molecules of alanine.
    (ii) In your answer to **d** (i), draw a circle round the peptide link.
    (iii) State the type of polymerisation taking place when peptides and proteins are formed from α-amino acids.

CHAPTER 6

Stereoisomerism in organic synthesis

By the end of this chapter you should be able to:

1 interpret and use the term *stereoisomerism* in terms of *cis–trans* and optical isomerism;

2 explain the term *chiral centre* and identify any chiral centres in a molecule of given structural formula (for example, amino acids and 2-hydroxypropanoic acid (lactic acid));

3 understand that chiral molecules prepared synthetically in the laboratory may contain a mixture of optical isomers, whereas molecules of the same compound produced naturally in living systems will often be present as one optical isomer only (for example L-amino acids);

4 understand that the *synthesis* of pharmaceuticals often requires the production of chiral drugs containing a single optical isomer, resulting in smaller doses (only half the drug is needed), reduced side-effects and improved pharmacological activity;

5 describe the two-stage synthesis of 2-hydroxypropanoic acid (lactic acid) by the addition of hydrogen cyanide to ethanal followed by acid hydrolysis and explain the use of such reactions in synthesis by providing a route for lengthening a carbon chain.

You will have already seen that many naturally occurring compounds are predominantly found as one of two isomeric forms. This type of isomerism is called optical isomerism.

It is not hard to find the reasons why only one of the two isomers predominates naturally. As life has evolved, the biochemical processes that take place in organisms have also evolved. Many of these processes require molecules of a specific shape for reactions to occur. For example, neuro-transmitters interact with sites on nerve cells that exactly accommodate both their shape and the intermolecular forces arising from the arrange-ment of atoms present. A different isomer of a specific neurotransmitter could not interact with these sites. Dopa is a neurotransmitter that exhibits optical isomerism. Only one form of

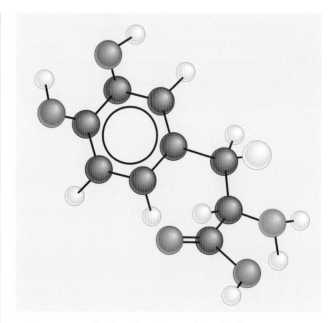

● **Figure 6.1** Ball-and-stick model of L-dopa.

dopa (L-dopa) is active in the brain. *Figure 6.1* shows a molecular model of L-dopa.

In this chapter, we shall look at examples of stereoisomerism. We shall also look at the stepwise synthesis of organic compounds. This provides an opportunity to bring together your knowledge and understanding of organic chemistry from both *Chemistry 1* and *Chemistry 2*. We shall also look at the way chemists are trying to mimic nature by selecting synthetic routes to produce only the active isomer when manufacturing a medicine.

Stereoisomerism

Stereoisomers contain the same atoms with the same order of bonds but with different spatial arrangements of atoms. Optical isomers and *cis–trans* isomers are examples of stereoisomers.

Cis-trans isomerism

You studied *cis–trans* isomerism in the *Chains and Rings* module in *Chemistry 1* (chapters 7 and 10). This type of isomerism occurs in alkenes where the carbon–carbon double bond, C=C, prevents rotation. Two identical atoms or groups on opposite sides of the double bond can then give rise to a *cis* isomer and a *trans* isomer. For example 1,2-dichloroethene has the following isomers.

cis-1,2-dichlorethene   *trans*-1,2-dichlorethene

SAQ 6.1

Which of the following compounds show *cis–trans* isomerism? Draw and label the *cis* and *trans* isomers where they exist.

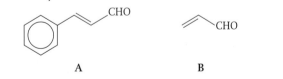

A   B

Optical isomerism

Optical isomers are molecules that are non-super-imposable mirror images of each other. Like other isomers they have the same molecular formulae. As stereoisomers, they have the same atoms and the same bonds between atoms. However, the bonds are arranged differently in space. The molecule CHBrClF provides a simple example of optical isomerism. The displayed formula of CHBrClF is shown below.

$$F - C - Br$$

with H above and Cl below the central C.

Displayed formulae give no indication of the spatial arrangement of the atoms in this molecule.

To display the optical isomers, we need to use three-dimensional formulae:

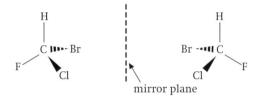

mirror plane

In these diagrams the solid wedge is coming towards you, the dashed wedge is away from you.

Rotation of the right-hand structure about the C–H bond produces

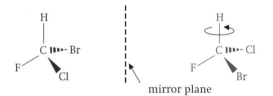

mirror plane

Notice that in the two structures the F, C and H atoms are in the same spatial position but the Br and Cl are interchanged. If the two isomers are placed on top of each other, as follows, they do not match. We say they are **non-superimposable**.

In effect, the molecules are rather like your right and left hands. Try rotating your right hand and place your left hand on top, they are non-superimposable images of each other. They might also be mirror images if you ignored warts, old nail varnish etc. Chemists use the term **chiral centre**, derived from the Greek for hand, to describe carbon atoms that exhibit optical isomerism. A key feature of a chiral centre in an organic molecule is the presence of four different groups on a carbon atom. The chiral centre in CHBrClF is labelled with an asterisk in the following diagram:

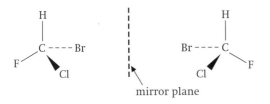

When drawing three-dimensional formulae by hand, it saves time to use a dotted line instead of the dashed wedge.

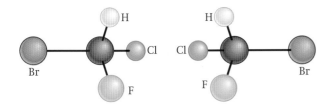

In this book we use the dashed wedge to provide a more three-dimensional effect. You will find it helps to visualise these structures if you use a model kit (or modelling software on a computer) to make these two isomers. (Use the colours shown in table 1.2 on page 4 for the different atoms). Molecular models of these isomers are shown in *figure 6.2*.

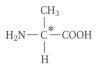

● **Figure 6.2** Ball-and-stick models of the optical isomers of CHBrClF.

With the exception of glycine, the α-amino acids all have a chiral centre at the α-carbon atom (the α-carbon atom is the one next to the carboxylic acid group). For example, alanine has the structure

$$H_2N - \overset{*}{\underset{H}{\overset{CH_3}{C}}} - COOH$$

Figure 6.3 shows molecular models of the two optical isomers.

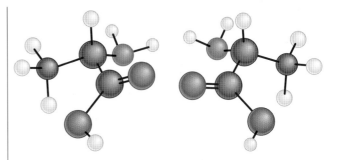

● **Figure 6.3** Ball-and-stick models of the two isomers of alanine.

SAQ 6.2

Draw three-dimensional formulae to show the two optical isomers of alanine.

SAQ 6.3

Draw the three-dimensional formula of L-dopa using the molecular model in *figure 6.1*. Alongside, mark a mirror plane and draw the three-dimensional formula of the isomer of L-dopa. Label this isomer D-dopa.

L-dopa is used in the treatment of Parkinson's disease. This disease causes much suffering and is characterised by tremors in the hands and loss of balance. The L-dopa must be free of D-dopa as the latter has many unpleasant side-effects. Increasingly, chemists are finding that, where a medicine has a chiral centre, one isomer is more beneficial than the other is. In some instances, as with D-dopa, one isomer has undesirable effects. Many chemical companies are seeking routes to produce chiral medicines containing only the beneficial isomer. A medicine containing only the beneficial isomer will require a smaller dose as only half the quantity of the medicine is needed. Pharmacological activity will be improved and side-effects reduced or even eliminated.

Undesirable effects proved to be a particular problem with the drug thalidomide, which was prescribed to pregnant women as a sedative during the early 1960s. Indeed, thalidomide was for a time the preferred sedative during pregnancy as the alternatives, such as valium, were addictive. Unfortunately, one of the isomers of thalidomide proved to have disastrous side-effects, causing babies to be born with congenital deformities (teratogenicity). Not surprisingly, thalidomide was quickly withdrawn from use. It is now mandatory for tests to be carried out on possible new medicines for teratogenicity.

How do we design molecules?

If we wish to design a molecule for a particular purpose, one approach is to identify the structural features that will achieve the desired result. The structural features of interest may be associated with the shape of the molecule or with the functional groups present. It is often possible to see a relationship between these structural features and the behaviour of the molecule in the body (**pharmacological activity**).

Some of the milder pain killers such as aspirin are derived from 2-hydroxybenzoic acid (salicylic acid). (These compounds are also used to reduce the effects of fevers.) Many modern medicines are related to naturally occurring compounds used in 'folk' medicine. For example, a derivative of salicylic acid, called salicin, is present in willow bark and willow leaves (*figure 6.4*). An infusion of willow leaves was recommended by Hippocrates (in 400 BC) for relieving pain whilst giving birth. A brew made from willow bark was used in the eighteenth century to reduce fever.

● **Figure 6.4** The leaves and bark of willow trees were used as a 'folk' medicine to reduce a fever and to relieve pain.

SAQ 6.4

The structures of aspirin, 2-hydroxybenzoic acid and salicin are:

aspirin

2-hydroxybenzoic acid (salicylic acid)

salicin

Copy these diagrams and circle the common structural feature.

The part of the molecules that you have circled in *SAQ 6.4* is the part which gives rise to their similar pharmacological activity. Such a structural feature is known as a **pharmacophore**. Investigation of other potential pain killers might focus on making similar molecules with this common structural feature.

SAQ 6.5

Which of these compounds might have potential as mild pain killers?

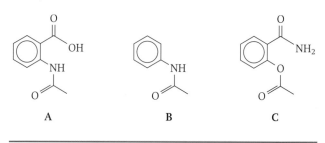

A   B   C

Medicines act by binding to **receptor molecules** present in the body. In order to bind to a receptor molecule and produce the desired pharmacological effect, the medicine molecule must have the following features.

■ A shape which fits the receptor molecule.
■ Groups which are capable of forming intermolecular bonds to complementary groups on the receptor molecules. These intermolecular bonds may involve hydrogen bonding, ionic attraction, dipole–dipole forces or instantaneous dipole–induced dipole forces.

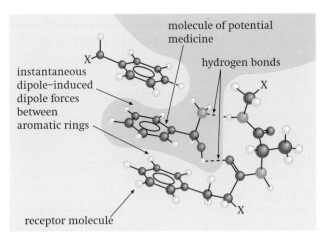

instantaneous dipole–induced dipole forces between aromatic rings

molecule of potential medicine

hydrogen bonds

X

X

X

receptor molecule

● **Figure 6.5** The interaction between a receptor molecule and a potential medicine.

Computers are now used to examine the relationship between a molecule and a receptor site. Such **molecular modelling** has greatly speeded up the process of designing new medicines; the interactions and fit of a potential medicine with a biological receptor molecule can be studied before the medicine is synthesised (*figure 6.5*). Before molecular modelling became available, the synthesis of a new medicine involved far more trial and error with many more compounds being prepared for testing. With molecular modelling, only those molecules that show potential after computer tests are made and tested. Molecular modelling on a computer thus provides a powerful tool for the design of medicines and many other compounds (such as pesticides or polymers).

SAQ 6.6
Which of these compounds would you choose to investigate for pharmacological activity at the receptor site shown in *figure 6.5*?

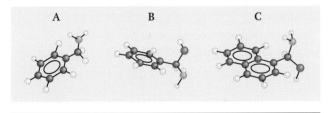

A

B

C

Routes to new molecules

Even simple molecules such as aspirin may have several functional groups present. There may be a suitable, readily available molecule with a structure very close to the one desired. If such a starting material exists, it may be possible to achieve the desired product in a **one-step synthesis**. A one-step synthesis involves converting the starting material to the product by means of a single reaction. For example, a natural penicillin may be modified to produce a new penicillin with enhanced antibacterial activity. However, it is much more likely that several separate reactions may be needed to convert a suitable starting compound to the desired product: a **multi-step synthesis** is required.

Planning a multi-step synthesis requires a sound knowledge of many different reactions. The reactions that you have met in your study of advanced chemistry provide you with the basis for planning the syntheses of a surprisingly wide range of organic compounds. We shall now review these reactions. This review should enable you to use reactions effectively in planning multi-step syntheses of your own, as well as helping you to learn the reactions more thoroughly. The reactions are best divided into two groups: aliphatic reactions and aromatic reactions.

Aliphatic reactions
You may have already seen a connection between the reactions of a number of functional groups. These are summarised in *figure 6.6*, which shows the names of the functional groups, together with arrows to indicate the interconversions possible.

Aromatic reactions
Figure 6.7 provides you with the framework for reactions involving aromatic compounds.

Try copying and displaying the reaction summaries (from *figures 6.6* and *6.7*) where you will look at them regularly – this will help you to learn the reactions and their conditions. Note the central role of halogenoalkanes in these synthetic routes (this was referred to in *Chemistry 1*, chapter 12). The frameworks given in *figures 6.6* and *6.7* are also suitable for making annotated charts to provide summaries of reaction mechanisms or for summaries of tests for the different groups.

You can use the reaction summaries to plan multi-step syntheses. Suppose we wish to convert ethene to ethanoic acid. A possible route is to convert ethene to ethanol, which is then oxidised to ethanoic acid. Alternatively, ethene could be converted to bromoethane, which is then hydrolysed to ethanol, and this is oxidised to ethanoic acid. This alternative involves an extra reaction step; you should usually try to complete a synthesis in as few steps as possible (remember that material is lost at each stage when preparing organic compounds: reaction yields seldom approach 100%).

SAQ 6.7

Outline how you might carry out the following conversions involving two- or three-step syntheses. Include the conditions required for the reactions. Start by drawing the structural formulae of the initial and final compounds.

a Ethene to ethylamine.
b Benzaldehyde to ethyl benzoate.
c 1-bromopropane to butanoic acid.
d Butan-2-one to 2-aminobutane.

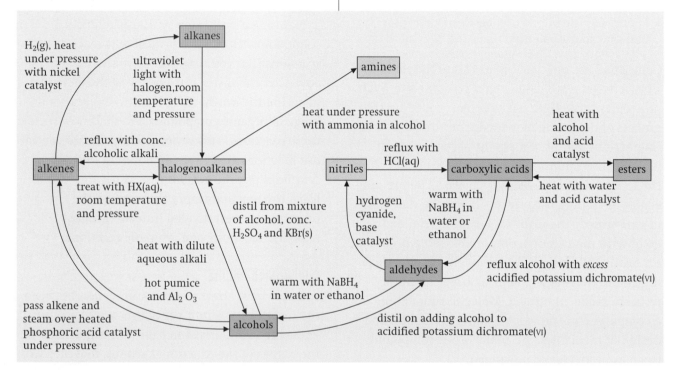

● **Figure 6.6** A summary of reactions of the functional groups.

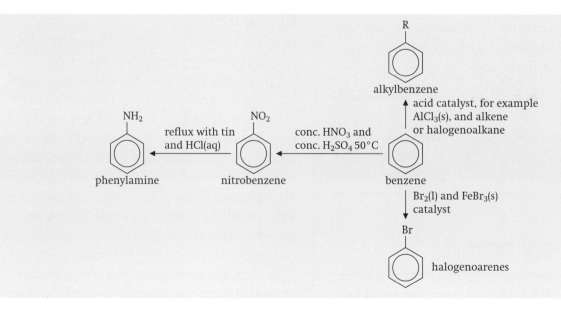

● **Figure 6.7** A summary of reactions involving aromatic compounds.

Carrying out a synthesis

The synthesis of a simple medicine, such as paracetamol or aspirin (*figure 6.8*), can provide an exciting basis for an investigation. The structures of paracetamol and aspirin are:

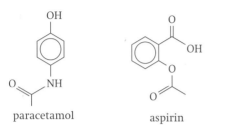

paracetamol   aspirin

When considering such an investigation, there are a number of criteria to consider. A good investigation will have sufficient scope to allow you to demonstrate your skills in planning, implementing, analysing evidence and drawing conclusions, evaluating evidence and procedures. As these skills all carry similar weight in the assessment of your investigation, it is important that you design your investigation in such a way as to allow you to address each skill.

SAQ 6.8

Outline a possible route from phenol to paracetamol.

If you have answered *SAQ 6.8*, you should have a three-step synthesis. At the end of the first step you will have a mixture of isomers to separate. As they are solids, this may be possible using fractional crystallisation. Alternatively, chromatography may be used. The second step involves a steam distillation. All this takes time, and in the limited amount of practical time that you have for your investigation you may only manage to complete this synthesis two (possibly three) times. As this will produce very limited results, you will have insufficient opportunity to discuss the effects of variables or to produce a well-developed discussion of your results. You may have made a couple of samples of paracetamol with yields and melting points to comment on, but little else.

A better approach for the purpose of an investigation is to concentrate on investigating the best conditions to optimise the yield at a particular step. Studying the effect of different conditions on a single reaction step will give a range of results for discussion. For example, the first step to paracetamol involves the nitration of phenol. Different conditions could be tried – a range of temperatures; a range of concentrations of nitric acid; different lengths of reaction time; and so on. Analysis of the products obtained in this first step may be carried out at intervals during the reaction using thin-layer chromatography. Comparisons may be made of product yield and purity. If you carry out an investigation in this way, you will be working in the same way as a process development chemist, repeating the reaction whilst making minor changes to achieve the optimum yield (you could even consider costs of energy and materials). You will have extensive results to discuss and you can still make a sample of paracetamol.

SAQ 6.9

Outline a possible conversion of ethanol to ethyl ethanoate via ethanoic acid. Suggest a possible sequence of experiments to investigate optimising the yield of the ester. Indicate which variables are being studied and which are being controlled.

Deciding on masses of reactants

If you choose to carry out an organic synthesis for your project, you will need to calculate the appropriate reacting masses (for liquids you may choose to use volumes, for solutions you will need to know the concentrations to decide on the volumes required). These will need to be

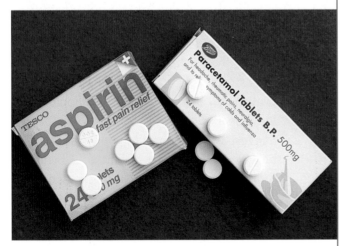

● **Figure 6.8** Aspirin and paracetamol are products of multi-step syntheses.

appropriate for the capacity of the reaction flask that you will use.

Calculate reacting quantities using the stoichiometric equation for the reaction. The approach is similar to that used in *Chemistry 1*, chapter 7, when deciding which reactant is in excess for the calculation of percentage yield. You may wish to use exact amounts or to have one (possibly cheaper) reagent in excess.

SAQ 6.10

Write a balanced equation for the conversion of ethanol to bromoethane using hydrogen bromide. Calculate the mass of ethanol required to react with 2.0 g of hydrogen bromide.

In *Chemistry 1*, chapter 7, we discussed the calculation of the yield of product after a single reaction step. To calculate the overall yield for a multi-step synthesis, you multiply the percentage yield of the last step by the fractional yield for the preceding steps. For example, if a three-step synthesis has yields of 70% at each step, the overall yield is:

$$\frac{70}{100} \times \frac{70}{100} \times 70\% = 34\%$$

Purifying and identifying the product

You will need to consider how to purify your product (called the **target molecule** in the pharmaceutical industry). Confirming that you have made the target molecule is called **characterisation**. This can be done in a variety of ways. Chromatography can be particularly useful for confirming purity as well as identity. Other methods of characterising a product include melting point and boiling point determinations, electrophoresis, mass spectrometry and the use of spectroscopic techniques. The spectroscopic techniques are described in chapter 8. You may have the opportunity to study them in more depth in the *Methods of Analysis and Detection* module.

Safety

Before you start any practical work, you must check your proposed experiments for hazards and establish the precautions that you need to take to work safely. This is called a **risk assessment** and your teacher will provide guidance on how to do this. Your teacher will also expect to check your risk assessment before allowing you to start practical work.

A two stage synthesis

2-Hydroxypropanoic acid (lactic acid) may be prepared by the addition of hydrogen cyanide to ethanal. However, due to the toxicity of hydrogen cyanide, you will not be performing this synthesis in school! The reaction is a good example of a nucleophilic addition reaction (see chapter 3, page 24). Following the addition of hydrogen cyanide, the product is hydrolysed by refluxing with aqueous hydrochloric acid.

The two stages of this reaction are as follows.

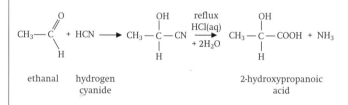

Note that, over the two stages of this reaction, the carbon chain length has grown by one carbon atom from two in ethanal to three in the 2-hydroxypropanoic acid. Reactions such as this provide synthetic chemists with a route for lengthening a carbon chain.

SAQ 6.11

a 2-hydroxypropanoic acid exists as two isomers. Identify the type of isomerism present and draw appropriate diagrams to illustrate the two isomers.

b (i) Describe, using structural formulae and curly arrows, the mechanism of the addition of HCN to ethanal.

(ii) Explain why the nucleophilic addition of HCN to ethanal is catalysed by a base.

(iii) Suggest, with reference to your answer to **b**(i), why an equimolar mixture of 2-hydroxypropanoic acid is formed in this nucleophilic addition reaction.

Designing molecules in industry

The use of molecular modelling in the design of a new medicine has already been mentioned, as have the many tools used by chemists in the characterisation of a compound. The use of all these tools has given us greatly increased capabilities in our search for new medicines. However, the search would not be possible without a wide range of other specialists including botanists, instrument designers and operators, computer scientists, biochemists, statisticians, geneticists and molecular biologists. All these specialists work with chemists in a team with a common goal. Any one of them might have the idea which provides the breakthrough to a new medicine. In terms of a career, working in such a team must be one of the most creative activities possible. Indeed, Lord Porter (winner of the 1967 Nobel Prize for Chemistry) has said: 'We chemists have not yet discovered how to make gold but, in contentment and satisfaction with our lot, we are the richest people on Earth.'

SUMMARY

- Stereoisomers contain the same atoms with the same order of bonds but with different spatial arrangements of the atoms. *Cis–trans* and optical isomers are examples of stereoisomers.

- *Cis–trans* isomers are found in alkenes where the carbon–carbon double bond, C=C, prevents rotation. The presence of two identical atoms or groups on opposite sides of the double bond can then give rise to *cis–trans* isomers.

- Optical isomers are molecules that are non-superimposable mirror images of each other. Such molecules contain a carbon atom which is a chiral centre. This chiral centre has four different atoms or groups attached to it. With the exception of glycine, α-amino acids exhibit optical isomerism.

- Both natural biochemicals and modern medicines contain chiral molecules. Generally, only one of the isomers is beneficial to living organisms. The other isomer may have undesirable effects. The beneficial isomer has the appropriate shape and pattern of intermolecular forces to interact with a receptor molecule in a living organism.

- Chemists are now producing medicines containing single isomers rather than a mixture of isomers. This enables the dose to be halved, improves pharmacological activity (behaviour of molecule in an organism) and reduces side-effects.

- Molecular design of a new medicine is made possible with a sound understanding of the structural features that produce medical effects. The computerised study of the interactions between molecules and biological receptors has become a powerful tool in the search for new medicines.

- Many multi-step syntheses can be planned using the reactions of the functional groups discussed in this book.

- The preparation of a new compound will involve safety considerations, making decisions on quantities of reagents to use, establishing what conditions provide the best yield, and purification and characterisation of the product.

- In the design and production of a new medicine, chemists work as part of a team that includes a wide range of other specialists such as molecular biologists, chemical engineers and computer scientists.

Questions

1   Alkenes provide the feedstock for the synthesis of many other compounds. Suggest reactants and conditions for the following conversions.

a

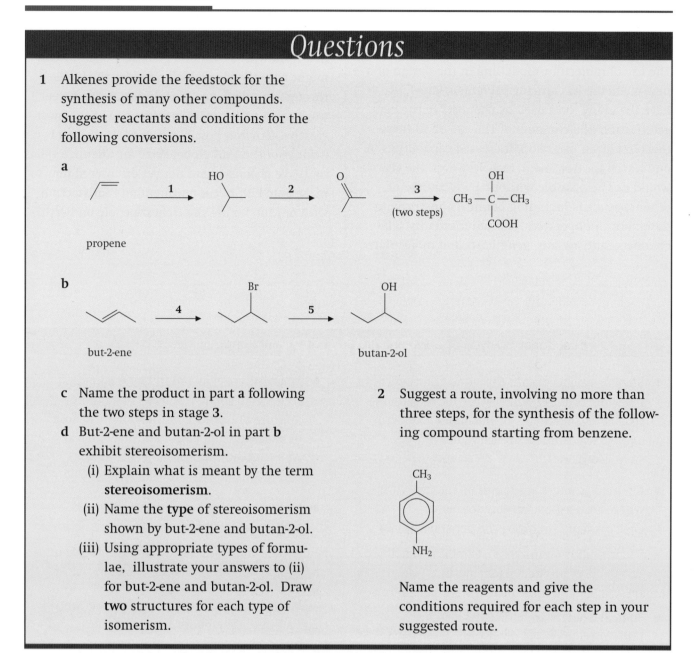

propene

b

but-2-ene   butan-2-ol

c Name the product in part **a** following the two steps in stage **3**.

d But-2-ene and butan-2-ol in part **b** exhibit stereoisomerism.
  (i) Explain what is meant by the term **stereoisomerism**.
  (ii) Name the **type** of stereoisomerism shown by but-2-ene and butan-2-ol.
  (iii) Using appropriate types of formulae, illustrate your answers to (ii) for but-2-ene and butan-2-ol. Draw **two** structures for each type of isomerism.

2   Suggest a route, involving no more than three steps, for the synthesis of the following compound starting from benzene.

Name the reagents and give the conditions required for each step in your suggested route.

CHAPTER 7

Polymers

By the end of this chapter you should be able to:

1 describe the characteristics of *addition polymerisation*, typified by poly(phenylethene);

2 identify that some alkenes, typified by propene, can produce addition polymers that are *atactic*, *isotactic* and/or *syndiotactic*;

3 describe the characteristics of *condensation polymerisation* in polyesters, in polyamides, typified by nylon-6,6 and Kevlar and in polypeptides and proteins;

4 suggest the type of polymerisation reaction from a given monomer or pair of monomers or from a given section of a polymer molecule;

5 deduce the *repeat unit* of a polymer obtained from a given monomer or pair of monomers;

6 identify, in a given section of polymer, the monomer(s) from which it was obtained;

7 state the use of *polyesters* and *polyamides* as fibres in clothing.

Polymers are macromolecules that are built up from very large numbers of small molecules known as monomers. Many natural polymers are known. For example, proteins are polymers of amino acids, natural rubber is a polymer of isoprene (see *Chemistry 1*, chapter 10) and DNA is a polymer of nucleotides. Nucleotides consist of an organic base, such as adenine in adenosine triphosphate (ATP, the chemical that carries energy within cells), bonded to a sugar, such as ribose, which is in turn joined to one or more phosphate ions:

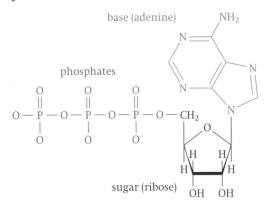

The polymer chain in DNA consists of a sugar–phosphate backbone. Two such backbones are linked by hydrogen bonds between pairs of bases to form a double helix.

Many polymers were discovered by chemists in the twentieth century. Some of these polymers were made by modifying naturally occurring materials. For example, cellulose is converted into cellulose ethanoate (acetate) by an esterification reaction:

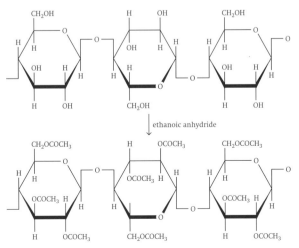

Other polymers were discovered by accident when the chemists concerned were pursuing a very different goal: examples include Bakelite® (*box 7A*), poly(tetrafluoroethene) and poly(ethene).

Nowadays, our understanding of the reactions and structures of polymers is much greater. Computer molecular modelling (page 49) is being used to design polymers with specific properties before the compounds are synthesised by chemists.

Polymer properties are dependent on a variety of factors such as chain length, crystallinity (crystallinity is greater when the molecules pack more closely), the degree of chain-branching or cross-linking and the strength of the intermolecular forces. The properties can be modified by the way the polymer is treated. For example, if the polymer is drawn (pulled through a small hole) whilst

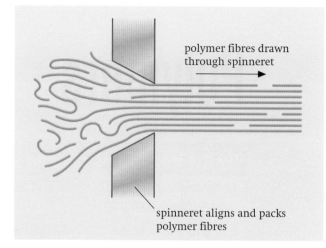

polymer fibres drawn through spinneret

spinneret aligns and packs polymer fibres

● **Figure 7.2** The packing of polymer chains increases the tensile strength of a fibre.

being formed into a fibre, the molecules tend to become more ordered. The intermolecular forces are increased because the polymer chains are more closely packed; the tensile strength of the fibre is therefore greater (*figure 7.2*). Properties are also modified by mixing the polymer with other materials. Glass fibre will produce a much stronger and more rigid material; plasticisers will produce a more flexible material. Canoes are made of glass-fibre-reinforced poly(phenylethene) (*figure 7.3a*). The bags and tubing for blood transfusions are made from a poly(chloroethene) composite containing a plasticiser (*figure 7.3b*).

The formation of polymers

Addition polymerisation

Alkenes polymerise by addition reactions. The alkene undergoes an addition to itself. As further molecules are added, a long molecular chain is built up. The reactions are initiated in various ways and an initiating chemical (**initiator**) may become incorporated at the start of the polymer chain. Ignoring the initiator, the empirical formula of an addition polymer is the same as the alkene it comes from. This type of reaction is called **addition polymerisation**. Many useful polymers are obtained via addition polymerisation of different alkenes.

Poly(ethene) was first produced accidentally by Eric Fawcett and Reginald Gibson in 1933. The reaction involves ethene adding to itself in a

---

Box 7A Bakelite®

In 1872, Adolf von Baeyer made a resin by heating phenol with an aldehyde. He threw this resin away because he could not see a use for the material. The resin was re-investigated by Leo Hendrik Baekeland who, in 1910, set up a company to manufacture the material (which he called Bakelite®) for use in making electrical sockets and plugs. Since Baekeland's day, the material used in these components has changed several times. In the 1990s, polyester, polycarbonate and acrylonitrilebutadiene styrene copolymer (ABS) are used for these components (*figure 7.1*). Once Bakelite® has been formed it cannot be melted, so it is a **thermosetting** polymer; the new materials can be melted and moulded many times (they are **thermoplastic** polymers), making fabrication much easier.

● **Figure 7.1** Electrical sockets and plugs are made from thermoplastic polymers.

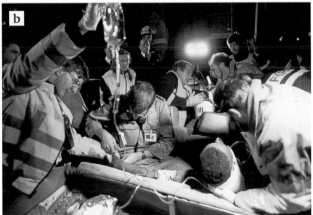

● **Figure 7.3**
a Canoes are often made from glass-reinforced poly(phenylethene).
b Blood bags are made from poly(chloroethene).

chain reaction. It is a very rapid reaction, with chains of up to 10 000 ethene units being formed in one second. The product is a high molecular mass, straight-chain alkane. It is a polymer and is a member of a large group of materials generally known as **plastics**. The alkene from which it is made is called the **monomer**, and the section of polymer that the monomer forms is called the **repeat unit** (often shown within brackets in structural formulae):

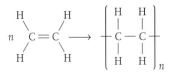

Skeletal formulae for two other important poly(alkene)s, poly(chloroethene) and poly(phenylethene), are:

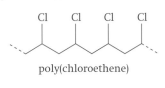

poly(chloroethene)

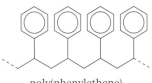

poly(phenylethene)

They are more commonly known as PVC and polystyrene, respectively. Note how the systematic name is derived by putting the systematic name of the monomer in brackets and prefixing this with 'poly'. The skeletal formulae of the monomers, chloroethene (old name vinyl chloride) and phenylethene (old name styrene), are as follows:

chloroethene   phenylethene

The synthesis of phenylethene from benzene is described on page 15.

SAQ 7.1

a Acrylic fibre is often used in furnishing fabric or as a wool substitute in sweaters. It is an addition polymer of propenenitrile, $CH_2{=}CHCN$ (also called acrylonitrile). Write a balanced equation for the polymerisation of propenenitrile. Use a displayed formula in your equation to indicate the repeat unit of this polymer.

b A polymer which is often used to make plastic boxes for food storage has the structure:

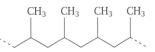

Draw displayed formulae to show (i) the repeat unit of this polymer and (ii) the monomer from which it is made. Label your diagrams with the appropriate systematic names.

There are several ways of bringing about the addition polymerisation of alkenes. These different methods produce polymers with different properties, which provide the wide variety of poly(alkene)s for the many applications of these versatile materials.

Stereoregular polymers

In 1953, a German chemist Karl Ziegler discovered a new catalyst which produced very long molecules of poly(ethene) with very little chain-branching. Before 1953, the poly(ethene) produced contained shorter polymer chains with many chain-branches present. Chain-branching in a polymer prevents close-packing of the polymer molecules. The molecules in Ziegler's polymer, with little chain-branching present, could pack more closely. The new polymer thus had a higher density and a higher melting point and was suitable for many new applications. It became known as high-density poly(ethene) or hdpe. The earlier polymer became known as ldpe (low-density poly(ethene)). Ziegler was able to patent his discovery and became a millionaire.

An Italian chemist Giulio Natta believed that Ziegler's catalyst would make it possible to synthesise polymers with a regular structure. In 1954, Natta developed Ziegler's catalyst to prepare poly(propene). Using different Ziegler-type catalysts he prepared three different forms of poly(propene). All contained long molecular chains. One form was highly crystalline with all the methyl groups ordered on one side of the polymer chain. Natta called this form **isotactic** poly(propene) (*figure 7.4a*). Natta's second form of poly(propene) was amorphous with the methyl groups randomly arranged along the polymer chain. He called this form **atactic** poly(propene) (*figure 7.4b*). A third form has the methyl groups alternating between one side of

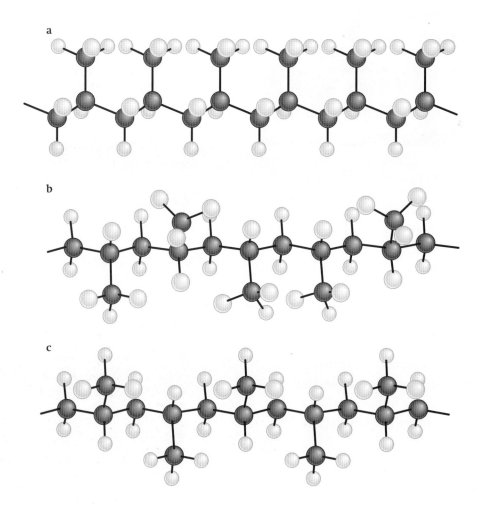

● **Figure 7.4** Molecular models of the three forms of poly(propene):
a isotactic poly(propene), **b** atactic poly(propene), **c** syndiotactic poly(propene).

Properties	Structure	Uses
Isotactic poly(propene): regular structure, a rigid, tough, crystalline polymer which can withstand heat	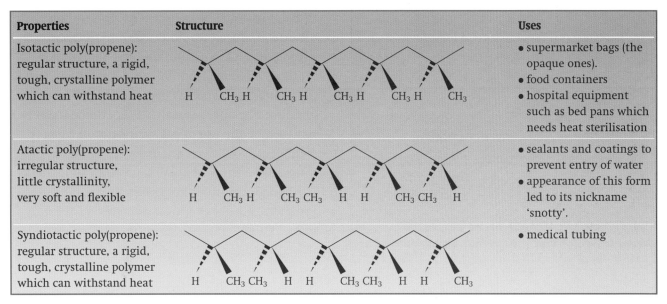	• supermarket bags (the opaque ones). • food containers • hospital equipment such as bed pans which needs heat sterilisation
Atactic poly(propene): irregular structure, little crystallinity, very soft and flexible		• sealants and coatings to prevent entry of water • appearance of this form led to its nickname 'snotty'.
Syndiotactic poly(propene): regular structure, a rigid, tough, crystalline polymer which can withstand heat		• medical tubing

• **Table 7.1** Structures, properties and uses of poly(propene).

the polymer chain and the other. This is known as **syndiotactic** poly(propene) (*figure 7.4c*). Only the isotactic and syndiotactic forms are stereoregular.

In *figure 7.4* molecular models of short sections of poly(propene) show the different structures of the three types. Ziegler and Natta shared the 1963 Nobel Prize for Chemistry for their work on these new polymerisation catalysts.

Table 7.1 shows the molecular structures, properties and uses of these three polymers.

SAQ 7.2

Atactic and isotactic forms of pvc are shown in the following molecular models.

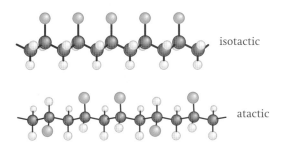

isotactic

atactic

a Draw three-dimensional formulae to show isotactic and atactic forms of pvc.

b How will isotactic and atactic forms of pvc differ in their:
 (i) hardness and rigidity
 (ii) resistance to heat?

c Explain your answers to part **b** in terms of inter-molecular forces.

Processing of poly(alkene)s

Poly(alkene)s are thermoplastic, so they are easily made into different products by a variety of techniques. The molten polymer may be forced under pressure into a mould (**injection moulding**) or forced through a die to form pipes or other continuously moulded shapes (**extrusion moulding**). Fibres are produced by forcing the molten polymer through a die with fine holes (a spinneret). The emerging polymer is cooled in an air current to produce a continuous filament which may be spun into a yarn (the process is called **melt spinning**). Alternatively, a softened polymer sheet can be moulded into a shape under reduced pressure (**vacuum forming**) or under increased air pressure (**blow moulding**). An example of one of these techniques is shown in *figure 7.5*.

• **Figure 7.5** A stage in the production of poly(ethene) film.

● **Figure 7.6** Polymer waste is not easy to dispose of – it is usually not biodegradable.

Disposing of poly(alkene)s

The use of poly(alkene)s has created a major problem when we wish to dispose of them. Sights like that shown in *figure 7.6* are only too familiar. As they are alkanes, they break down very slowly in the environment. They are resistant to most chemicals and to bacteria (they are non-biodegradable). It would be sensible to collect waste poly(alkene)s, sort them and recycle them into new products (*figure 7.7*). However, the current costs of recycling (in terms of the energy used in collecting and reprocessing the material) are often greater than those required for making new material. One alternative is to burn the poly(alkene)s to provide energy. They are potentially good fuels as they are hydrocarbons, and they would reduce the amount of oil or other fossil fuels burned. They could be burnt with other combustible household waste, saving considerable landfill costs and providing a substantial alternative energy source. Modern technology is such that the waste could be burnt cleanly and with less pollution than from traditional, fossil-fuel power stations. The carbon dioxide produced would not add to the total emissions of this 'greenhouse gas' but would replace emissions from burning fossil fuels. Other pollutant gases, such as hydrogen chloride (produced by burning poly(chloroethene)), can be removed by the use of gas scrubbers. In a gas scrubber, acidic gases are dissolved and neutralised in a spray of alkali. European Union legislation requires household waste incinerators to use them. A second option is to subject the polymers to high-temperature pyrolysis. This enables the polymers to be broken down into smaller, useful molecules. This is a process similar to the cracking of alkanes (*Chemistry 1*, chapter 8).

SAQ 7.3

Suggest some small molecules that might be produced by pyrolysis of poly(ethene). Explain how your suggestions would be useful.

Condensation polymerisation

Polyester formation

A significant proportion of clothing is made using polyester fibre. Polyester is also used to make plastic bottles for drinks (*figure 7.8*). Polyester is made by polymerising ethane-1,2-diol with benzene-1,4-dicarboxylic acid (terephthalic acid). As each ester link is made, a water molecule is lost – a condensation reaction occurs. So the formation of a polyester is an example of **condensation polymerisation**. The reaction requires a catalyst

● **Figure 7.7** Recycling polymers is one way of combating the problem of polymer waste.

● **Figure 7.8** Poly(ethylene terephthalate), a polyester, is widely used for drinks bottles as a replacement for glass.

such as antimony(III) oxide at about 280 °C. An equation for the reaction is:

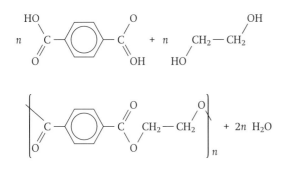

The resulting polymer is fairly rigid because of the 1,4 links across the benzene ring. The 1,4 links produce a more linear polymer, which enables the polymer chains to pack more closely. Close-packing produces strong intermolecular forces, which enable the polymer to be spun into strong threads for the clothing industry.

SAQ 7.4

The external mirror housings of some vehicles have been made from PBT, or poly(butylene terephthalate). This material provides excellent protection to the mirror glass whilst driving off-road. The structure of PBT is:

Draw displayed formulae to show the two monomers used to make PBT. Write an equation for the reaction.

Polyamide formation

Wallace Carothers carried out research for Du Pont in 1928 in order to find new polymers that might be used for making fabric. At that time, it was known that wool and silk were proteins and that they contained the peptide linkage, −NHCO−. Because of this, Carothers set out to make polymers systematically, using condensation reactions involving amines and carboxylic acids.

In order to make a polymer, he realised that he needed monomers which had two functional groups present. The monomer could have an amino group at one end and a carboxylic acid

group at the other. Alternatively, two monomer units could be used, one with an amino group at both ends, the other with a carboxylic acid group at both ends. Both approaches led to the discovery of new polymers, which are now widely used to make fibres.

Use of the diamine, 1,6-diaminohexane, together with the dicarboxylic acid, hexanedioic acid (commonly called adipic acid) produces a nylon called nylon-6,6. An amino group undergoes a condensation reaction with a carboxylic acid group. A water molecule is released and a C−N bond is formed. This can occur at each end of the two monomer molecules, so a condensation polymerisation is possible:

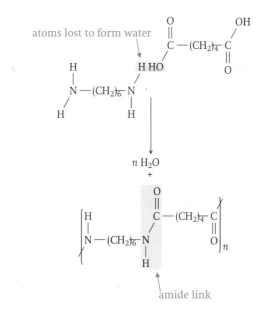

The product is a long chain of alternating monomer residues linked by amide groups, −NHCO−. Such polymers are called **polyamides**. Notice that each of the two monomer units contains six carbon atoms. This is why it is called nylon-6,6. Nylons are given names that indicate the number of carbon atoms in each monomer unit.

Nylon-6 is made from a single monomer containing six carbon atoms. This monomer is caprolactam, a cyclic amide. The caprolactam ring is polymerised to nylon-6 by heating:

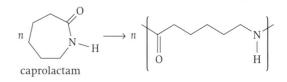

caprolactam

Caprolactam is formed from 6-aminohexanoic acid by a condensation reaction:

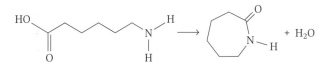

SAQ 7.5

Kevlar is a polyamide made by Du Pont. It has some remarkable properties, including fire resistance and a much higher tensile strength than steel. Kevlar is being used to make protective clothing for fire-fighters, bullet-proof vests, crash helmets for motor cyclists and tail fins for jumbo jets, and it is used instead of steel in radial tyres. The structure of this remarkable polymer is:

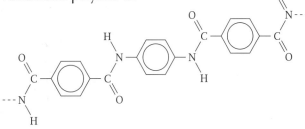

Draw a displayed formula to show the repeat unit in Kevlar and label the amide link clearly. Draw displayed formulae of the two monomer units required to make Kevlar. Write a balanced equation for the reaction.

Nylon forms a very strong fibre by melt spinning, during which the molecules become oriented along the axis of the fibre. This increases the opportunities for hydrogen bonds to form between the molecules. The hydrogen bonds also provide nylon with greater elasticity than is present in fibres without hydrogen bonds (such as poly(propene)). The hydrogen bonds tend to pull the molecules back to their original positions after the fibre has been stretched. This is why nylon is the most popular fibre for making tights. Tights made from many other fibres would tend to sag and lose their shape. The combination of strength and elasticity are also important properties in a climbing rope (*figure 7.9*).

Proteins and polypeptides

Twenty α-amino acids occur naturally in the human body. These make up a wide variety of natural polymers known as peptides and proteins. Peptides are smaller molecules than proteins. *Figure 7.10* shows the structure of a protein.

Peptides and proteins are formed by condensation polymerisation. A peptide link is formed between two amino acids with the loss of a water molecule. A peptide link may also be called an amide link. Hence both polyamides and proteins contain monomer units joined by the same link. You can find more about peptides and proteins in chapter 5.

● **Figure 7.9** Alex climbing Quietus on Stanage Edge, UK. He is using nylon rope and slings for protection. Nylon has a very high tensile strength, coupled with considerable elasticity. Climbers rely on these properties to minimise the effects of a fall.

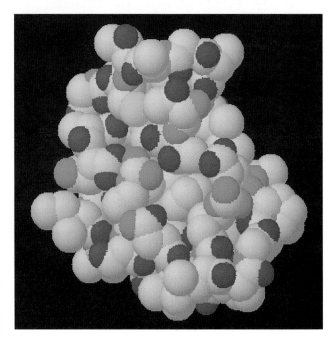

● **Figure 7.10** Structure of a relatively small protein. You can explore protein structures by visiting http://www.rcsb.org/pdb/

SUMMARY

- Polymers are macromolecules that are built up from a very large number of small molecules known as monomers.

- Natural polymers include proteins, DNA and rubber. Many synthetic polymers have been discovered by accident (for example, poly(ethene) and Bakelite®). Polymers are now being designed to fulfil specific functions.

- The properties of polymers depend on chain length, intermolecular forces, degree of chain branching, crystallinity and additives.

- Addition polymerisation occurs when a monomer joins to itself by an addition reaction. Alkenes polymerise in this way. Poly(ethene), poly(chloroethene) and poly(phenylethene) are important alkene polymers.

- Propene may be polymerised by Ziegler–Natta catalysts to produce stereo-regular polymers described as isotactic or syndiotactic. Isotactic poly(propene) has all the methyl groups on one side. In syndio-tactic poly(propene), the methyl groups alternate from one side of the chain to the other. Such polymers have very regular structures with closely packed chains. Intermolecular forces are greater than in atactic poly(propene). The methyl groups in atactic poly(propene) are arranged ran-domly on each side of the polymer chain, preventing close packing. Isotactic and syn-diotactic poly(propene) are denser, harder and more rigid than other forms of poly(propene). Atactic poly(propene) is soft, flexible and melts at a lower temperature than isotactic or atactic poly(propene).

- Poly(alkene)s are non-biodegradable and are also very resistant to chemical decomposi-tion. Disposal of poly(alkene) waste has become a problem. The waste may be buried or recycled and reprocessed. Alternatively, poly(alkene) waste may be incinerated as a 'clean' fuel. Gas scrubbers are required to remove polluting gases such as hydrogen chloride from poly(chloroethene) incineration.

- Condensation polymerisation involves the loss of a small molecule (usually water) in the reaction between two monomer mole-cules. Both polyesters and polyamides are formed by condensation polymerisation.

- Polyester is formed by condensation poly-merisation of benzene-1,4-dicarboxylic acid with ethane-1,2-diol.

- Polyamides are formed by condensation polymerisation between an amine group and a carboxylic acid group. These groups may be at either end of the same monomer or on different monomers. Nylon-6,6 is formed in a condensation polymerisation between 1,6-diaminohexane and hexane-dioic acid. Nylon-6 is formed by heating caprolactam, which is produced from 6-aminohexanoic acid in a condensation reaction. The numbers in the names for nylons refer to the number of carbon atoms present in the monomers.

- Condensation polymerisation between the amino and carboxylic acid groups in amino acids produces a polypeptide or protein. The amide links in these polymers are known as peptide links.

Questions

1   Perspex is an acrylic polymer produced from the monomer methyl 2-methyl-propenoate, shown below.

$$\begin{array}{c} H \\ \diagdown \\ \diagup \\ H \end{array} C = C \begin{array}{c} COOCH_3 \\ \diagup \\ \diagdown \\ CH_3 \end{array}$$

methyl 2-methylpropenoate

   a   (i) Suggest the type of polymerisation undergone by methyl 2-methyl-propenoate.
       (ii) Draw a section of the Perspex polymer chain produced by the polymerisation of methyl 2-methyl-propenoate. On your diagram, circle the repeating unit in the polymer.
   b   Identify the **types** of intermolecular forces in Perspex and in poly(propene).
   c   Atactic poly(propene) has randomly arranged polymer chains. It is a soft, flexible material which melts at a low temperature. Isotactic poly(propene) is a rigid, tough, heat-resistant polymer.
       (i) Explain, with the aid of structural formulae, the meaning of the terms **atactic** and **isotactic**.
       (ii) Suggest why a close-packed poly-mer is tougher and has greater resistance to heat than a randomly arranged polymer.

2   Kevlar is formed by a condensation polymerisation reaction.
   a   Explain the term **condensation polymerisation**.
   b   A section of Kevlar is shown below.

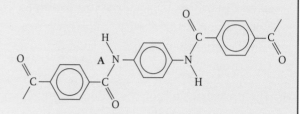

       (i) Identify the functional group at **A**.
       (ii) Use brackets to show the smallest repeating unit in the polymer chain.
       (iii) Draw the structural formulae of the two monomers used to form Kevlar.

CHAPTER 8

Spectroscopy

By the end of this chapter you should be able to:

1 use a simple *infrared spectrum* to identify the presence of functional groups in a molecule (limited to alcohols, OH, carbonyl compounds, C=O, carboxylic acids, COOH, and esters, COOR);

2 use the *molecular ion peak* in a *mass spectrum* to determine the relative molecular mass of an organic molecule;

3 predict, from the *high-resolution n.m.r. spectrum* of a simple molecule containing carbon, hydrogen and/or oxygen, the different types of proton present from *chemical shift* values, the relative numbers of each type of proton present from the relative peak area, the number of protons adjacent to a given proton from the *spin–spin splitting pattern*, limited to splitting patterns up to a quadruplet only, and possible structures for the molecule;

4 predict the chemical shifts and splitting patterns of the protons in a given molecule;

5 describe the use of D_2O to identify the n.m.r. signal from –OH groups.

Before the last century, the determination of organic structures was a difficult and time-consuming process. One trial-and-error approach was to build the suggested structure of a compound by synthesising it from simpler compounds of known structure. The synthetic product was then compared to the compound for which a structure was required. If both compounds had the same physical and chemical properties, they were likely to have the same structure.

Chemists now have a wide range of physical methods available for identifying the structure of a compound. In *Chemistry 1*, you met two of these methods, mass spectrometry and infrared spectroscopy. In particular, in *Chemistry 1*, chapter 2, you saw how mass spectrometry could be used to determine the mass number and percentage of each isotope present in a sample of an element. From such data, we can determine the relative atomic mass of the element. In *Chemistry 1*, chapter 11, infrared spectroscopy was used to identify the functional groups >C=O and –OH in simple organic compounds such as alcohols or carboxylic acids.

Infrared spectroscopy

The technique of infrared spectroscopy declined as n.m.r. spectrometers (see page 69) became more sophisticated. However, the introduction of modern infrared spectrometers has led to a resurgence of use of this once popular analytical technique. Modern infrared spectrometers (*figure 8.1*, overleaf) are able to make use of sophisticated mathematical processing that enables spectra to be obtained from a much wider range of specimens. No special preparation is required with the most recent spectrometers and an infrared spectrum can, for example, be obtained from the surface of a solid sample. Earlier infrared spectrometers required time-consuming preparation of the sample before a spectrum could be recorded. In particular, modern infrared spectrometers are finding use in many areas, such as

- in forensic science, for example to identify paint samples following hit-and-run accidents – a knowledge of the composition of a paint sample can narrow the search for the driver of a car which failed to stop;

● **Figure 8.1** This infrared spectrometer is used to monitor levels of NO_2 in the atmosphere.

- to rapidly identify different samples of polymers – this could help recycling, enabling separation of different polymers;
- to identify compounds absorbed by a surface – This might be used to monitor health and safety in a laboratory where, for example, potential new medicines or pesticides were being synthesised, as both the flooring material and the surface of the bench can be checked for contamination.

In a modern infrared spectrometer, a beam of infrared radiation is passed through a sample. Computer analysis enables the absorbance of radiation to be measured at different frequencies. Study of the resulting spectrum enables the presence (or absence) of particular functional groups to be established. *Figure 8.2* shows the infrared spectrum of 2-hydroxybenzoic acid, which has the following structure:

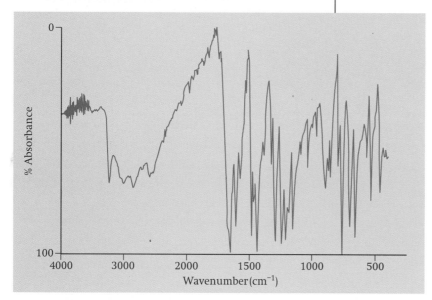

● **Figure 8.2** The infrared spectrum of 2-hydroxybenzoic acid.

Notice in *figure 8.2* that absorbance is shown increasing in a downward direction. An unusual unit is used to measure frequency, the wavenumber or cm^{-1} (in other words, the number of waves in 1 cm).

Table 8.1 shows the absorptions which we shall use in this chapter.

Look again at the infrared spectrum of 2-hydroxybenzoic acid in *figure 8.2*. Most of the absorptions are sharp, some overlap. The absorptions of interest are

1 the medium very broad absorption between 2500 and 3200 cm^{-1}, which is due in part to the presence of the carboxylic acid O–H group;

2 the sharper absorption at about 3250 cm^{-1}, which is likely to be due to the phenolic O–H group, free of hydrogen bonding;

Bond	Location	Wavenumber (cm^{-1})	Absorbance
O–H	hydrogen-bonded alcohols and phenols	3200–3600	strong, broad
O–H	free of hydrogen bonds in alcohols	3580–3670	medium–strong
O–H	hydrogen-bonded carboxylic acids	2500–3300	medium, very broad
C–O	alcohols, esters	1000–1300	strong
C=O	aldehydes, ketones, carboxylic acids and esters	1680–1750	strong, sharp

● **Table 8.1** Infrared absorption frequencies.

3 the sharp absorption at about 1660 cm^{-1}, due to the carboxylic acid >C=O group;

4 the strong absorptions between 1000 and 1300 cm^{-1} – as there are several of these we cannot be certain which is due to the carboxylic acid C–O group.

If 2-hydroxybenzoic acid is refluxed with ethanoic anhydride, (CH$_3$CO)$_2$O, in the presence of concentrated sulphuric acid as a catalyst, aspirin (see page 51) is formed:

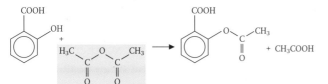

How do we know that aspirin is present? The infrared spectrum of a sample of aspirin is shown in *figure 8.3*. Note the presence of the following absorptions:

1 the strong broad absorption between 2500 and 3100 cm^{-1}, as in 2-hydroxybenzoic acid – again this is due in part to the presence of the carboxylic acid O–H group.

2 the two absorptions at 1690 and 1760 cm^{-1} due to the presence of two carboxyl >C=O groups. each in a different environment.

Note the absence of the sharp absorption at 3250 cm^{-1} from the O–H group in 2-hydroxybenzoic acid – this group is no longer present in aspirin.

SAQ 8.1

Explain how the two carboxyl groups in aspirin lead to a different environment for the two >C=O groups.

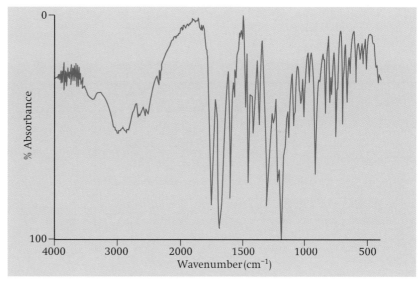

● **Figure 8.3** The infrared spectrum of aspirin.

SAQ 8.2

Figure 8.4 shows the infrared spectrum and a molecular model for paracetamol. Like aspirin, paracetamol is a widely used analgesic (pain killer).

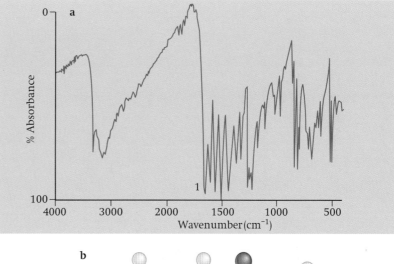

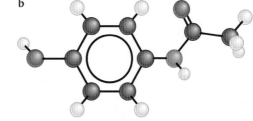

● **Figure 8.4a** The infrared spectrum of paracetamol. **b** Molecular model of paracetamol.

a Using the molecular model of paracetamol in *figure 8.4b*, draw the structural formula of paracetamol.

b Use the infrared spectrum in *figure 8.4a* to record the frequency of the absorption labelled **1**. Identify the bond that you would give rise to this absorption by labelling it '**1**' on your structure.

Mass spectrometry

In *Chemistry 1*, chapter 2, you were introduced to the use of a mass spectrometer for the determination of relative atomic masses from relative isotopic masses and percentage abundance. A mass spectrometer may also be used to determine relative molecular masses. When a molecular compound is placed in a mass spectrometer, it is also ionised. The molecule will lose one electron, a positive ion will be formed and this can be detected. This ion, which will have a mass equal to the M_r of the compound is called the **molecular ion**.

Figure 8.5 shows the mass spectrum of dodecane. The molecular ion is shown by the peak with the highest mass/charge ratio. Hence the relative molecular mass of dodecane is shown by peak *M*, which has a mass/charge ratio of 170. The molecular formula of dodecane is $C_{12}H_{26}$ and the formula of the ion at peak *M* is $C_{12}H_{26}^+$. When writing the formula of an ion, remember to include the positive charge. You will see that the mass spectrum of dodecane shows the presence of many other ions of lower mass/charge ratios. These correspond to fragment ions with the formulae shown on the spectrum. You will learn more about the use of such ions in determining the structure of an organic compound if you study the *Methods of Analysis and Detection* optional module.

In some larger molecules, care is needed in selecting the molecular ion. This may occur when the relative abundance of the molecular ion is high compared to the fragment ions. The presence of about 1% of naturally occurring carbon-13 often means a smaller peak is visible at one mass unit above the molecular ion peak. An example is shown in the mass spectrum of another hydrocarbon shown in *figure 8.6*. The small peak is labelled the *M* + 1 peak to help distinguish it from the main molecular ion peak. The *M* + 1 peak shows the percentage abundance of molecules with one carbon-13 atom present in place of a carbon-12 atom.

SAQ 8.3

Using the mass spectrum in *figure 8.6*, determine the relative molecular mass of the hydrocarbon present. Be careful to use the larger peak, labelled *M*.

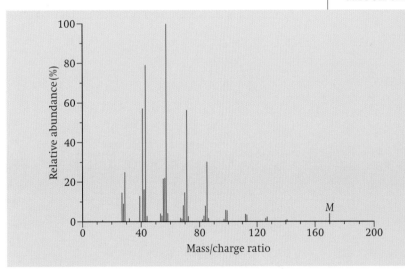

● **Figure 8.5** The mass spectrum of dodecane.

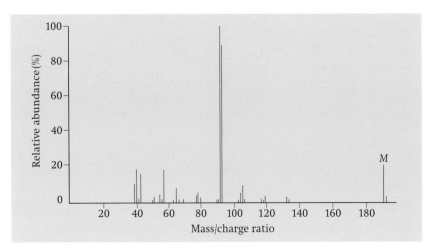

● **Figure 8.6** The mass spectrum of a hydrocarbon.

● **Figure 8.7** A mobile mass spectrometer used for environmental chemical analysis.

Analytical applications of the mass spectrometer

Water analysis

The very tiny amounts of industrial and agricultural organic chemicals that find their way into our water supplies can be monitored by means of a mass spectrometer. *Figure 8.7* shows a modern portable mass spectrometer that has been developed for this purpose. It is comforting to know that these instruments are capable of detecting such pollutants at levels well below the point where the pollutants might harm us. An example comes from SAC Scientific who have developed analytical methods for determining the concentration of triazine herbicides, which have been found in ground-water. These herbicides have been used to control weeds on railway lines, but less persistent herbicides such as glyphosphate (Tumbleweed), which rapidly breaks down in soil into harmless products, are now being used.

Drug analysis

In most sports competitions, a careful watch is kept for athletes who may have taken drugs to enhance their performance (*figure 8.8*). Mass spectrometry is linked with gas–liquid chromatography to provide a rapid method of detecting tiny quantities of a drug in a sample of blood or urine.

● **Figure 8.8** Drug analysis is needed to detect the use of performance-enhancing drugs by athletes.

Nuclear magnetic resonance spectroscopy

Nuclear magnetic resonance spectroscopy (n.m.r. spectroscopy) is a particularly powerful tool for the determination of the structure of a compound. In only a few minutes, it is possible for a chemist to have established the absolute structure for a simple organic compound. The technique can even be used to determine the structures of quite complex organic compounds. For this reason, it is a very popular method among chemists.

N.m.r. spectroscopy was developed from work by both chemists and nuclear physicists. The technique relies on the interaction between magnetic properties of certain nuclei and their chemical environment. Some nuclei (with odd mass numbers such as ^1H or ^{13}C) have a property called 'spin' (like electrons). This spin gives the nuclei magnetic properties so that they behave like very small bar magnets. When a sample of a compound containing such nuclei is placed in a large magnetic field, a small majority of nuclei will line up in the same direction as the magnetic field (parallel to the field). The remaining nuclei will line up in the opposite direction (anti-parallel).

The nuclei aligned parallel to the magnetic field are at a lower energy to those aligned anti-parallel. The difference in energy is of the same frequency as electromagnetic radiation in the radio-frequency range. By subjecting the sample to a pulse of radio-frequency radiation, some of the nuclei will flip from the parallel to the anti-parallel alignment (*figure 8.9* overleaf).

Because electrons surround the nuclei, the energy needed for resonance varies slightly, depending on the local chemical environment. This slight variation is the key to structure determination. In the following section we shall focus on the use of proton n.m.r spectroscopy. This will enable the positions of protons (hydrogen atoms) in a compound to be determined.

Use of n.m.r. to determine the structure of ethanol

A low-resolution n.m.r spectrum of ethanol consists of three lines, as shown in *figure 8.10*. You will notice several features in this spectrum:

■ Unusually, the horizontal scale increases from right to left.
■ The scale is labelled in terms of chemical shift, δ (ppm). The

small peak at 0 ppm is due to a compound, tetramethylsilane, (TMS, $(CH_3)_4Si$), which is used as a reference standard.

■ The spectrum consists of three sharp peaks. The numbers at the top of each peak show the relative areas of each peak. The relative numbers of each type of proton are shown by relative peak areas.

Ethanol has protons in three different chemical environments. Look at the structure of ethanol: CH_3CH_2OH. There are three protons on the first carbon, two on the second carbon and one on the oxygen atom. Each atom has different neighbours and so has a different chemical environment. Notice that these numbers correspond to the relative peak areas in the n.m.r. spectrum of ethanol. The peak at about 1.2 ppm is due to the CH_3- protons; that at about 3.7 ppm is due to the $-CH_2-$ protons and that at about 5.4 ppm to the $-OH$ proton. For ethanol, a low-resolution spectrum confirms the structure.

It is not always so easy to establish a structure from a low-resolution spectrum. Indeed such spectra are not usually recorded. More information can be obtained from a high-resolution spectrum, as we shall see.

The high-resolution spectrum of ethanol is shown in *Figure 8.11*. Notice that there are still three main groups of peaks, with areas in

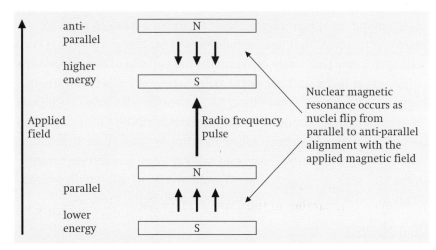

● Figure 8.9 A nucleus may flip from parallel to anti-parallel alignment on absorption of energy from radio frequency radiation.

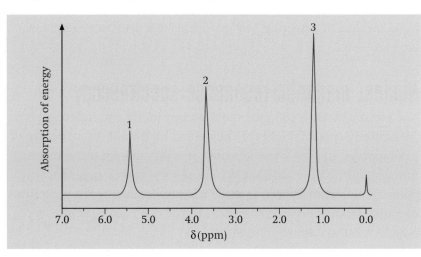

● Figure 8.10 Low-resolution n.m.r. spectrum of ethanol.

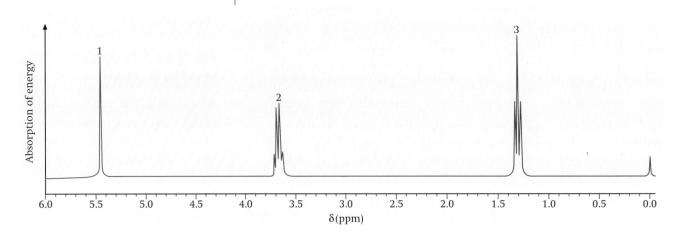

● Figure 8.11 High-resolution n.m.r. spectrum of ethanol.

the same ratio. However, two of the peaks are split. The CH_3- peak is split into a triplet, whilst the $-CH_2-$ peak is split into a quartet. This splitting is caused by spins of protons on adjacent carbon atoms coupling with each other. A proton on an adjacent carbon will produce a small difference in the magnetic field experienced by a proton. The difference depends on whether the spin of the adjacent proton is parallel or anti-parallel to the applied magnetic field. Protons on the same carbon atom are equivalent and do not affect each other.

Consider a single proton, for example the $-CH-$ proton in $CH_3CH(OH)COOH$. In this compound (lactic acid) there are three equivalent methyl (CH_3-) protons. The signal for these will be split into two signals (a doublet) of almost equal intensity as slightly more than half of the $-CH-$ protons will have parallel spins, the rest being anti-parallel.

However, if we consider the arrangements of spin for the $-CH_2-$ protons in ethanol, CH_3CH_2OH, we find more possibilities arise. We find that the methyl protons (CH_3-) are now split into a triplet of ratio 1:2:1. This ratio reflects the possible arrangements, shown in *figure 8.12*.

There is a general rule for predicting the number of signals in the splitting pattern of

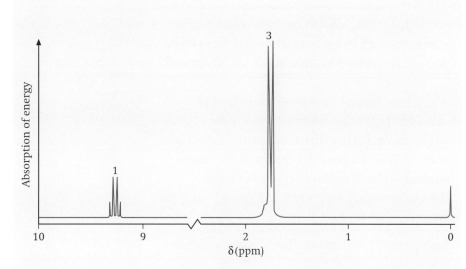

● **Figure 8.13** The n.m.r spectrum of an unknown molecule, C_2H_4O.

protons on a carbon atom by protons on an adjacent carbon. It is known as the $n + 1$ rule, where n = number of protons on the adjacent carbon. Hence for a $-CH-$ proton, $n = 1$ so $n + 1 = 2$, and a doublet is produced. For $-CH_2-$, a triplet results and for CH_3-, a quartet.

Type of proton	Chemical shift, δ (ppm)
$R-CH_3$	0.7–1.6
$R-CH_2-R$	1.2–1.4
R_3CH	1.6–2.0
$-\overset{O}{\overset{\|}{C}}-CH_3$ $-\overset{O}{\overset{\|}{C}}-CH_2-R$	2.0–2.9
⬡$-CH_3$ ⬡$-CH_2-R$	2.3–2.7
$-O-CH_3$ $-O-CH_2-R$	3.3–4.3
$R-OH$	3.5–5.5
⬡$-OH$	6.5–7.0
⬡$-H$	7.1–7.7
$R-\overset{O}{\overset{\|}{C}}-H$ ⬡$-\overset{O}{\overset{\|}{C}}-H$	9.5–10
$-\overset{O}{\overset{\|}{C}}-OH$	11.0–11.7

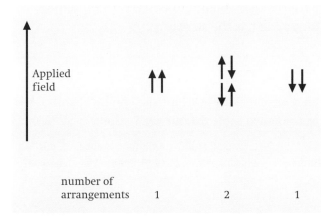

● **Figure 8.12** The arrangements possible for the two protons in $-CH_2-$. In ethanol, the $-CH_2-$ protons cause the CH_3- peak to be split into a triplet with a 1:2:1 ratio.

● **Table 8.2** Chemical shifts for some types of proton in n.m.r. spectra. All chemical shifts are relative to tetramethylsilane (TMS), $\delta = 0$ ppm. The symbol 'R' represents an alkyl group.

SAQ 8.4

By considering the possible arrangements of spin for the protons in a CH_3- group, show that the splitting of the $-CH_2-$ protons in ethanol is a 1:3:3:1 quartet.

We will now look at the interpretation of the n.m.r. spectrum of an unknown molecule of molecular formula, C_2H_4O. The spectrum is shown in *figure 8.13. Table 8.2* provides information on the chemical shifts of different types of proton.

The information contained in *figure 8.13* may be summarised in *table 8.3*.

Chemical shift, δ (ppm)	Relative number of protons	Splitting pattern
2.2	3	doublet
9.8	1	quartet

● **Table 8.3**

From the splitting patterns given, the following can be deduced:

■ to produce a quartet the single proton at chemical shift 9.8 must be adjacent to a $-CH_3$ group.

■ to produce a doublet the three protons at chemical shift 2.2 must be adjacent to a $-CH-$ proton.

The types of proton are shown in *table 8.4*.

Chemical shift, δ (ppm)	Type of proton
2.2	$\begin{matrix} & O \\ & \| \\ CH_3- & C-R \end{matrix}$
9.8	$\begin{matrix} & O \\ & \| \\ R- & C-H \end{matrix}$

● **Table 8.4**

The structure of the compound is thus CH_3CHO (ethanal), which agrees with the molecular formula of C_2H_4O.

SAQ 8.5

A compound has the molecular formula $C_4H_8O_2$. The n.m.r. spectrum of this compound is shown in *figure 8.14*. The compound shows a strong sharp absorption in its infrared spectrum at $1750\,cm^{-1}$.

a Summarise the information from the n.m.r. spectrum in a table similar to *table 8.3*.

b From the splitting patterns, deduce which protons are on adjacent carbon atoms.

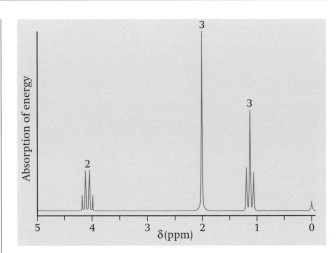

● **Figure 8.14** The n.m.r. spectrum of the compound with molecular formula $C_4H_8O_2$.

c Use *table 8.2*, together with the infrared data given above, to identify the types of proton present.

d Deduce the structural formula for this compound.

Predicting an n.m.r. spectrum

When chemists set out to synthesise a compound, they may predict the n.m.r. spectrum of the desired compound. They can then compare the spectrum of the product with that of their desired compound. Computer programs are now available to make predictions of n.m.r. spectra from chemical structures. However, you will not be able to use such a program in an examination when you are asked to predict the spectrum of a simple compound. Fortunately, the process is quite straightforward for simple compounds, as the following example shows.

Suggest the chemical shifts and splitting patterns that you might observe for butanone. Butanone has the structure

$$CH_3 \diagdown \underset{CH_2}{} \overset{\overset{\textstyle O}{\textstyle\|}}{C} \diagdown CH_3$$

First we check *table 8.2* for the chemical shifts. We can create a table for our predictions.

Type of proton	Chemical shift, δ (ppm)	Relative number of protons	Splitting pattern
CH_3-R	1.2	3	triplet
$\begin{matrix} O \\ \| \\ -C-CH_3 \end{matrix}$	2.0–2.9	3	singlet
$\begin{matrix} O \\ \| \\ -C-CH_2-R \end{matrix}$	2.0–2.9	2	quartet

The n.m.r. spectrum for butanone is shown in *figure 8.15*. Note that both –CH_3 protons are outside the range given in *table 8.2*. The ranges given in *table 8.2* may not always be appropriate. The chemical shift for a particular group of protons can be affected by factors outside the molecule such as the solvent used to run the spectrum.

SAQ 8.6

Suggest the chemical shifts and splitting patterns that you might observe for methyl propanoate.

Identifying the –OH signal

The –OH signal in the high-resolution n.m.r. spectrum of ethanol appears as a single peak. You may have wondered why the signal is not split by the protons on the neighbouring –CH_2– group. The reason for this is that the –OH proton exchanges very rapidly with protons in traces of water (or acid) present as follows. The hydrogen atoms involved in this reversible exchange have been coloured red and blue to help you to see what takes place.

$$CH_3CH_2OH + H_2O \rightleftharpoons CH_3CH_2OH + HOH$$

This exchange is so rapid that the signal for the –OH protons becomes a single peak.

Table 8.2 shows that –OH signals range from a chemical shift of 3.5–5.5 (for R–**OH** protons) through 6.5–7.0 (for phenol protons) to 11.0–11.7 (for carboxylic acid protons). Some of these ranges overlap with the signals for other protons and can make an n.m.r. spectrum less clear.

Fortunately, there is a simple remedy to this lack of clarity. The signal for the –OH group can be easily removed from the spectrum by adding a small amount of deuterium oxide, D_2O, to the n.m.r. sample. The deuterium atoms in D_2O exchange reversibly with the protons in the –OH groups:

$$-OH + D_2O \rightleftharpoons -OD + HOD$$

Deuterium atoms (^2H) do not absorb in the same region of the spectrum as protons (^1H). The –OH signal disappears from the n.m.r. spectrum. This enables the –OH signal in the n.m.r. spectrum from the D_2O-free sample to be identified and any overlapping signals clarified.

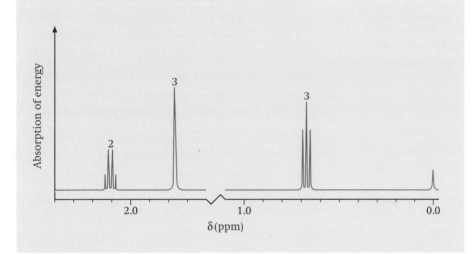

● **Figure 8.15** The n.m.r spectrum of butanone. Note that the chemical shift values differ from the predicted values. Such variation is not uncommon.

SUMMARY

◆ The infrared spectrum of a compound enables the presence of different functional groups to be established. Groups such as >C=O or –O–H absorb radiation at different frequencies in the infrared. In infrared spectroscopy frequency is measured in units of cm^{-1} (called wavenumbers).

◆ The mass spectrum of a compound enables the molecular mass of the compound to be determined using the molecular ion peak. The molecular ion peak, *M*, is the peak produced by the loss of one electron from a molecule of the compound.

◆ The n.m.r. spectrum of a compound provides detailed information about the structure of the compound. In particular, the spectrum for the protons, ^1H, in a compound can provide a complete determination of the compound's structure.

◆ Protons in different chemical environments produce signals at different chemical shifts. The chemical shift provides information about the type of proton present.

◆ The area ratios of the signals correspond to the numbers of protons in the different chemical environments.

◆ Protons on neighbouring carbon atoms cause signals to be split. The splitting pattern establishes which groups of protons are on adjacent carbon atoms. The $n + 1$ rule predicts the splitting pattern.

◆ Protons on −OH can be identified by the addition of D_2O to the n.m.r. sample, which collapses the signal due to an −OH proton.

Questions

1 The empirical formula of compound A is $C_3H_6O_2$. The mass spectrum of compound A is shown below.

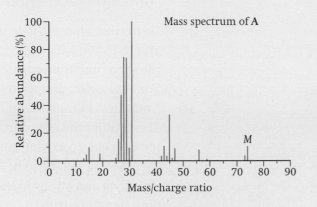

Mass spectrum of A

a Use the molecular ion peak, M, to show that the molecular formula of A is the same as its empirical formula.

The infrared spectrum of A is shown below.

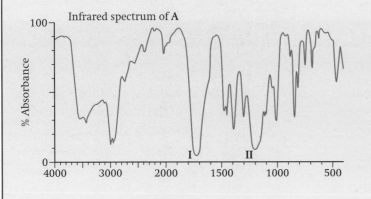

Infrared spectrum of A

b (i) Identify the types of bond which give rise to the absorptions labelled I and II in this infrared spectrum.

(ii) Draw three structural isomers of A which contain the bonds identified in part b.

The n.m.r. spectrum of A is shown below.

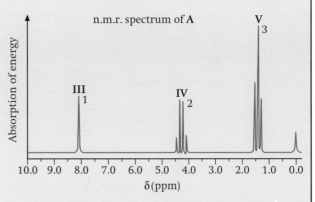

n.m.r. spectrum of A

c Suggest the identity of the protons responsible for the groups of signals labelled III, IV and V in this n.m.r. spectrum. Use the number of protons present in each group, the splitting pattern and the chemical shift to explain your reasoning.

d Suggest a possible structure for this compound, using information that you have obtained in parts a, b and c.

2 Compound **B** is an aromatic hydrocarbon
   with the molecular formula $C_8H_{10}O$.
   The infrared spectrum of **B** is given below.

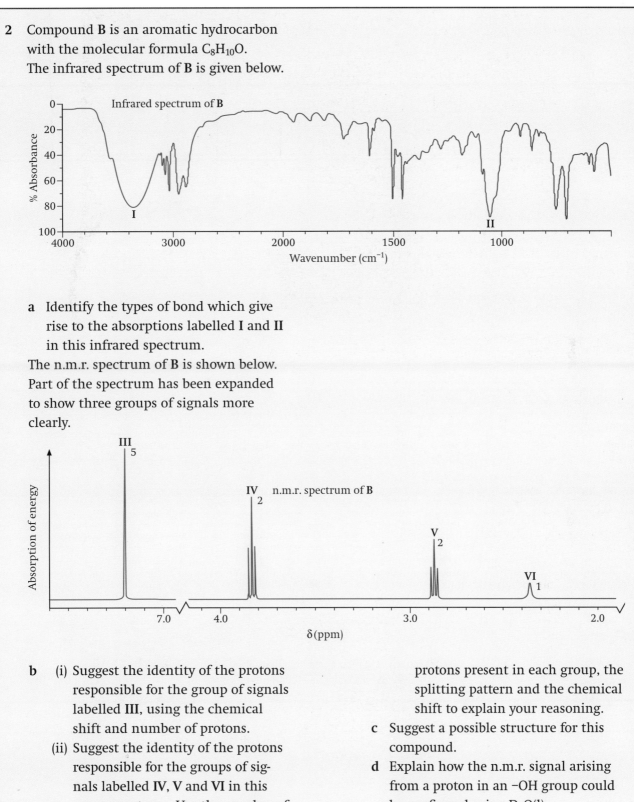

Infrared spectrum of **B**

Wavenumber (cm^{-1})

a Identify the types of bond which give
   rise to the absorptions labelled **I** and **II**
   in this infrared spectrum.

The n.m.r. spectrum of **B** is shown below.
Part of the spectrum has been expanded
to show three groups of signals more
clearly.

n.m.r. spectrum of **B**

δ (ppm)

b (i) Suggest the identity of the protons
      responsible for the group of signals
      labelled **III**, using the chemical
      shift and number of protons.
   (ii) Suggest the identity of the protons
      responsible for the groups of sig-
      nals labelled **IV, V** and **VI** in this
      n.m.r. spectrum. Use the number of
      protons present in each group, the
      splitting pattern and the chemical
      shift to explain your reasoning.
   c Suggest a possible structure for this
      compound.
   d Explain how the n.m.r. signal arising
      from a proton in an –OH group could
      be confirmed using $D_2O(l)$.

Part 2: Trends and Patterns

CHAPTER 9

Lattice enthalpy

By the end of this chapter you should be able to:

1 explain the term *lattice enthalpy* of an ionic solid;

2 construct a *Born–Haber cycle* for an ionic solid;

3 name all the enthalpy changes in a Born–Haber cycle;

4 calculate lattice enthalpy from a Born–Haber cycle;

5 explain how the charge on an ion affects its lattice enthalpy;

6 explain how the size of an ion affects its lattice enthalpy;

7 state that magnesium oxide has a large lattice enthalpy and is used as a refractory lining;

8 describe the trend in the *decomposition temperatures* of the Group II carbonates ($MgCO_3$ to $BaCO_3$);

9 explain this trend by considering the effects of the charge density of the metal cations and the *polarisation* of the carbonate anion.

Ionic compounds are familiar to all of us, chemists as well as non-chemists, probably because three of them have been used through-out history – salt (NaCl), washing soda (Na_2CO_3) and caustic soda (NaOH).

■ Salt was used to pay Roman soldiers in AD 43 and the word 'salary' is derived from the Latin for salt, *salerium argentinium*. Nowadays we are cautious about taking too much salt in our diet because this has been linked to high blood pressure, but salt has always been recognised as necessary to life. One of the most famous of Gandhi's protests against British rule in India was the Salt March of 1930, when he and his followers marched on a salt factory as a protest against the Salt Tax that prevented them mak-ing their own salt. As the marchers moved for-ward in columns they were beaten to the ground, offering no resistance.

■ Washing soda has been used for centuries to soften water for bathing and washing, and it is still used as a common household chemical today.

■ Caustic soda is used in huge quantities in the paper and soap industries and many other industries too – for instance 17 million tonnes are used every year as part of the production process for aluminium.

You have already studied the ionic bonding and lattice structure of sodium chloride (see *Chemistry 1*, chapter 3). It is important to realise that solid ionic compounds do not form as a result of the transfer of electrons only – overall, forming the ions actually *requires* energy, as you can see if you look at the energy changes involved:

$$Na(g) \rightarrow Na^+(g) + e^- \qquad \Delta H^\ominus = +496 \, kJ \, mol^{-1}$$
$$Cl(g) + e^- \rightarrow Cl^-(g) \qquad \Delta H^\ominus = -349 \, kJ \, mol^{-1}$$
$$\overline{Na(g) + Cl(g) \rightarrow Na^+(g) + Cl^-(g) \quad \Delta H^\ominus = +147 \, kJ \, mol^{-1}}$$

Yet most ionic solids form easily from their elements. So if transferring electrons is not the reason why ionic compounds form, what is? It is the *huge release in energy* that occurs when the two ions of opposite charge combine to form a solid. This is the **lattice enthalpy**, $\Delta H^{\ominus}_{latt}$.

> The lattice enthalpy, $\Delta H^{\ominus}_{latt}$ is the enthalpy change when 1 mole of an ionic compound is formed from its gaseous ions under standard conditions (298 K, 100 kPa).

The *gaseous* ions are important here – the equation representing the lattice enthalpy of sodium chloride is

$$Na^+(g) + Cl^-(g) \rightarrow NaCl(s); \qquad \Delta H^{\ominus}_{latt} = -781\ kJ\ mol^{-1}$$

You can see that the process of bringing together the separate ions in the gaseous state and putting them together into a regular lattice structure releases a large amount of energy. This large exothermic value indicates that the sodium chloride lattice is very stable, and cannot easily be pulled apart again. Of course, to actually do this process *experimentally* is impossible – how can gaseous sodium ions and chloride ions be mixed together so that a solid forms?

The way in which we measure the lattice enthalpy is by using a **Born–Haber cycle**, which is a particular type of Hess's law enthalpy cycle (see *Chemistry 1*, chapter 13). In a Born–Haber cycle every step from the elements to the ionic compound can be measured, except the lattice enthalpy. The lattice enthalpy can therefore be calculated in the usual way in a Hess's law cycle.

The lattice enthalpy is an exothermic change and always has a negative value.

SAQ 9.1

Explain what is meant by the terms:
a enthalpy change
b exothermic reaction
c endothermic reaction.

SAQ 9.2

State Hess's law.

The Born–Haber cycle

Let's go through the Born–Haber cycle for lithium fluoride step by step, as shown in *figure 9.1*.

We begin with the elements in their standard states, metallic lithium, Li(s) and gaseous diatomic fluorine, $F_2(g)$. From these we can follow two routes to obtain lithium fluoride, LiF(s).

■ Route 1 is the direct combination of the elements to give LiF(s); this is the standard enthalpy change of formation, $\Delta H^{\ominus}_f$. You have used this enthalpy change earlier (*Chemistry 1*, chapter 13).

■ Route 2 is the multi-step cycle which includes the lattice enthalpy and also gives LiF(s).

From Hess's law, we know that both paths have the same overall enthalpy change, so in route 1 $\Delta H^{\ominus}_f$ = sum of $\Delta H^{\ominus}$ for the steps in route 2.

Route 1 involves only one step, so is easily dealt with. This step is the *standard enthalpy change of formation of lithium fluoride*. The enthalpy change of formation is defined as the enthalpy change when 1 mole of a compound is formed from its elements in their standard states under standard conditions.

$$Li(s) + \tfrac{1}{2}F_2(g) \rightarrow LiF(s); \qquad \Delta H^{\ominus}_f = -617\ kJ\ mol^{-1}$$

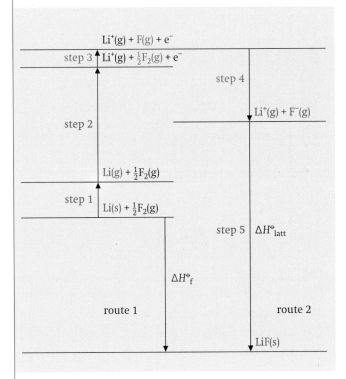

● **Figure 9.1** Born–Haber cycle for lithium fluoride.

The overall changes that take place in route 2 can be summarised as follows (see *figure 9.1*):

■ the elements are converted to individual gaseous atoms (steps 1 and 3);

■ these atoms are converted to gaseous ions (steps 2 and 4);

■ the ions form the solid (step 5).

Step 1 Converting solid lithium into separate gaseous lithium atoms is called the **standard enthalpy change of atomisation**, $\Delta H_{at}^{\ominus}$. This requires energy, so it is an endothermic change.

$$Li(s) \rightarrow Li(g); \qquad \Delta H_{at}^{\ominus} = +161\,kJ\,mol^{-1}$$

> The **standard enthalpy change of atomisation** of an element is the enthalpy change when one mole of gaseous atoms are formed from the element in its standard state.

Step 2 This step involves removing 1 mole of electrons from 1 mole of Li to form 1 mole of Li^+. Once again, this is an endothermic change. It is called the **ionisation energy**, $\Delta H_{i1}^{\ominus}$. (You met ionisation energies in *Chemistry 1*, chapter 1.)

$$Li(s) \rightarrow Li(g) + e^-; \qquad \Delta H_{i1}^{\ominus} = +520\,kJ\,mol^{-1}$$

Step 3 This is another enthalpy change of atomisation, but this time half a mole of fluorine *molecules*, $\frac{1}{2}F_2(g)$, are being converted into 1 mole of fluorine *atoms*, $F(g)$. This again is an endothermic change and it is equal to half the bond enthalpy of F_2. (You met bond enthalpies in *Chemistry 1*, chapter 13.)

$$\tfrac{1}{2}F_2(g) \rightarrow F(g); \qquad \Delta H_{at}^{\ominus} = \tfrac{1}{2}(+159) = +79.5\,kJ\,mol^{-1}$$

Step 4 Adding an electron to F to form F^- is the **electron affinity**, $\Delta H_{ea1}^{\ominus}$. This is an exothermic change – the only exothermic change in this path of the Born–Haber cycle.

$$F(g) + e^- \rightarrow F^-(g); \qquad \Delta H_{ea1}^{\ominus} = -328\,kJ\,mol^{-1}$$

> The **first electron affinity**, $\Delta H_{ea1}^{\ominus}$, is the enthalpy change when one electron is added to each gaseous atom in one mole, to form one mole of 1– gaseous ions:
>
> $$X(g) + e^- \rightarrow X^-(g)$$

> The **second electron affinity**, $\Delta H_{ea2}^{\ominus}$, is the enthalpy change when one electron is added to each 1– gaseous ion in one mole, to form one mole of gaseous 2– ions:
>
> $$X^-(g) + e^- \rightarrow X^{2-}(g)$$

Step 5 This step represents the **lattice enthalpy**. The two gaseous ions come together to form the ionic solid, and this is an exothermic change.

$$Li^+(g) + F^-(g) \rightarrow LiF(s)$$

The enthalpy change for this step is usually unknown and has to be calculated.

How to calculate the lattice enthalpy from a Born–Haber cycle

According to Hess's law,

$$\Delta H_f^{\ominus} = \Delta H_{at}^{\ominus}(Li(g)) + \Delta H_{at}^{\ominus}(F(g)) + \Delta H_{i1}^{\ominus} + \Delta H_{ea1}^{\ominus} + \Delta H_{latt}^{\ominus}$$

This can be rearranged;

> lattice enthalpy = $\Delta H_f^{\ominus} - \Delta H_{at}^{\ominus}(Li(g)) - \Delta H_{at}^{\ominus}(F(g)) - \Delta H_{i1}^{\ominus} - \Delta H_{ea1}^{\ominus}$

In words, the formula is:

lattice enthalpy = heat of formation – heats of atomisation – ionisation energy – electron affinity

Putting in the figures:

lattice enthalpy = $(-617) - (+161) - (+79.5) - (+520)$
$- (-328)$
$= -1049.5\,kJ\,mol^{-1}$

SAQ 9.3

Write equations to represent the following enthalpy changes:

a the atomisation of oxygen gas;

b the first ionisation energy of caesium;

c the enthalpy change of formation of potassium chloride;

d the first electron affinity of iodine;

e the atomisation of barium.

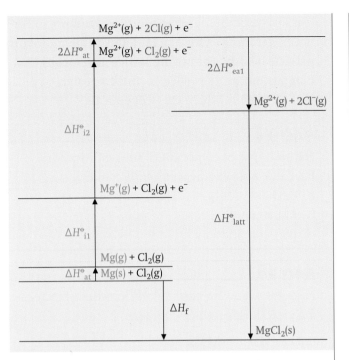

- **Figure 9.2** Born–Haber cycle for magnesium chloride.

SAQ 9.4

a Draw a Born–Haber cycle for sodium chloride, naming each step.

b Calculate the lattice enthalpy for sodium chloride, given that

$$
\begin{aligned}
\Delta H_f^\ominus \,(\text{NaCl}) &= -411\,\text{kJ mol}^{-1} \\
\Delta H_{at}^\ominus \,(\text{Na(g)}) &= +107\,\text{kJ mol}^{-1} \\
\Delta H_{at}^\ominus \,(\text{Cl}_2(\text{g})) &= +242\,\text{kJ mol}^{-1} \\
\Delta H_{i1}^\ominus \,(\text{Na(g)}) &= +496\,\text{kJ mol}^{-1} \\
\Delta H_{ea1}^\ominus \,(\text{Cl(g)}) &= -348\,\text{kJ mol}^{-1}
\end{aligned}
$$

The Born–Haber cycle for magnesium chloride

It is important that you know the Born–Haber cycle for sodium chloride, so make sure you have done *SAQ 9.4* and checked the answer. Another Born–Haber cycle you must know is the one shown for magnesium chloride (*figure 9.2*). It is essentially the same as before, with the same type of steps in each path. However, the magnesium ion is Mg^{2+}, so the gaseous magnesium atom is ionised *in two stages*:

$$Mg(g) \rightarrow Mg^+(g) + e^-$$
the first ionisation energy, $\Delta H_{i1}^\ominus$

$$Mg^+(g) \rightarrow Mg^{2+}(g) + e^-$$
the second ionisation energy, $\Delta H_{i2}^\ominus$

Whenever an ion is formed, it is done in stages, losing or gaining one electron at a time. So, to get to Al^{3+}, you will use three ionisation energies:

$$Al(g) \xrightarrow{\Delta H_{i1}^\ominus} Al^+(g) + e^- \xrightarrow{\Delta H_{i2}^\ominus} Al^{2+}(g) + 2e^- \xrightarrow{\Delta H_{i3}^\ominus} Al^{3+}(g) + 3e^-$$

The same principle applies to anions. To form O^{2-}, you will use two electron affinities:

$$O(g) + e^- \xrightarrow{\Delta H_{ea1}^\ominus} O^-(g); \qquad O^-(g) + e^- \xrightarrow{\Delta H_{ea2}^\ominus} O^{2-}(g)$$

One other difference to remember is that two Cl^- ions are present in $MgCl_2$, hence $2\Delta H_{at}^\ominus$ is required in the Born–Haber cycle for $MgCl_2$.

SAQ 9.5

Draw Born–Haber cycles for **a** MgO; **b** Na_2O.

Trends in the lattice enthalpy

The lattice enthalpy is the result of electrostatic attractions between ions of opposite charge. The properties of the ions can therefore affect the value of the lattice enthalpy. We will look at two different ways that the lattice enthalpy is affected.

Size of the ions

The lattice enthalpy becomes *less exothermic* as the size of the ion *increases*.

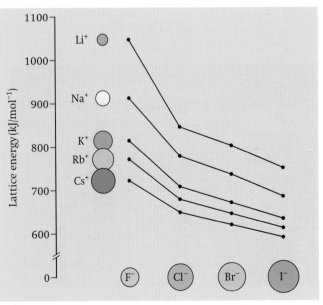

- **Figure 9.3** Lattice enthalpies of the Group I halides.

This applies to both cations and anions. The reason is that as the radius of the ion increases, the attraction between the ions decreases, so the lattice energy is less exothermic. You can see this in *figure 9.3*. The trends in the size of both the cations and the anions are shown, and you can see that the trend in lattice enthalpy is in the opposite direction.

Charge of the ions

The lattice enthalpy becomes *more exothermic* as the charge on the ion *increases*.

The effect of the charge of the ion on lattice enthalpy can be seen by comparing LiF with MgO. Both solids have the same structure, the Li^+ ion is about the same size as the Mg^{2+} ion, and the F^- ion is about the same size as the O^{2-} ion. The only difference between the two solids is the *charge* on the ions. Look at the lattice enthalpies for these two compounds:

$$LiF \quad \Delta H^{\ominus}_{latt} = -1050 \, kJ \, mol^{-1}$$
$$MgO \quad \Delta H^{\ominus}_{latt} = -3923 \, kJ \, mol^{-1}$$

They are very different. The lattice enthalpy for magnesium oxide is much more negative, which shows that doubly charged ions attract each other more strongly than singly charged ions.

This exceptionally high exothermic value for the lattice enthalpy of magnesium oxide means it is a very useful compound in certain situations. The lattice is so strong that it takes a great deal of heat to decompose it (the melting point is 2853 °C), and this means magnesium oxide is used to line furnaces – we say it is a **refractory lining** (*figure 9.4*).

● **Figure 9.4** Magnesium oxide is used as a lining in furnaces.

It is also used in high-temperature windows in furnaces, ceramics, wire coatings and flame-retardant particle boards. The strong lattice also means that magnesium oxide is used in anti-corrosion coatings in tankers which carry chemicals.

SAQ 9.6
For each pair of compounds, suggest which will have the most exothermic lattice enthalpy.
a CaO and $CaCl_2$
b KCl and K_2O
c BaI_2 and SrI_2

SAQ 9.7
Place the following compounds in order of increasingly exothermic lattice enthalpy.

Li_2O LiF   MgO

Explain why you have placed them in this order.

The stability of the Group II carbonates to heat

You have already studied the Group II elements magnesium to barium (see *Chemistry 1*, chapter 5). You looked at
■ the reaction of magnesium carbonate with acids;
■ the thermal decomposition of calcium carbonate;
■ the formation of calcium carbonate when carbon dioxide gas is bubbled through lime water.
We will now look at the decomposition of the Group II carbonates when they are heated, and see what role the lattice enthalpy plays in determining the temperature at which this decomposition takes place.

The reaction showing the thermal decomposition of the Group II carbonates is

$$MgCO_3(s) \rightarrow MgO(s) + CO_2(g)$$

This reaction is the same for all the Group II metals.

Figure 9.5 shows that the trend is increasing decomposition temperatures as the group is descended. $MgCO_3$ decomposes at 350 °C, $BaCO_3$ at 1450 °C. Let's think about this trend. What can we suggest about the lattice enthalpies of magnesium carbonate and barium carbonate?

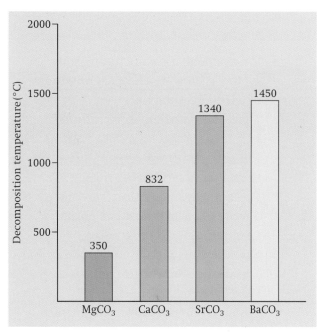

- **Figure 9.5** Decomposition temperatures of group II carbonates.

- $MgCO_3$ has the smallest cation and therefore the *most exothermic* lattice enthalpy ($-3123 \, kJ \, mol^{-1}$).
- $BaCO_3$ has the largest cation and therefore the *least exothermic* lattice enthalpy ($-2556 \, kJ \, mol^{-1}$).
  But these lattice enthalpies suggest that $MgCO_3$ has the strongest lattice and should therefore have the highest decomposition temperature.

Another factor must be considered – it is the effect of the cation's charge density on the large carbonate anion. The lattice structure of magnesium carbonate is weaker than the lattice structure of barium carbonate, and this is caused by the charge density of the cation **polarising** the anion. You have met this polarisation of the anion before in *Chemistry 1*, chapter 3. Let's go through the reasons for this again.

- The small magnesium cation has a large charge density and so it has the greatest ability to polarise the carbonate ion. The cation pulls electron density from the O atoms of the CO_3^{2-} ion towards it:

  (Mg^{2+}) (CO_3^{2-}) small Mg2+ ion polarises larger CO_3^{2-} ion

- The larger barium cation has a lower charge density so it polarises the carbonate anion to a lesser extent:

  (Ba^{2+}) (CO_3^{2-}) ions same size – no polarisation

- The greater the polarising power of the cation, the more distorted the CO_3^{2-} ion becomes.
- The distorted CO_3^{2-} breaks up into CO_2 and O^{2-} more readily.
- As a result, the $MgCO_3$ lattice is less strong than the $BaCO_3$ lattice and decomposes at a lower temperature.

SAQ 9.8

Explain why the decomposition temperature of calcium nitrate is higher than the decomposition temperature of magnesium nitrate.

SUMMARY

- The lattice enthalpy of an ionic solid is the energy change when gaseous ions form a solid lattice.

- Lattice enthalpies are exothermic. A strong lattice has a more exothermic lattice enthalpy than a weak lattice.

- Lattice enthalpies can be calculated from a Born–Haber cycle, which is a type of Hess's law cycle.

- Each step of the Born–Haber cycle is a separate enthalpy change.

- The standard enthalpy change of atomisation of an element is the enthalpy change when one mole of gaseous atoms are formed from the element in its standard state.

- The value of the lattice enthalpy is affected by the size of the ions making up the lattice, and also by their charge.

- Magnesium oxide is an example of an ionic solid with a large exothermic lattice enthalpy, and therefore it has many uses.

- The Group II carbonates decompose at increasingly high temperatures as the group is descended.

- The reason for this trend can be explained by considering the charge density of the cation and the degree of polarisation of the anion.

Questions

1 a In ionic compounds with certain metals, hydrogen exists as the hydride ion, H^-. Calculate the electron affinity of hydrogen (ΔH° for the reaction $H(g) + e^- \rightarrow H^-(g)$) by constructing a Born–Haber cycle for sodium hydride, NaH. Name each enthalpy change in the cycle.

$Na(s) \rightarrow Na(g)$
$\quad \Delta H^\circ = +108 \, kJ \, mol^{-1}$
$H_2(g) \rightarrow 2H(g)$
$\quad \Delta H^\circ = +436 \, kJ \, mol^{-1}$
$Na(g) \rightarrow Na^+(g) + e^-$
$\quad \Delta H^\circ = +496 \, kJ \, mol^{-1}$
$Na(s) + \frac{1}{2}H_2(g) \rightarrow NaH(s)$
$\quad \Delta H^\circ = -57 \, kJ \, mol^{-1}$
$Na^+(g) + H^-(g) \rightarrow NaH(s)$
$\quad \Delta H^\circ = -812 \, kJ \, mol^{-1}$ (lattice enthalpy)

b State and explain how the lattice enthalpies of KH and MgH_2 compare with the lattice enthalpy of NaH.

2 a Write an equation, including state symbols, showing the decomposition of barium carbonate.

b The decomposition temperature of barium carbonate is 1450°C. Estimate the decomposition temperature of magnesium carbonate.

c Explain why magnesium carbonate has a **more exothermic** lattice enthalpy than barium carbonate.

d Explain why magnesium carbonate has a **lower decomposition temperature** than barium carbonate.

e (i) Give one use of the compound magnesium oxide.
  (ii) Explain why it is suitable for this use.

CHAPTER 10

Period 3 of the Periodic Table

By the end of this chapter you should be able to:

1 describe in general terms how the oxides and chlorides of the Period 3 elements are prepared;

2 describe the reactions of magnesium, aluminium and sulphur with oxygen;

3 describe what happens when these oxides react with water, and know the pH of the resulting solutions;

4 explain the trend in the reactions of magnesium, aluminium and sulphur with oxygen and of the oxides with water in terms of the structure and bonding of the oxides;

5 describe the reactions of sodium, magnesium, aluminium, silicon and phosphorus with chlorine;

6 describe what happens when these chlorides react with water, and know the pH of the resulting solutions;

7 explain the trend in the reactions of sodium, magnesium, aluminium, siilicon and phosphorus with chlorine and of the chlorides with water in terms of the structure and bonding of the chlorides;

8 describe the reactions of magnesium and sodium with water and explain why the pH values of the resulting solutions are different.

Recurring patterns occur everywhere in the natural world, from the beat of the heart to the movement of the planets. You have already looked at the periodic variation of properties such as metallic character and ionisation energies of elements (see *Chemistry 1*, chapter 4). In this chapter you will see how some compounds of Period 3 elements also show periodic variations. The compounds you will study are predominantly the oxides and the chlorides. Chemists have studied these compounds extensively because they are usually easy to prepare and they show how the structure and bonding of a compound affect its reactions. Some of them are important in ways most people find unexpected.

In chapter 9 you learnt that magnesium oxide is a very useful substance because it has such a high melting point and can withstand corrosive chemicals. Another important use of magnesium oxide is as an additive to cattle feed, as without magnesium as a trace element cattle rapidly become ill.

Aluminium oxide is also important, but in quite a different way – aluminium is a very reactive metal so when it is exposed to air a layer of aluminium oxide rapidly forms on the surface of the metal. This layer prevents the rest of the metal reacting, which means that aluminium foil is safe to use next to food, aluminium cans do not dissolve into the drink they contain and aeroplanes will not dissolve in water when they fly through a rain cloud (*figure 10.1*, overleaf). This oxide layer is so important that it is sometimes made thicker by a process called anodising. Without it, aluminium would not be the widely used metal it is today.

Another very useful oxide is the gas sulphur dioxide, SO_2. It is a vital part of the Contact process, producing sulphuric acid. Sulphuric acid

Period 3 oxides

Preparation of the oxides

The elements of Period 3 form oxides by direct combination with oxygen. We are only interested here in four of these oxides: magnesium oxide, aluminium oxide, sulphur dioxide and sulphur trioxide.

- **Magnesium oxide** (see also *Chemistry 1*, chapter 5)

  Magnesium burns very vigorously (once the reaction has started) with a bright white flame, producing a white solid which is magnesium oxide.

  $$2Mg(s) + O_2(g) \rightarrow 2MgO(s)$$

- **Aluminium oxide**

  Aluminium oxide forms easily at room temperature, as mentioned earlier, and is a useful protection for the metal underneath. Powdered aluminium can catch fire and burn, but solid lumps of aluminium will not do this. Aluminium oxide, like magnesium oxide, is a white solid.

  $$4Al(s) + 3O_2(g) \rightarrow 2Al_2O_3(s)$$

- **Sulphur dioxide** and **sulphur trioxide**

  Solid sulphur burns easily with a blue flame and produces sulphur dioxide gas. Sulphur dioxide can be made to react with more oxygen in the presence of a heated vanadium pentoxide, V_2O_5, catalyst to give sulphur trioxide, which is a solid with a melting point of 17 °C.

  $$S(s) + O_2(g) \rightarrow SO_2(g)$$

  $$2SO_2(g) + O_2(g) \xrightarrow[V_2O_5]{\text{heat}} 2SO_3(g)$$

● **Figure 10.1** Uses of aluminium, made possible by the layer of aluminium oxide on the surface of the object.

is not just a useful laboratory chemical, but it is used in huge quantities and so it is produced in huge quantities. Without it we would not have many of the paints, pigments, fertilisers, plastics, fibres and other products we enjoy today.

Sodium chloride needs no introduction; as salt it is both well known and well used. What about other chlorides of Period 3? Magnesium chloride is the source of magnesium metal – it is electrolysed to give magnesium and chlorine gas. Carbon tetrachloride, CCl_4, was previously used as a dry-cleaning fluid because it dissolves grease so well, but this use has been discontinued as it has toxic fumes. Silicon(IV) chloride, $SiCl_4$, is used to produce pure silicon for integrated circuits, one of the purest materials used routinely, without which the computer industry could not function.

So these oxides and chlorides have a variety of uses, but chemically we will be looking at the trends in properties which they show. You will not study all the oxides and chlorides of the Period 3 elements – you need to know just those which are covered in this chapter.

SAQ 10.1

Suggest what observations you would make if a piece of calcium was burnt in air. Construct an equation for this reaction.

SAQ 10.2

As part of the industrial preparation of sulphuric acid, sulphur is burnt in air to form sulphur dioxide. When the sulphur dioxide is passed over a heated V_2O_5 catalyst, further reaction occurs. Write an equation showing the overall reaction.

Structure and bonding of the oxides, and their reactions with water

Magnesium oxide has a *giant ionic lattice structure* with *ionic bonding*. When it reacts with water it produces the alkali magnesium hydroxide in aqueous solution, but this product is not highly soluble, so the pH is around 9–11.

$$MgO(s) + H_2O(l) \rightarrow Mg(OH)_2(aq)$$

Aluminium oxide has a *giant ionic lattice structure* with a significant amount of *covalent bonding*. It is described as having *intermediate bonding*. It does not react with water – it is insoluble.

Both sulphur dioxide and sulphur trioxide have *simple molecular structures* with *covalent bonding*. In solid sulphur trioxide van der Waals' forces operate between the molecules; in sulphur dioxide gas there are no forces between the molecules (as molecules in a gas are widely separated). Both these oxides react with water to give acids.

$$SO_3(g) + H_2O(l) \rightarrow H_2SO_4(aq)$$

We can see certain trends emerging here (*figure 10.2*).

- Metal oxides (on the left of the Periodic Table) have giant ionic lattice structures with ionic bonding and react with water to give alkalis. They are **basic oxides**.

- Non-metal oxides (on the right of the Periodic Table) have simple molecular structures with covalent bonding and react with water to give acids. They are **acidic oxides**.

- Oxides in the centre of the Periodic Table have intermediate properties. They are **amphoteric oxides**.

SAQ 10.3

Predict the structure of:

a barium oxide;

b nitrogen dioxide;

c lithium oxide.

SAQ 10.4

Write equations for the reactions with water of:

a magnesium oxide;

b sulphur dioxide.

Predict the pH of the resulting solutions.

Period 3 chlorides

Preparation of the chlorides

The elements of Period 3 form chlorides by direct combination with chlorine. We are only interested here in five of these chlorides: sodium chloride, magnesium chloride, silicon(IV) chloride, phosphorus(III) chloride and phosphorus(V) chloride.

- **Sodium chloride**
  Sodium burns in chlorine gas to give white sodium chloride.

$$2Na(s) + Cl_2(g) \rightarrow 2NaCl(s)$$

- **Magnesium chloride**
  Like sodium, magnesium burns in chlorine gas to give white magnesium chloride.

$$Mg(s) + Cl_2(g) \rightarrow MgCl_2(s)$$

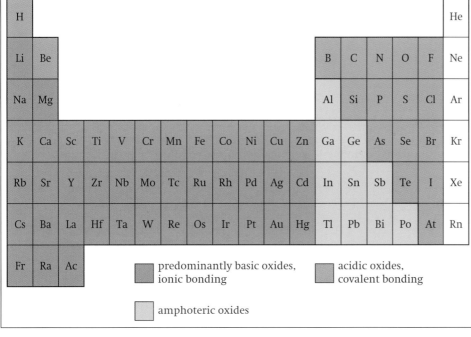

● **Figure 10.2** The Periodic Table and types of oxides.

■ **Silicon(IV) chloride**

Silicon(IV) chloride is a volatile liquid, which is produced by heating silicon in chlorine gas.

$$Si(s) + 2Cl_2(g) \rightarrow SiCl_4(l)$$

■ **Phosphorus(III) chloride** and **phosphorus(V) chloride**

Phosphorus(III) chloride is a volatile colourless liquid which is made by exposing phosphorus to chlorine gas – no heating is required. If excess chlorine is present then the phosphorus(III) chloride reacts with chlorine to give phosphorus(V) chloride, which is a pale yellow solid.

$$P_4(s) + 6Cl_2(g) \rightarrow 4PCl_3(l)$$

followed, in excess chlorine, by

$$PCl_3(l) + Cl_2(g) \rightarrow PCl_5(s)$$

SAQ 10.5

Construct an equation for the reaction between chlorine and calcium.

SAQ 10.6

What observation would you make if chlorine was passed over solid phosphorus?

Structure and bonding of the chlorides, and their reactions with water

Sodium chloride and magnesium chloride have *giant ionic lattice structures* with *ionic bonding*. Sodium chloride simply dissolves in water to give a *neutral* solution, pH 7. Magnesium chloride also dissolves in water but the solution here is *very slightly acidic*, pH 6.5.

The liquids silicon(IV) chloride and phosphorus(III) chloride have *simple molecular structures* with *covalent bonding*. PCl$_5$ in the gaseous state is a covalent molecule.

These chlorides react vigorously with water in an exothermic reaction giving off white fumes of hydrogen chloride gas. This is called a **hydrolysis** reaction, and the solution remaining is *acidic*, pH 2.

■ **Hydrolysis of silicon(IV) chloride**

The reaction is

$$SiCl_4(l) + 2H_2O(l) \rightarrow SiO_2(s) + 4HCl(g)$$

■ **Hydrolysis of phosphorus(III) chloride**

$$PCl_3(l) + 3H_2O(l) \rightarrow H_3PO_3(aq) + 3HCl(g)$$

H$_3$PO$_3$ is known as phosphonic acid.

Again, as with the oxides, we can see certain trends emerging here (*figure 10.3*).

■ Metal chlorides (on the left of the Periodic Table) have giant ionic lattice structures with ionic bonding and react with water to give neutral (or slightly acidic) solutions. They are **neutral chlorides**.

■ Non-metal chlorides (on the right of the Periodic Table) have simple molecular structures with covalent bonding and react with water to give acids. They are **acidic chlorides**.

SAQ 10.7

Predict the pH value of a solution formed by dissolving lithium chloride in water.

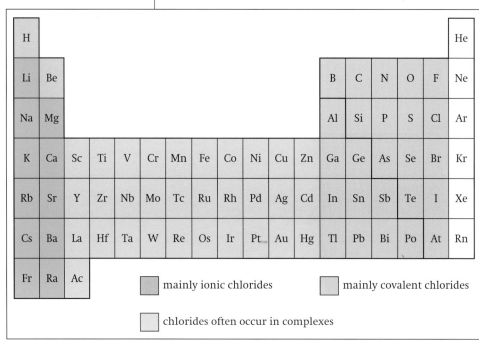

● **Figure 10.3** The Periodic Table and types of chlorides.

SAQ 10.8

Carbon tetrachloride does not mix or react with water, but silicon tetrachloride, $SiCl_4$, reacts violently.

a State what type of reaction this is.

b Write an equation showing this reaction.

c Give three observations you would make watching this reaction.

The reactions of sodium and magnesium with water

The reactions of sodium and magnesium with water are redox reactions, in which the metal is oxidised and hydrogen gas is produced. The remaining solution is an alkali.

When a piece of sodium is placed onto the surface of water it floats and fizzes about. If it gets stuck in one place it can become so hot that it catches fire, burning with an orange flame.

$$2Na(s) + 2H_2O(l) \rightarrow 2NaOH(aq) + H_2(g)$$

The solution of sodium hydroxide remaining has a high pH of 12–14. Because sodium hydroxide is very soluble, there is a high concentration of $OH^-(aq)$ ions present in solution.

When a piece of magnesium is placed into water it sinks and at first nothing appears to happen. However, if an inverted test-tube full of water is placed over the magnesium and left, after a few days you can see a gas has collected – this is hydrogen. So magnesium does react with water in the cold, but the reaction is very slow. Magnesium hydroxide is not as soluble as sodium hydroxide so the pH of the resulting solution is lower, around 9–11. As you may predict, magnesium reacts faster with steam, but the product here is magnesium oxide.

$$Mg(s) + 2H_2O(l) \rightarrow Mg(OH)_2(aq) + H_2(g)$$
$$Mg(s) + H_2O(g) \rightarrow MgO(s) + H_2(g)$$

We can see that sodium and magnesium react with water to give *alkaline solutions*, but there are two differences in these reactions.

■ Sodium is more reactive with water than magnesium is.

■ Aqueous sodium hydroxide is a stronger alkali than aqueous magnesium hydroxide because NaOH is more soluble in water.

SAQ 10.9

Show, by writing equations, the different products obtained when magnesium reacts with

a steam;

b cold water.

SUMMARY

- The elements of Period 3 react directly with oxygen to give oxides, and with chlorine to give chlorides.

- Metal oxides have giant ionic lattice structures and ionic bonding. They are basic oxides that react with water to give hydroxides, which are basic.

- Non-metal oxides have simple molecular structures and covalent bonding. They are acidic oxides with a pH value in aqueous solution of around 1–2.

- Metal chlorides have giant ionic lattice structures and ionic bonding. They are neutral with a pH value in aqueous solution of 7 (or slightly higher).

- Non-metal chlorides have simple molecular structures with covalent bonding. They are acidic with a pH value in aqueous solution of around 2.

- Sodium and magnesium react with water to give the aqueous hydroxides. Sodium reacts more vigorously than magnesium.

- Aqueous sodium hydroxide has a pH of 12–14, aqueous magnesium hydroxide has a pH of 9–11. Aqueous magnesium hydroxide is a weaker alkali than aqueous sodium hydroxide because it is less soluble in water.

Questions

1 Describe the acid–base nature of the solutions obtained when the following compounds are added to water. Use equations to illustrate your answer.
   a sodium chloride
   b sulphur trioxide
   c sodium oxide
   d phosphorus(v) chloride.

2 a (i) Write an equation to show the reaction of magnesium with water.
     (ii) Predict and explain the pH of the resulting solution.
   b When magnesium is added to water, the reaction is very slow. In contrast, phosphorus trichloride reacts vigorously with water.
     (i) Write an equation, including state symbols, showing the reaction of phosphorus trichloride with water.
     (ii) Predict the pH of the solution obtained.
     (iii) State one observation a student watching the reaction would make.

CHAPTER 11

The transition elements

By the end of this chapter you should be able to:

1 give a description of a *transition element*;

2 work out the *electronic configuration* of the first row transition element atoms and ions;

3 use iron and copper to explain the *multiple oxidation states* of transition elements in compounds, the formation of coloured ions and why transition elements are good catalysts;

4 describe the reactions of aqueous Fe^{2+}, Fe^{3+} and Cu^{2+} with aqueous sodium hydroxide;

5 explain the terms *complex ion* and *ligand*;

6 describe *ligand substitution* of H_2O in $[Cu(H_2O)_6]^{2+}$ by the chloride ion and ammonia;

7 describe ligand substitution of H_2O in $[Fe(H_2O)_6]^{3+}$ by the thiocyanate ion;

8 predict the shape of a complex from its formula;

9 describe how you would determine the formula of a complex using *colorimetry*;

10 predict the colour of a complex from its *visible spectrum*;

11 construct *redox equations* involving transition metals or ions using half-equations;

12 describe *redox titrations* involving transition metal ions and perform calculations with data obtained from such titrations.

Transition elements are a popular area of experimental chemistry because their compounds are coloured, and so experiments involve blue, yellow, pink and green solutions (*figure 11.1*). This property means compounds of these elements are used in pigments for many applications such as traffic lane paints (*figure 11.2*, overleaf), ceramic glazes and oil paints.

Transition elements are metals, and include the metals which most people recognise because they are used so frequently – gold and silver jewellery, copper wiring, chromium car bumpers, iron pipes (*figure 11.3*). Iron is also well known for the role of its ions in haemoglobin.

Other transition metals are not as well known but also have very important uses. Most light bulbs have tungsten filaments. Drill bits are made from tungsten carbide. A mixture of platinum,

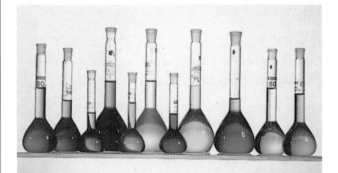

● **Figure 11.1** From left to right, the strongly coloured solutions of the following transition elements: Ti^{3+}, V^{3+}, VO^{2+}, Cr^{3+}, $Cr_2O_7^{2-}$, Mn^{2+}, MnO_4^-, Fe^{3+}, Co^{2+}, Ni^{2+} and Cu^{2+}.

● **Figure 11.2** Yellow road markings contain pigments made from the transition element chromium.

rhodium and palladium is used in catalytic converters on car exhausts. Zirconium is used in nuclear reactors.

Many transition elements are important in the diets of living organisms as trace elements – only needed in small quantities, but necessary for life. In humans, vanadium ions are needed in fat metabolism, chromium for glucose utilisation, manganese and copper for cell respiration as well as the iron we all know is necessary as part of the haemoglobin in blood. An interesting trace element is zinc, part of the enzyme alcohol dehydrogenase, which metabolises ethanol. People with low levels of zinc ions get drunk on very little alcohol because their bodies cannot metabolise the alcohol away.

Transition metals are so important to mankind that most reserves will be used up within the next fifty years or so. This means that other sources of transition metals must be found, and one source

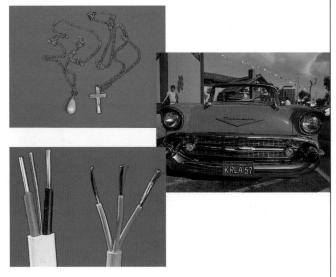

● **Figure 11.3** Transition elements have many uses.

which may be used is on the ocean floor. Here nodules have been found over large areas, some a few millimetres and some a few metres in diameter, containing mostly manganese and iron oxides but also many other transition metal oxides in smaller quantities. Altogether there are billions of tonnes of these nodules on the ocean floors, but there are two problems linked with using them. The first problem is the technical expertise required to mine from such an inhospitable place. The second problem is that, legally, the ocean floors are international property, so ownership of the nodules and the wealth associated with them must be carefully worked out.

Did you know that the d-block metal mercury, the only liquid metal at room temperature and pressure, is responsible for one of literature's most famous characters – the Mad Hatter in *Alice in Wonderland*? A hatter made hats from felt, and felt was made from animal hair by a process involving mercury compounds. These compounds are toxic, so people who made felt and inhaled the dust of the mercury compounds suffered personality disorders and shaking. This was called 'hatter's shakes', and gives us a rather sinister explanation of the zany personality of the Mad Hatter.

This chapter deals with the chemistry of the first row of the transition elements, which are found in the d-block of the Periodic Table, located between Groups II and III. There is a precise definition of a transition element:

> A transition element is an element that forms at least one ion with a partly filled d orbital.

The transition elements have certain common *physical properties*:
- they have high densities;
- they are metals with high melting points;
- they are hard and rigid, and so are useful as construction materials;
- they are good conductors of electricity.

They also have certain common *chemical properties*:
- they can show several different oxidation states in their compounds;
- they are good catalysts;
- they form coloured compounds;
- they form **complexes** with **ligands** (these terms may be new to you – they are explained on page 96).

The physical properties of the transition elements can all be explained by the strong metallic bonding that exists in these elements (see *Chemistry 1*, chapter 3). There are more electrons in the outer shell of atoms of transition elements than in the outer shell of Group I and Group II metals, so the delocalised sea of electrons typical of metallic bonding produces a strong force holding the positive ions together. The melting points of the transition elements are high because it takes a lot of energy to disrupt this strong metallic bonding. This bonding also explains the good electrical conductivity, as there are many mobile electrons present. The hardness of the transition elements is caused by the atoms being held firmly in place by the metallic bonding.

Electronic structures

The electronic structures of the d-block elements dictate their chemistry, and so are extremely important.

Chemists have a shorthand to show the full subshells in electronic configurations – they use the symbol of the noble gas with the full subshells in square brackets, like this: $[Ar]3d^0 4s^0$.

scandium	Sc	$[Ar]3d^1 4s^2$
titanium	Ti	$[Ar]3d^2 4s^2$
vanadium	V	$[Ar]3d^3 4s^2$
chromium	Cr	$[Ar]3d^5 4s^1$
manganese	Mn	$[Ar]3d^5 4s^2$
iron	Fe	$[Ar]3d^6 4s^2$
cobalt	Co	$[Ar]3d^7 4s^2$
nickel	Ni	$[Ar]3d^8 4s^2$
copper	Cu	$[Ar]3d^{10} 4s^1$
zinc	Zn	$[Ar]3d^{10} 4s^2$

Where [Ar] is $1s^2 2s^2 2p^6 3s^2 3p^6$

If you look at these electronic configurations, you will see that the d subshell is being filled as we move from scandium to zinc, hence the term 'd-block' – scandium has one d electron, and zinc has ten, a full d subshell. The 4s level is filled before the 3d level but the two levels remain very close in energy. We see this closeness illustrated in chromium and copper. Chromium, instead of having a $[Ar]3d^4 4s^2$ structure, has $[Ar]3d^5 4s^1$; it has two half-filled subshells, which gives it greater stability. This exchange is made possible by the closeness of the two subshells. Similarly, copper has a full d subshell and a half-filled 4s shell: $[Ar]3d^{10} 4s^1$.

As the transition elements are metals they all form *positive* ions, so electrons are *lost* from a transition metal atom when an ion is formed. So the electronic configuration of Fe^{2+} is two electrons less than the electronic configuration of Fe. These electrons are lost from the 4s orbital first, and then the 3d orbital, which means the electronic configuration of Fe^{2+} is $1s^2 2s^2 2p^6 3s^2 3p^6 3d^6$.

As you will see in the next section, transition metals can form several different ions, and iron can form Fe^{3+} as well as Fe^{2+}. The electronic configuration of Fe^{3+} is $1s^2 2s^2 2p^6 3s^2 3p^6 3d^5$.

SAQ 11.1

Write down the electronic configurations of
a Cr **b** Cr^{3+} **c** Cu **d** Cu^{2+} **e** Mn **f** Mn^{2+}.

Take a look at the electronic configurations of the first element, scandium, and the last d-block element, zinc. For scandium the only observed oxidation state is +3, so the ion is Sc^{3+}, with the electronic configuration $1s^2 2s^2 2p^6 3s^2 3p^6$. This ion has no d electrons, so does not satisfy the definition of a transition element – scandium is a d-block element but is not a transition element. Now look at zinc. The only observed oxidation state is Zn^{2+}, with the electronic configuration $1s^2 2s^2 2p^6 3s^2 3p^6 3d^{10}$. This ion has a completely filled, not a partially filled, d subshell – so zinc is not a transition element. This is the reason why the compounds of zinc and scandium are white, and not coloured like those of transition elements (see page 95).

Variable oxidation states

Transition elements occur in **multiple oxidation states**. The most common oxidation state is +2, which occurs when the two 4s electrons are lost (for example Fe^{2+} and Cu^{2+}). But because the 3d electrons are very close in energy to the 4s electrons they can quite easily be lost too, so one element can form several different ions by losing different numbers of electrons, and all the ions will be almost equally stable. This closeness in energy between the 3d and 4s electrons also explains why the transition elements have such similar properties to each other.

Table 11.1 shows the main oxidation states of the first row of the d-block elements. The commonly occurring oxidation states are highlighted. It is worth noting that the highest oxidation state for the first five elements is the same as the total number of 4s and 3d electrons for the element; and for the second five elements, a common oxidation state is +2. It is important that you know the oxidation states of iron and copper in particular, and be able to give the electronic configurations of all their ions. *Box 11A* shows you how to determine oxidation numbers.

In transition element chemistry, the changes in oxidation state of the ions are often shown by changes in the colour of the solutions. For example, potassium dichromate(VI) is often used in titrations:

$$Cr_2O_7^{2-}(aq) + 14H^+(aq) + 6e^- \rightarrow 2Cr^{3+}(aq) + 7H_2O(l)$$
orange   green

Element	Oxidation states					
Sc		+3				
Ti	+2	+3	+4			
V	+2	+3	+4	+5		
Cr	+2	+3	+4	+5	+6	
Mn	+2	+3	+4	+5	+6	+7
Fe	+2	+3	+4	+5	+6	
Co	+2	+3	+4	+5		
Ni	+2	+3	+4			
Cu	+1	+2	+3			
Zn		+2				

● **Table 11.1** Main oxidation states of the first row d-block elements.

Box 11A How to determine oxidation states

■ Oxidation states are usually calculated as the number of electrons that atoms have to lose, gain or share, when they form ionic or covalent bonds in compounds.

■ The oxidation state of uncombined elements is always zero. For example, each atom in $H_2(g)$ or $O_2(g)$ or $Na(s)$ or $S_8(s)$ has an oxidation state of zero; otherwise, the states are always given a sign, + or –.

■ For a monatomic ion, the oxidation state of the element is simply the same as the charge on the ion. For example:

ion	Na^+	Ca^{2+}	Cl^-	O^{2-}
ox. state	+1	+2	–1	–2

■ In a chemical species (compound or ion), with atoms of more than one element, the most electronegative element is given the negative oxidation state. Other elements are given positive oxidation states. For example, in the compound disulphur dichloride, S_2Cl_2, chlorine is more electronegative than sulphur. The two chlorine atoms each have an oxidation state of –1, and thus the two sulphur atoms each have the oxidation state of +1.

■ The oxidation state of hydrogen in compounds is always +1, except in metal hydrides (e.g. NaH), when it is –1.

■ The oxidation state of oxygen in compounds is always –2, except in peroxides (e.g. H_2O_2), when it is –1, or in OF_2, when it is +2.

■ The sum of all the oxidation states in a neutral compound is zero. In an ion, the sum equals the overall charge. For example, the sum of the oxidation states in $CaCl_2$ is 0; the sum of the oxidation states in OH^- is –1.

SAQ 11.2

What is the oxidation state of chromium in
a $Cr_2O_7^{2-}$ and **b** Cr^{3+}?

Transition elements as catalysts

A catalyst is a substance that speeds up a chemical reaction, without itself being permanently changed in a chemical way (see *Chemistry 1*, chapter 14). Many transition elements are effective catalysts, and are used in reactions both in the laboratory and in industry.

In the laboratory, you may have seen the decomposition of hydrogen peroxide to water and oxygen:

$$2H_2O_2(l) \rightarrow 2H_2O(l) + O_2(g)$$

At room temperature this reaction is very slow. However, if manganese(IV) oxide is added it acts as a catalyst, and the reaction becomes very rapid.

In industry, one of the best-known reactions that depends on a catalyst is the Haber process, in which nitrogen and hydrogen react to give ammonia (see *Chemistry 1*, chapter 15).

$$N_2(g) + 3H_2(g) \rightleftharpoons 2NH_3(g)$$

The catalyst used in this reaction is finely divided *iron*.

Transition elements make efficient catalysts for two reasons.

- They can have several different oxidation states, so they can easily transfer electrons. This provides an alternative route for a reaction in a way that lowers the activation energy and so speeds up the reaction.
- They provide sites at which reactions can take place. Transition elements can bond to a wide range of ions and molecules, and can have different numbers of bonds, so the reacting molecules can be held in place while the reaction occurs (see *Chemistry 1*, page 174).

Coloured compounds

Transition metal ions in aqueous solution are frequently coloured; some examples are

Fe^{2+}	green	Co^{2+}	pink
Fe^{3+}	yellow	Ti^{3+}	purple
Cu^{2+}	blue	Cr^{3+}	violet
Ni^{2+}	green	Mn^{2+}	pink

This colour is related to the presence of partly filled d orbitals; for this reason, an ion with a *full* d orbital will not be coloured. So compounds of zinc, where zinc is in the form Zn^{2+} with an electronic configuration $1s^2 2s^2 2p^6 3s^2 3p^6 3d^{10}$ are white. Similarly, compounds with an empty d orbital, such as TiO_2, are also white. Here the titanium has an oxidation state of +4 so its electronic configuration is $1s^2 2s^2 2p^6 3s^2 3p^6 3d^0 4s^0$.

Visible spectroscopy of transition metal ions

Transition metal ions are coloured because they absorb radiation in the visible region of the electromagnetic spectrum. The spectrum produced shows us the colour of the transition metal ion. If you study the *Transition Elements* option you will study this phenomenom more closely.

Visible spectroscopy is also called absorption spectroscopy. *Figure 11.4* shows the absorption spectrum of the hydrated Cu^{2+} ion in aqueous solution (it has the formula $[Cu(H_2O)_6]^{2+}$ as it is a complex, see page 96). The solution is a blue colour. The spectrum shows us that incoming yellow and red light are absorbed. We see the colour that is transmitted, which is blue. *Table 11.2* provides information on wavelength, absorbed colour and observed colour.

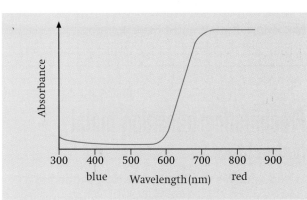

- **Figure 11.4** The visible spectrum of $[Cu(H_2O)_6]^{2+}$(aq), showing that incoming yellow and red light are absorbed and other wavelengths are transmitted.

Absorbed colour	λ nm	observed colour	λ nm
violet	400	green-yellow	560
blue	450	yellow	600
blue-green	490	red	620
yellow-green	570	violet	410
yellow	580	dark blue	430
orange	600	blue	450
red	650	green	520

- **Table 11.2** The relation between absorbed and observed colours.

SAQ 11.3

Figure 11.5 shows the visible spectrum of a transition metal ion in aqueous solution.

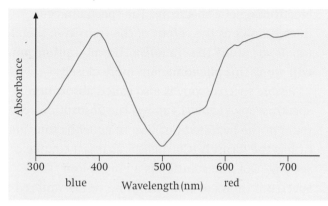

● **Figure 11.5**

a Make a copy of the spectrum, and write the colours of the visible spectrum underneath the appropriate wavelengths.

b Deduce the colour of the solution.

c Suggest the identity of the transition metal ion.

Precipitating transition metal hydroxides

When aqueous sodium hydroxide is added to a solution of a transition metal ion, a precipitate of the transition metal hydroxide is formed. These precipitates resemble a jelly so are called **gelatinous** and their colour can identify the transition metal ion.

$$Cu^{2+}(aq) + 2OH^-(aq) \rightarrow Cu(OH)_2(s) \quad \text{pale blue}$$
$$Fe^{2+}(aq) + 2OH^-(aq) \rightarrow Fe(OH)_2(s) \quad \text{green}$$
$$Fe^{3+}(aq) + 3OH^-(aq) \rightarrow Fe(OH)_3(s) \quad \text{rust}$$
$$Mn^{2+}(aq) + 2OH^-(aq) \rightarrow Mn(OH)_2(s) \quad \text{cream}$$
$$Cr^{3+}(aq) + 3OH^-(aq) \rightarrow Cr(OH)_3(s) \quad \text{grey-green}$$

Note that gelatinous precipitates can also be formed when ammonia solution is added to the aqueous transition element ion. This is because ammonia is a weak base that exists in equilibrium with the hydroxide ion in aqueous solution:

$$NH_3(aq) + H_2O(l) \rightleftharpoons NH_4^+(aq) + OH^-(aq)$$

This means that aqueous ammonia is a source of hydroxide ions. For example, aqueous ammonia added to $Mn^{2+}(aq)$ gives a cream precipitate of $Mn(OH)_2$.

SAQ 11.4

Write equations to predict the reactions between aqueous sodium hydroxide and aqueous solutions of **a** Ni^{2+} **b** Ti^{3+}.

Complexes

Transition elements form **complexes**, or **coordination compounds**, with ligands. **Ligands** are **electron-pair donors** and they form *dative* or *coordinate* covalent bonds with a central transition element ion or atom. Ligands can be either anions or neutral molecules. *Figure 11.6* shows the complex formed between Cu^{2+} ions and water ligands.

The formula of a complex is always written with the central transition element ion first, followed by the ligands (*table 11.3*), and with the overall charge of the ion at the end, for example $[Ni(CN)_4]^{2-}$ and $[Cr(H_2O)_4Cl_2]^+$. Note the use of square brackets. The overall charge on the complex is simply the individual charges of the transition element ion and the ligands added together. In these two examples, we know that the ligands must be CN^-, Cl^- and H_2O, so we can work out that the transition element ions are Ni^{2+} and Cr^{3+}.

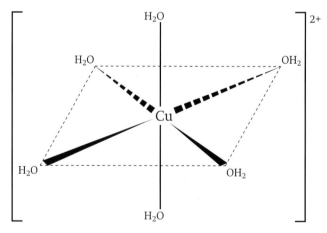

● **Figure 11.6** The shape of $[Cu(H_2O)_6]^{2+}(aq)$.

Type of ligand	Formula	Name
monodentate	H_2O	water
	NH_3	ammonia
	Cl^-	chloride ion
	CN^-	cyanide ion
	SCN^-	thiocyanate ion

● **Table 11.3** Some of the more common ligands.

Key:
L = ligand
E = transition element ion
Z = charge on ion

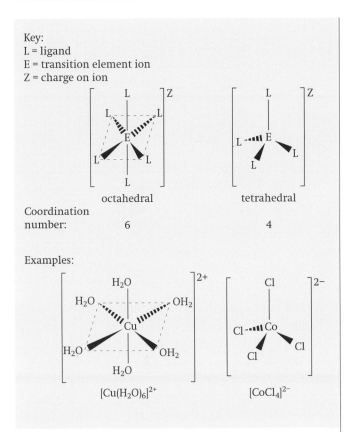

octahedral   tetrahedral

Coordination
number: 6   4

Examples:

$[Cu(H_2O)_6]^{2+}$ $[CoCl_4]^{2-}$

● **Figure 11.7** the shapes of transition element complexes.

SAQ 11.5

State the formulae and charges of the complexes made from:

a one iron(III) ion and four chloride ions;

b one titanium(III) ion and six water molecules.

Shapes of complexes

There are two main shapes adopted by transition element complexes – **octahedral** and **tetrahedral** (*figure 11.7*). These names show the shape of the outside 'surfaces' of the complex.

- An octahedral complex has a *six* ligands surrounding the metal.
- A tetrahedral complex has *four* ligands surrounding the metal.

One of the best-known complexes is formed in a solution of copper(II) sulphate, $CuSO_4$. In aqueous solution the copper ion is not isolated, but forms a complex with six water molecules. The complex has an octahedral shape, as shown in *figures 11.6* and *11.7*. This complex is responsible for the blue colour associated with a copper sulphate solution.

SAQ 11.6

Predict the shape of the following complexes:

a $[Co(NH_3)_5Cl]^{2+}$

b $[Cr(H_2O)_4Cl_2]^+$

c $[FeCl_4]^-$

Ligand substitution

The water ligands in the copper complex of aqueous copper(II) sulphate can be **substituted** by other ligands to form a more stable complex. When concentrated hydrochloric acid is added drop by drop, the solution turns yellow as a new complex is formed – the water ligands are substituted by four chloride ion ligands to give $[CuCl_4]^{2-}$:

$$[Cu(H_2O)_6]^{2+}(aq) + 4Cl^-(aq) \rightarrow [CuCl_4]^{2-}(aq) + 6H_2O(l)$$

Sodium chloride can also be used as a source of chloride ions in this reaction.

The chloride ion ligands are similarly replaced by ammonia ligands when concentrated ammonia solution is added, producing a deep-blue solution:

$$[CuCl_4]^{2+}(aq) + 4NH_3(aq) + 2H_2O(l)$$
$$\rightarrow [Cu(NH_3)_4(H_2O)_2]^{2+}(aq) + 4Cl^-(aq)$$

Of course, if the ammonia solution is added dropwise and you watch the solution carefully, you will see a pale blue precipitate of $Cu(OH)_2$ appear first and then this will dissolve as the deep blue complex between Cu^{2+} and NH_3 is formed. *Figure 11.8* shows the structure of the octahedral complex.

Figure 11.9 summarises this series of reactions. This sequence of ligand replacement means that we can list the complexes in order according to their stability (*table 11.4*).

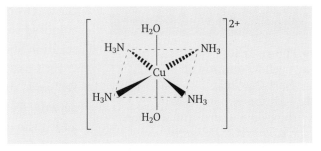

● **Figure 11.8** The structure of $[Cu(NH_3)_4(H_2O)_2]^{2+}$.

Complex	
$[Cu(H_2O)_6]^{2+}$	
$[CuCl_4]^{2-}$	increasing
$[Cu(NH_3)_4(H_2O)_2]^{2+}$	stability

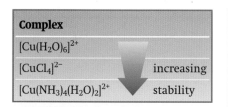

● **Table 11.4** The stability of copper complexes.

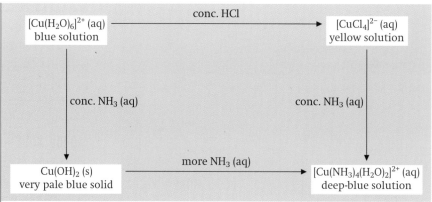

● **Figure 11.9** Ligand substitution reactions of various copper complexes.

Another striking colour change that can be seen when one ligand substitutes for another is the reaction of aqueous Fe^{2+} ions with thiocyanate ions, SCN^-. Here one H_2O ligand in each complex ion is replaced by an SCN^- ligand, and the colour changes from yellow to deep blood-red (*figure 11.10*).

$$[Fe(H_2O)_6]^{3+}(aq) + SCN^-(aq) \rightarrow [Fe(H_2O)_5SCN]^{2+}(aq) + H_2O(l)$$

yellow   blood-red

SAQ 11.7

The $[Ni(H_2O)_6]^{2+}$ ion is *green* in aqueous solution. Concentrated ammonia was added dropwise to this solution, which turned *dark blue*. Suggest an explanation for these observations.

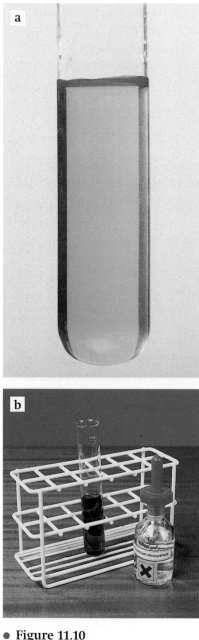

● **Figure 11.10**

a A yellow solution of $[Fe(H_2O)_6]^{3+}(aq)$.

b Addition of potassium thiocyanate turns the solution red. One H_2O ligand is substituted by a SCN^- ligand to form $[Fe(H_2O)_5SCN]^{2+}(aq)$.

Finding the formula of a complex by colorimetry

The colour of a transition metal ion can change as the ligand is changed, as we have seen above. We can use this change in colour to find the ratio of ligand to metal in a complex, using a colorimeter. In a colorimeter a narrow beam of light passes through the solution under test towards a sensitive photocell (*figure 11.11*). The wavelength of this light can be selected by using an appropriate filter. The current generated in the photocell is proportional to the amount of light transmitted by the solution, which depends on the colour of the solution. The colorimeter is usually calibrated to show the fraction of light absorbed by the solution – the most intensely coloured solution absorbs the most light, and the faintest coloured solution absorbs the least light.

Let's use an example to see how this method works. A solution of Fe^{3+} ions, such as aqueous $FeCl_3$, is yellow. The complex ion is actually $[Fe(H_2O)_6^{3+}]$. When aqueous sodium thiocyanate, NaSCN, is added the complex turns blood-red as the thiocyanate ligands (SCN^-) displace the water ligands. How do we work out the formula of the Fe^{3+}/SCN^- complex? Ten tubes are prepared which contain

Tube	1	2	3	4	5	6	7	8	9	10
vol. in cm³ of 0.1 mol dm⁻³ Fe³⁺(aq)	10	10	10	10	10	10	10	10	10	10
vol. in cm³ of 0.1 mol dm⁻³ SCN⁻(aq)	2	4	6	8	10	12	14	16	18	20
vol. in cm³ of H₂O added to make final volume 40 cm³	28	26	24	22	20	18	16	14	12	10

● **Table 11.5**

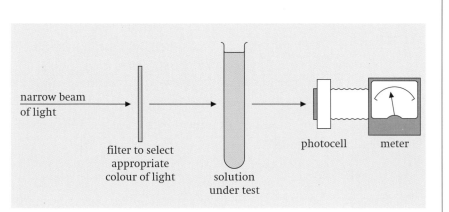

● **Figure 11.11** Using a colorimeter.

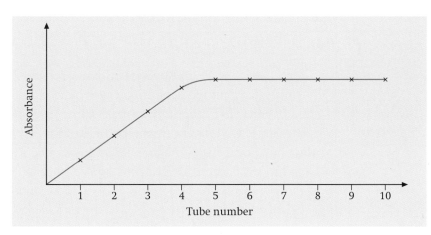

● **Figure 11.12** Experimental results.

different amounts of Fe^{3+} and SCN^-. The tube with the most intense colour, as read by the colorimeter, contains the maximum amount of ligand molecules to metal ions. *Table 11.5* contains details of one method you can follow. The principles of the method are always the same, although the volumes and concentrations of the metal ion and ligand solutions can change. What is extremely important is to use the *same volume of solution* in each tube.

The Fe^{3+} and SCN^- solutions are measured as accurately as possible into the tubes. The final solution from each tube in turn is then placed in a test-tube or cuvette and placed in the colorimeter. The complex is red so it absorbs in the blue region of the spectrum, so a blue filter is used, showing that the complementary colour to the complex is used in the filter. The absorbance reading is taken. The results are shown in *figure 11.12*.

As you can see, the absorbance readings taken on the colorimeter go up as the red colour gets more intense, and finally the readings level out. The point where the horizontal line is reached shows the number of moles of Fe^{3+} and SCN^- which form the complex. In this case it is at tube 5. In this experiment, this solution contains 10 cm³ of 0.1 mol dm⁻³ Fe^{3+} and 10 cm³ of 0.1 mol dm⁻³ SCN^-(aq). From these values you can work out the amount in moles of each species:

0.001 mol Fe^{3+} and
0.001 mol SCN^-
So the ratio is 1 Fe^{3+} : 1SCN^-

The formula of the complex is therefore $[Fe(H_2O)_5(SCN)]^{2+}$.

SAQ 11.8

In the colorimetry experiment described opposite, what pieces of apparatus are used for measuring out
a the Fe^{3+} solution
b the SCN^- solution?

SAQ 11.9

The results in *figure 11.13* were obtained from a colorimetry experiment to find the formula of a Ni^{2+} complex with the ligand known as edta. *Table 11.6* shows the details of the solutions. Show that the ratio of Ni^{2+} to ligand in this complex is 1 : 1.

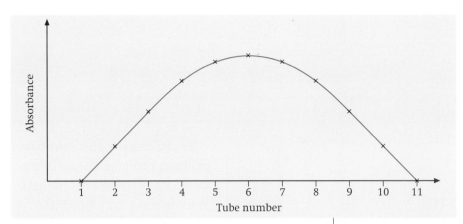

● Figure 11.13

Test tube number	Vol of 0.1 mol dm^{-3} Ni^{2+} solution (cm^3)	Vol of 0.1 mol dm^{-3} edta solution (cm^3)
1	0.0	5.0
2	0.5	4.5
3	1.0	4.0
4	1.5	3.5
5	2.0	3.0
6	2.5	2.5
7	3.0	2.0
8	3.5	1.5
9	4.0	1.0
10	4.5	0.5
11	5.0	0.0

● Table 11.6

Redox behaviour

Transition metals have a variety of different oxidation states and so they can be readily oxidised or reduced. Their redox reactions are an important part of their chemistry, especially as they are used in titrations for many different types of analysis.

Redox reactions

[Note: in this section state symbols have not been put into the equations, to make the species involved stand out more clearly.]

There are many redox reactions involving transition metal ions. One which you must know is the reaction between iron(II) ions (Fe^{2+}) and manganate(VII) ions (MnO$_4^-$) in acidified aqueous solution. Here is the equation for this reaction:

$$5Fe^{2+} + MnO_4^- + 8H^+ \rightarrow Mn^{2+} + 5Fe^{3+} + 4H_2O$$
purple   pink

The colour change, as you can see, is from purple aqueous MnO$_4^-$ to pale pink aqueous Mn^{2+}, but this pale pink is usually so faint that the solution simply appears to be decolorised. (You may wonder why the Fe^{3+} does not colour the solution yellow. Again, it is such a faint colour that it usually cannot be noticed. The green colour of Fe^{2+} is masked by the strong purple colour of MnO$_4^-$.) This colour change is often used as an indicator in a redox titration (see page 101).

This type of redox equation can be constructed from two half-equations:

■ the half-equation showing oxidation of Fe(II) in Fe^{2+} to Fe(III) in Fe^{3+}:
$$Fe^{2+} \rightarrow Fe^{3+} + e^-$$

■ the half-equation showing reduction of Mn(VII) in MnO$_4^-$ to Mn(II) in Mn^{2+} in the presence of acid:
$$MnO_4^- + 8H^+ + 5e^- \rightarrow Mn^{2+} + 4H_2O$$

To construct the final equation, write the two half-equations so that the number of electrons in each is the same. This means the first half-equation is multiplied by 5. Then the half-equations can be added together and the electrons on each side of the arrow cancel:

$$5Fe^{2+} \rightarrow 5Fe^{3+} + 5e^-$$
$$MnO_4^- + 8H^+ + 5e^- \rightarrow Mn^{2+} + 4H_2O$$
$$\overline{5Fe^{2+} + MnO_4^- + 8H^+ \rightarrow 5Fe^{3+} + Mn^{2+} + 4H_2O}$$

This method can be used for finding the redox equation between any two half-equations. Another example is the reaction between aqueous Fe^{2+} ions and hydrogen peroxide, H$_2$O$_2$. The Fe^{2+} ions are oxidised to Fe^{3+} ions, and the hydrogen peroxide is reduced to water.

$$Fe^{2+} \rightarrow Fe^{3+} + e^-$$
$$H_2O_2 + 2H^+ + 2e^- \rightarrow 2H_2O$$

This time the top half-equation is multiplied throughout by 2. The final redox equation is:

$$2Fe^{2+} + H_2O_2 + 2H^+ \rightarrow 2Fe^{3+} + 2H_2O$$

Another useful half-equation shows the reduction of orange Cr(VI) in the dichromate ion, $Cr_2O_7^{2-}$, to blue-green Cr(III) in Cr^{3+}. This is another reaction that requires acid:

$$Cr_2O_7^{2-} + 14H^+ + 6e^- \rightarrow 2Cr^{3+} + 7H_2O$$

orange   green

This is the reaction that occurs when primary and secondary alcohols are oxidised to aldehydes and ketones respectively (see *Chemistry 1*, chapter 11). Aqueous potassium dichromate(VI) is a common oxidising agent in organic chemistry.

SAQ 11.10

Construct the redox equation showing the reaction between dichromate(VI) ions and Fe(II) ions in aqueous solution, given:

$$Fe^{2+} \rightarrow Fe^{3+} + e^-$$

and

$$Cr_2O_7^{2-} + 14H^+ + 6e^- \rightarrow 2Cr^{3+} + 7H_2O$$

Redox titrations

The colour changes of redox reactions involving transition metal ions in aqueous solutions can be used to show when a titration has reached the end-point. A good example of this is the redox titration between Fe^{2+} and MnO_4^- in aqueous acid solution:

$$5Fe^{2+} + MnO_4^- + 8H^+ \rightarrow 5Fe^{3+} + Mn^{2+} + 4H_2O$$

The purple aqueous MnO_4^- is added from the burette into the acidified aqueous Fe^{2+}, and immediately turns pale pink or colourless as it reacts. The end-point of the titration is when all the Fe^{2+} has reacted and a permanent pink colour can be seen.

- This redox titration can be used for calculating how much Fe^{2+} is contained in an iron tablet.
- It can also be used for **standardising** a solution of aqueous $KMnO_4$. It is not possible to weigh out solid $KMnO_4$ to make up into a solution of accurate concentration because the solid $KMnO_4$ is not pure. However, it is possible to find the mass of a piece of pure iron and then

to use this reaction to calculate the concentration of the aqueous $KMnO_4$.

Example
A piece of iron wire with a mass of 0.14 g was converted into Fe^{2+} by reaction with acid, and titrated against aqueous $KMnO_4$. The titre obtained was 26.2 cm³. Calculate the concentration of the aqueous $KMnO_4$.

$$\text{Amount of Fe} = \frac{0.14\,g}{56\,g\,mol^{-1}}$$
$$= 0.0025\,mol$$

Amount of Fe^{2+} = Amount of Fe
$$= 0.0025\,mol$$

From the equation, 5 moles of Fe^{2+} react with 1 mole of MnO_4^-

$$5Fe^{2+} + MnO_4^- + 8H^+ \rightarrow 5Fe^{3+} + Mn^{2+} + 4H_2O$$

So amount of $KMnO_4$ in the titre $= \dfrac{0.0025}{5}$

$$= 0.0005\,mol$$

Concentration of $KMnO_4(aq) = \dfrac{0.0005\,mol}{26.2 \times 10^{-3}\,dm^3}$

$$= 0.019\,mol\,dm^{-3}$$

SAQ 11.11

A piece of iron ore was treated with acid so that the iron was oxidised to aqueous Fe^{2+} ions, and then titrated against 0.040 mol dm⁻³ aqueous potassium manganate(VII). The titre was found to be 25.0 cm³.

a Calculate the mass of iron in the sample.

b If the mass of the iron ore was 0.42 g, calculate the percentage mass of iron in the iron ore.

SUMMARY

- The transition elements are metals with similar physical and chemical properties.

- The electronic configurations of the elements includes electrons in the 3d subshell.

- A transition element is defined as having a partly filled 3d subshell in at least one of its ions.

- When a transition element is oxidised, it loses electrons from the 4s subshell first and then the 3d subshell.

- Transition elements can exist in several oxidation states.

- Transition elements are good catalysts because they can transfer electrons easily and provide a site for the reaction to take place.

- Transition metal compounds are often coloured, The colour can be recorded by visible spectroscopy.

- Transition elements react with aqueous hydroxide ions to give precipitates. The colour of the precipitate depends on the transition metal ion.

- Transition elements form complexes by combining with ligands. A strong ligand can displace a weak ligand in a complex. This can result in a change of colour.

- The formula of a complex can be found by colorimetry.

- Many reactions involving transition elements are redox reactions. Some redox reactions are used in titrations to determine concentrations.

Questions

1   A student investigated ligand substitution in complexes experimentally. He divided a solution of aqueous copper sulphate into two portions. He then added concentrated hydrochloric acid to one portion and concentrated ammonia solution to the other.

   a   Explain the meaning of the terms **ligand** and **complex**.

   b   Describe any observations the student made and explain them in terms of ligand substitution.

   c   Use these reactions to discuss different shapes of transition metal complexes.

2   a   Copy and complete the electronic configuration of Cu^{2+}:
       $1s^2\, 2s^2\, 2p^6\, 3s^2\, 3p^6$

   b   Transition metals are frequently used as catalysts in industrial reactions.
       (i) Give one example of such a catalyst.
       (ii) Explain why transition metals are good catalysts.

   c   Transition metal compounds are also found as waste products in industry. To test if the chromate ion, CrO_4^{2-}, is present in waste water from a chrome-plating plant, sodium dithionite, $Na_2S_2O_4$, is used:

   $$3S_2O_4^{2-}(aq) + 2CrO_4^{2-}(aq) + 2H_2O(l) + 2OH^-(aq) \rightarrow 6SO_3^{2-}(aq) + 2Cr(OH)_3(s)$$

   In this test, $22\,cm^3$ of waste water reacted exactly with $50\,cm^3$ of standard $0.2\,mol\,dm^{-3}$ aqueous sodium dithionite. Calculate
       (i)   the amount of sodium dithionite used in the reaction;
       (ii) the amount of chromate ion used in the reaction;
       (iii) the concentration of chromate ions in the waste water;
       (iv) the oxidation number of S in $S_2O_4^{2-}$ and SO_3^{2-}.

Part 3: Unifying Concepts

CHAPTER 12

How fast?

By the end of this chapter you should be able to:

1. explain and use the terms: *rate of reaction*, *order*, *rate constant*, *half-life*, *rate-determining step*;

2. deduce, from a concentration–time graph, the rate of a reaction and the half-life of a first-order reaction;

3. recall that the half-life of a first-order reaction is independent of the concentration;

4. deduce, from a rate–concentration graph, the order (0, 1 or 2) with respect to a reactant;

5. calculate, using the *initial-rates method*, the order (0, 1 or 2) with respect to a reactant;

6. construct a *rate equation* of the form: rate $= k[A]^m[B]^n$, for which m and n are 0, 1 or 2;

7. calculate a rate constant from a rate equation;

8. explain qualitatively, the effect of temperature change on a rate constant and hence the rate of a reaction;

9. for a multi-step reaction, predict an expression for the rate equation, given the rate-determining step, know that a rate equation enables a rate-determining step to be proposed, and use a rate equation and the balanced equation for a reaction to suggest possible steps in a *reaction mechanism*.

In *Chemistry 1* you were introduced to the more qualitative aspects of reaction rates. For example, you saw how collision theory can be used to explain the effect of changing concentration, pressure or temperature on reaction rate. Quantitative aspects were limited to making measurements during rate experiments and using activation energy to explain the effect of temperature changes or catalysts on reaction rate.

A knowledge and understanding of the rate of a reaction for the production of a chemical is essential before work begins on the design of a manufacturing plant. In *Chemistry 1*, you saw how the work of Haber led to the process for making ammonia that bears his name.

Over the past 25 years, the study of atmospheric chemistry has developed. There are many different chemical species naturally present in the atmosphere. Many more chemical species are present due to the activities of man. Studies of the atmosphere have shown that the variety of reactions between these species is very large indeed. Many of these reactions require ultraviolet radiation. Some are only possible in the upper atmosphere (*figure 12.1*), others occur under the different conditions present close to the surface of the Earth.

Where the reaction rates are particularly fast, the study of these reactions has required new techniques. Ronald Norrish and George Porter won the 1967 Nobel Prize in Chemistry for their work in Cambridge on the development of a technique to follow fast reactions. Their technique, known as 'flash-photolysis' used a flashlight to 'freeze' reactions and observe intermediates with

● **Figure 12.1** The Northern Lights (aurora borealis) are the result of many complex reactions taking place in the upper atmosphere. A knowledge of reaction rates is needed to understand the natural reactions involved and how these might be disturbed by man-made emissions.

lifetimes of 10^{-6} to 10^{-3} s. Porter (*figure 12.2*) subsequently refined the technique and developed the use of a laser to study reactions. The reaction is started by a very short, intense flash from the laser. This is very quickly followed by a second flash which allows the composition of the mixture to be studied spectroscopically.

● **Figure 12.2** George Porter, who, with Ronald Norrish, won a Nobel Prize in 1967 for their work on measuring fast reaction rates.

The 1986 Nobel Prize for Chemistry went to Dudley Herschbach, Yuan Lee and John Polanyi, who used a crossed molecular beam technique to enable even faster reactions, with lifetimes of intermediates in picoseconds (ps, 10^{-12} s), to be studied. Most recently, the Egyptian chemist Ahmed Zewail won the 1999 Nobel Prize for measurements of even faster reactions taking place in femtoseconds (fs, 10^{-15} s). Zewail's technique allows chemists to follow vibrations of individual bonds, which last 10–100 fs, for reactions which are complete in less than 200 fs.

SAQ 12.1
a Which region of the electromagnetic spectrum would enable the vibrations of individual bonds to be identified?
b Write 200 fs in seconds using standard form.

In this chapter you will find out about the quantitative aspects of reaction rates. In particular, you will meet the rate equation for a reaction and learn how to determine rate equations from measurements made whilst following a reaction.

You will also, like the Nobel Prizewinners mentioned above, find out how a study of reaction rates leads to ideas for the intermediates present in reaction mechanisms. However, the reactions that you will study take place over several minutes rather than in split seconds!

The rate equation

A simple example of a rate equation is provided by the isomerisation of cyclopropane to propene.

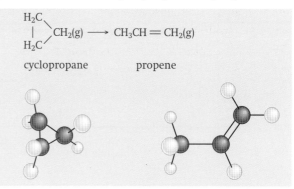

cyclopropane   propene

Table 12.1 shows the change in concentration of cyclopropane at 500 °C. As temperature affects the rate of reaction, the measurements in *table 12.1*

Time (min)	0	5	10	15	20	25	30	35	40
[cyclopropane](mol dm^{-3})	1.50	1.23	1.00	0.82	0.67	0.55	0.45	0.37	0.33
[propene](mol dm^{-3})	0.00	0.27	0.49	0.68	0.83	0.95	1.08	1.13	1.20

● **Table 12.1** Concentrations of reactant (cyclopropane) and product (propene) at 5 min intervals (temperature = 500 °C (773 K)).

were all made at the same temperature. *Figure 12.3* shows a plot of the cyclopropane concentration against time, using the data from *table 12.1*. Note the square brackets round 'cyclopropane'. These square brackets are the symbols that chemists use to indicate concentration, in this case of cyclopropane. More usually, the brackets will be round the formula of the chemical species, but sometimes it is more helpful to write the name of the compound.

The rate of a chemical reaction can be found by dividing the change in concentration by time. (Remember speed is distance travelled divided by time taken.) For the cyclopropane reaction, writing Δ[cyclopropane] for a change in concentration over a time interval Δt, the rate of reaction is shown by the following expression:

$$\text{rate of decrease of cyclopropane concentration} = \frac{\Delta[\text{cyclopropane}]}{\Delta t}$$

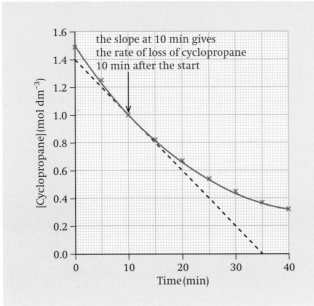

● **Figure 12.3** The rate of decrease of cyclopropane concentration over time as isomerisation proceeds. The rate of reaction at a given time can be found by drawing a tangent and measuring its gradient.

Figure 12.3 shows a method for measuring the reaction rate for the cyclopropane isomerisation. A tangent is drawn at a chosen point on the graph. This is drawn so as to *just touch* the curve of the concentration against time plot. The two angles between the straight line and the curve should look very similar. Note that the tangent is then extended to meet the axes of the graph. By extending the tangent to the axes, we reduce the error in the measurements made from the graph. The slope of the tangent is a measure of the rate of reaction.

Ten minutes after the start of the reaction, the slope of the tangent is:

$$\text{slope} = \frac{1.4 - 0.0 \,\text{mol dm}^{-3}}{35 \times 60 \,\text{s}}$$

$$= 6.67 \times 10^{-4} \,\text{mol dm}^{-3}\,\text{s}^{-1}$$

= rate of decrease of cyclopropane concentration.

Notice the units for rate of reaction are (change in) concentration per second; compare them to the typical units for the speed of a runner, metres per second (m s^{-1}).

Take another look at *figure 12.3*. Notice that, as time passes, the concentration of cyclopropane falls – hardly surprising. The question to ask is: 'In what way does it fall?' Does it fall in a predictable way? Is there a mathematical way of describing it?

Figure 12.4 supplies some answers. We will use it to calculate the rate of reaction at different concentrations: 1.5 mol dm^{-3}, 1.0 mol dm^{-3}, and 0.5 mol dm^{-3}. (Again, we can measure the rate at any point on a graph by drawing the tangent to the curve and measuring its slope at that point.)

The three measurements are shown in *table 12.2* and are represented by the graph in *figure 12.5*.

The data and *figure 12.5* show that the rate of the reaction does depend directly upon the concentration of cyclopropane as we predicted. If

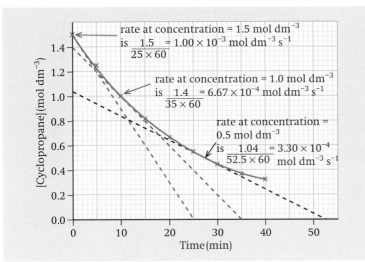

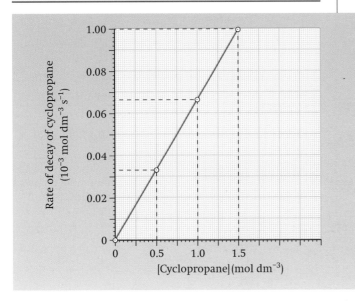

The third line in *table 12.2* shows that rate/concentration is a number that is pretty well constant ($6.7 \times 10^{-4}\,\text{s}^{-1}$). This can be expressed mathematically:

rate of reaction = $k \times$ [cyclopropane]

The proportionality constant, k, is called the **rate constant**. For the reaction above, it has the units of rate divided by concentration, s^{-1}. For the data of *table 12.2* the rate constant is $6.7 \times 10^{-4}\,\text{s}^{-1}$.

SAQ 12.3

a Plot the data in *table 12.1* for yourself. Measure the rate after 10 minutes by drawing a tangent which is about 5 cm in length and not extended to the axes. Mark the horizontal and vertical measurements on your graph and calculate a value for the rate of reaction. Compare your value with the value given in *table 12.2*. Which value do you consider to be more reliable? Explain your answer.

b Draw two further tangents at the following cyclopropane concentrations: 1.25 and $0.75\,\text{mol dm}^{-3}$. Extend these tangents to meet both axes. Use the data from these measurements, together with the data in *figure 12.4* to plot your own version of *figure 12.5*. Your data should also lie on, or close to, the straight line.

More rate equations

We already have a rate equation for the decomposition of cyclopropane:

rate = k [cyclopropane]

This rate equation was found by experiment – not by theoretical calculation.

The reaction between hydrogen gas and nitrogen monoxide, NO, at $800\,^\circ\text{C}$ produces water and nitrogen gas:

$$2H_2(g) + 2NO(g) \rightarrow 2H_2O(g) + N_2(g)$$

• **Figure 12.4** Calculations of the rate of decay of cyclopropane, made at regular intervals.

concentration (mol dm^{-3})	1.5	1.0	0.5
rate (mol dm^{-3} s^{-1})	1.00×10^{-3}	6.67×10^{-4}	3.30×10^{-4}
$\dfrac{\text{rate}}{\text{concentration}}$ (s^{-1})	6.7×10^{-4}	6.7×10^{-4}	6.6×10^{-4}

• **Table 12.2** Rates of decay for cyclopropane at different concentrations, calculated from *figure 12.4*.

the concentration of cyclopropane drops to two thirds, so does its reaction rate.

SAQ 12.2

Consider the cyclopropane reaction described above. What would happen to the reaction rate if the concentration of cyclopropane was halved?

• **Figure 12.5** The rate of decay of cyclopropane. Note how the gradient (rate/concentration) is constant.

Experiment shows that doubling the concentration of hydrogen doubles the rate of reaction, tripling $[H_2]$ triples the rate, and so on. So

$$\text{rate} \propto [H_2] \qquad \text{or} \qquad \text{rate} = k_1 \times [H_2]$$

Further experiment shows that doubling the concentration of nitrogen monoxide quadruples the rate of reaction (2^2), tripling $[NO]$ increases it by a factor of nine (3^2), and so on. Therefore

$$\text{rate} \propto [NO]^2 \qquad \text{or} \qquad \text{rate} = k_2 \times [NO]^2$$

The two equations can be combined as follows:

$$\text{rate of reaction} \propto [H_2][NO]^2$$
$$\text{or} \qquad \text{rate of reaction} = k_1 \times k_2 \times [H_2] \times [NO]^2$$
$$= k \times [H_2] \times [NO]^2$$

(where $k_1 \times k_2 = k$), which can be written as

$$\text{rate of reaction} = k[H_2][NO]^2$$

More rate equations are shown in *table 12.3*. They were all found by experiment. They cannot be predicted from the equation – so don't assume they can. The units for k may be different for each reaction; they must be worked out for each reaction. For example:

$$k[H_2][NO]^2 = \text{rate of reaction in mol dm}^{-3}\,\text{s}^{-1}$$

$$\text{so } k \text{ is in } \frac{(\text{mol dm}^{-3}\,\text{s}^{-1})}{(\text{mol dm}^{-3}) \times (\text{mol dm}^{-3})^2}$$

i.e. k's units are $\text{dm}^6\,\text{mol}^{-2}\,\text{s}^{-1}$.

Order of reaction

The order of a reaction gives us an idea of how the concentration of a reagent affects the reaction rate. It is defined as follows: the **order of a reaction** is the power to which we have to raise the concentration to fit the rate equation.

The easiest way to explain order is to use an example.

- Chemical equation:
  $$2NO(g) + O_2(g) \rightarrow 2NO_2(g)$$

- Experimental rate equation:
  $$\text{rate of reaction} = k[NO]^2[O_2]^1 = k[NO]^2[O_2]$$

The order of the reaction as far as nitrogen monoxide (NO) is concerned is 2. It is the power of 2 in $[NO]^2$. We say the reaction is 'second order with respect to nitrogen monoxide'.

The order of reaction as far as oxygen is concerned is 1. We say the reaction is 'first order with respect to oxygen'.

Overall, the order of reaction is $2 + 1 = 3$. Note how careful you should be when you talk about reaction orders. Always ask yourself the question: 'Order with respect to *what*?'

SAQ 12.4

What is the order of reaction for the decomposition of cyclopropane to propene? The rate equation is

$$\text{rate of reaction} = k[\text{cyclopropane}]$$

Zero-order reactions

Ammonia gas decomposes on a hot tungsten wire.

$$2NH_3(g) \xrightarrow{\text{W}} N_2(g) + 3H_2(g)$$

The rate of decomposition does not depend upon the concentration of ammonia gas. The rate of reaction is fixed. Doubling and tripling the concentration of ammonia makes no difference to the rate at which the ammonia decomposes. Thus

$$\text{rate of reaction} = k$$

which can be written as

$$\text{rate of reaction} = k[NH_3]^0$$

(since anything to the power 0 equals 1). When a graph of rate of reaction against concentration is plotted for a zero-order reaction, a horizontal straight line is obtained as shown in *figure 12.6*.

First-order reactions

The gas dinitrogen oxide, N_2O, decomposes on a heated gold surface:

$$2N_2O(g) \xrightarrow{\text{Au}} 2N_2(g) + O_2(g)$$

Equation for the reaction	Rate equation	Units for k
$2H_2(g) + 2NO(g) \rightarrow 2H_2O(g) + N_2(g)$	rate = $k[H_2][NO]^2$	$\text{dm}^6\,\text{mol}^{-2}\,\text{s}^{-1}$
$H_2(g) + I_2(g) \rightarrow 2HI(g)$	rate = $k[H_2][I_2]$	$\text{dm}^3\,\text{mol}^{-1}\,\text{s}^{-1}$
$NO(g) + CO(g) + O_2(g) \rightarrow NO_2(g) + CO_2(g)$	rate = $k[NO]^2$	$\text{dm}^3\,\text{mol}^{-1}\,\text{s}^{-1}$

- **Table 12.3** Rate equations for some reactions.

The rate of reaction depends directly upon the concentration of N_2O. If its concentration is doubled, its reaction rate doubles. Thus

rate of reaction = $k[N_2O]$

which can be written as

rate of reaction = $k[N_2O]^1$

(since anything to the power 1 is unchanged).
When a graph of rate of reaction against concentration is plotted for a first-order reaction, an inclined straight line is obtained as shown in *figure 12.6*.

Second-order reactions

Ethanal vapour (CH_3CHO) decomposes at 800 K:

$$CH_3CHO(g) \rightarrow CH_4(g) + CO(g)$$

The rate of reaction depends directly upon the square of the concentration of CH_3CHO. If its concentration is doubled, its rate of reaction quadruples. Thus

rate of reaction = $k[CH_3CHO]^2$

When a graph of rate of reaction against concentration is plotted for a second-order reaction, a curved line is obtained as shown in *figure 12.6*.

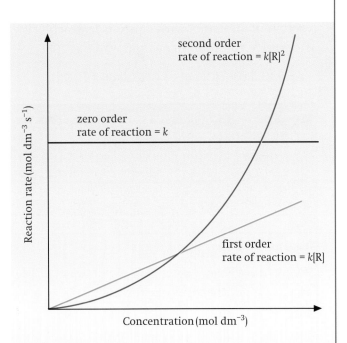

● **Figure 12.6** Zero-, first- and second-order reactions: how changes in the concentration of a reactant affect the reaction rate.

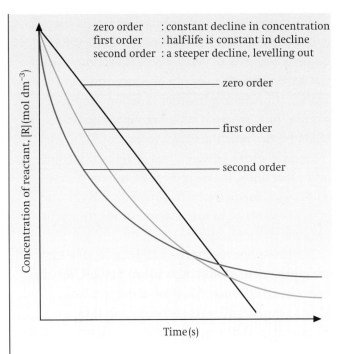

● **Figure 12.7** Zero-, first- and second-order reactions: how changes in the concentration of a reactant affect the time taken for a reaction to proceed.

An alternative method of distinguishing between these three types is shown in *figure 12.7*.

Figure 12.7 shows the differences between the concentration against time graphs for zero-, first- and second-order reactions. The zero-order data is immediately recognisable as it is a straight line. However, both the first- and second-order data produce a curve. In the next section you will see how we can distinguish between these curves, so we can identify a first-order reaction.

A generalised form of the rate equation for the reaction

$$A + B \rightarrow products$$

is

rate of reaction = $k[A]^m[B]^n$

The powers m and n show the order of the reaction with respect to reactants A, B.

Half-life and reaction rates

In chemical reactions half-life ($t_{\frac{1}{2}}$) refers to concentrations of reactants − it is the time taken for the concentration of a reactant to fall to half its original value.

A feature of a first-order reaction is that the half-life is independent of concentration. This is not true for zero- or second-order reactions. As you have just seen, a graph of concentration against time for a zero-order reaction produces a straight line, whereas such graphs for first- and second-order reactions are curves.

To distinguish between first-order and second-order reactions, measurement of two (or more) half-lives is made from the graph. *Figure 12.8* and *table 12.4* show such measurements for the cyclopropane isomerisation reaction.

The three figures for the half-lives in *table 12.4* are quite close, producing a mean half-life for this reaction of 17.0 min. A second-order reaction shows significant increases when half-lives are measured in this way. A zero-order reaction shows significant decreases in half-lives. As this book deals only with orders of 0, 1 or 2 with respect to an individual reagent, you may assume that a concentration–time curve with a half-life which increases with decreasing concentration is a second-order reaction. In general, this is not a satisfactory way of identifying a second-order reaction as orders of reaction other than 0, 1 or 2 do exist. For example, orders of −1 or fractional orders are known. Much less common are third-order reactions. Concentration against time graphs for these other orders may also be curves.

You will only be expected to identify orders of 0, 1 or 2 from rate measurements.

Finding the order of reaction using raw data

We are now going to proceed to a more complex example. Keep clear in your mind the meanings of the terms 'rate of reaction', 'rate constant', and 'order of reaction'. It helps also to keep an eye on the units you will use.

We can identify a sequence of steps in the processing of the experimental results:
- summarising the raw data in a table;
- plotting a graph of raw data;
- finding the rate at a particular concentration;
- tabulating rate data;
- plotting a graph of rate/concentration data.

Table 12.5 gives rate and concentration data for the reaction of methanol with aqueous hydrochloric acid to give chloromethane and water at 298K:

$$CH_3OH(aq) + HCl(aq) \rightarrow CH_3Cl(aq) + H_2O(l)$$

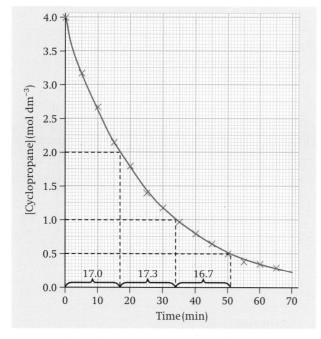

● **Figure 12.8** Measurement of half-life for cyclopropane isomerisation.

Δ[cyclopropane] (mol dm^{-3})	Half-life (min)
4.0 to 2.0	17.0
2.0 to 1.0	34.3 − 17.0 = 17.3
1.0 to 0.5	51.0 − 34.3 = 16.7

● **Table 12.4**

Time (min)	[HCl] (mol dm^{-3})	[CH$_3$OH] (mol dm^{-3})
0	1.84	1.84
200	1.45	1.45
400	1.22	1.22
600	1.04	1.04
800	0.91	0.91
1000	0.81	0.81
1200	0.72	0.72
1400	0.66	0.66
1600	0.60	0.60
1800	0.56	0.56
2000	0.54	0.54

● **Table 12.5** Data for the reaction between methanol and hydrochloric acid.

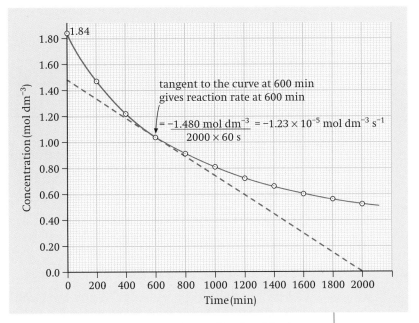

The labels and annotations within the figure read:

1.84

tangent to the curve at 600 min
gives reaction rate at 600 min

$= \dfrac{-1.480 \text{ mol dm}^{-3}}{2000 \times 60 \text{ s}} = -1.23 \times 10^{-5} \text{ mol dm}^{-3} \text{ s}^{-1}$

Concentration (mol dm^{-3})

Time (min)

● **Figure 12.9** The concentrations of hydrochloric acid and methanol fall at the same rate as time elapses.

SAQ 12.5

The data in *table 12.5* could have been obtained by titrating small samples of the reaction mixture with a standard strong base. What would have been found like this? How else might the reaction have been monitored?

Figure 12.9 shows a graph of these data, and the beginnings of an exploration of the data.

First look to see if there is a consistent half-life for this reaction. Half of the initial amount of each reagent is $1.84/2 \text{ mol dm}^{-3} = 0.92 \text{ mol dm}^{-3}$. The half-life is 780 min. However, this amount, 0.92 mol dm^{-3}, does not halve again in another 780 min. The second half-life (from 0.92 to 0.46 mol dm^{-3}) is off the graph at around 1400–1500 min. The concentration–time graph has a long 'tail' at low concentration which is typical of a second-order graph. The half-life increases

– so the overall order of reaction is likely to be 2.

As with the previous reaction, we can draw tangents to the curve to derive approximate rates at different times. This is shown for $t = 600$ min in *figure 12.9*. Other values have been calculated from these data and are shown in *table 12.6*. You can draw your own graph using the data in *table 12.5* to find out what results *you* obtain – they should vary a bit owing to the difficulty of drawing an accurate tangent by eye.

By examining the data in *table 12.6* you can see that the rate of reaction diminishes with time – unlike a zero-order reaction. A graph (*figure 12.10*, overleaf) shows that it most closely resembles a second-order plot (see *figure 12.6*, page 109).

SAQ 12.6

a Look again at the raw data in *table 12.5*. Notice that the concentrations of both CH_3OH and HCl are changing.

   (i) Are both reactants affecting the rate or is only one reactant responsible for the data in *table 12.5*?

   (ii) Suggest how the experiment might be re-designed to obtain data that would provide evidence for the effect of changing the HCl concentration whilst controlling the CH_3OH concentration.

b Further experiments have shown that the rate of this reaction is first order with respect to each of methanol, hydrogen ions and chloride ions. Suggest how these experiments could be carried out.

Time (min)	Concentration (mol dm^{-3})	Rate from graph (mol dm^{-3} min^{-1})	Rate from graph (mol dm^{-3} s^{-1})
0	1.84	2.30×10^{-3}	3.83×10^{-5}
200	1.45	1.46×10^{-3}	2.43×10^{-5}
400	1.22	1.05×10^{-3}	1.75×10^{-5}
600	1.04	0.74×10^{-3}	1.23×10^{-5}
800	0.91	0.54×10^{-3}	0.90×10^{-5}

● **Table 12.6** Values calculated for the reaction between methanol and hydrochloric acid.

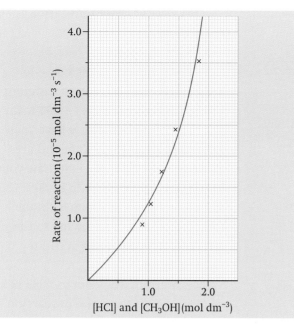

● **Figure 12.10** A graph showing how concentration changes of hydrochloric acid or methanol affect reaction rate. The curve show that the reaction is likely to be second order.

The results in *table 12.7* show that over a range of times during the reaction, k is constant. (Although the figures are not exactly equal, they are fairly close considering that tangents were estimated from a graph.)

Time (min)	Rate constant k $(10^{-5}\,\mathrm{dm^3\,mol^{-1}\,s^{-1}})$
0	1.13
200	1.16
400	1.18
600	1.14
800	1.09

● **Table 12.7** Calculations for the rate constant k assuming that the reaction is first order with respect to each of the starting reagents.

The initial-rates method

We have seen that the rate of a reaction changes as the reactants are used up. For some reactions, measuring these changes over time may not be the best method for determining the rate equation. For instance, if the rate is quite slow, then obtaining a useful set of measurements would take an inconvenient amount of time. However, we usually know the initial concentrations of the reactants that we mix together in the reaction flask, and we can measure the initial rate of

Initial concentration $[N_2O_5]\,(\mathrm{mol\,dm^{-3}})$	Initial rate $(10^{-5}\,\mathrm{mol\,dm^{-3}\,s^{-1}})$
3.00	3.15
1.50	1.55
0.75	0.80

● **Table 12.8** Data for the decomposition of dinitrogen pentoxide.

reaction. (For example, look again at the graph in *figure 12.4*, page 107: the rate we calculated at the concentration of $1.5\,\mathrm{mol\,dm^{-3}}$ is the initial rate.) If we carry out several experiments with different initial concentrations of reactants, and we measure the initial rates of these experiments, then we can determine the rate equation. The best way to illustrate this is with an example.

Dinitrogen pentoxide decomposes to nitrogen dioxide and oxygen:

$$2N_2O_5(g) \rightarrow 4NO_2(g) + O_2(g)$$

Table 12.8 gives the values of the initial rate as it varies with the concentration of dinitrogen pentoxide. A graph of the data (*figure 12.11*) shows that the initial rate of reaction is directly proportional to the initial concentration:

$$\text{Rate of reaction} \propto [N_2O_5]$$
$$= k[N_2O_5]$$

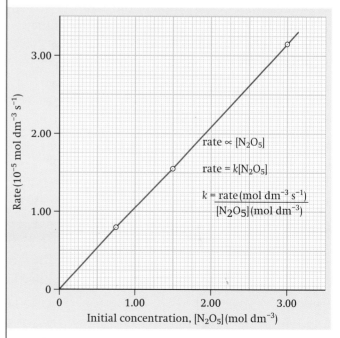

● **Figure 12.11** The initial rate of decomposition of dinitrogen pentoxide is directly proportional to the initial concentration.

SAQ 12.7

a What is the order of reaction for the decomposition of dinitrogen pentoxide?

b Use the data for $3.00\,mol\,dm^{-3}$ N_2O_5 to calculate a value for the rate constant for this decomposition.

Another example of the use of initial rates is provided by data from experiments to follow the acid-catalysed reaction of iodine with propanone.

$$CH_3COCH_3 + I_2 \rightarrow CH_3COCH_2I + HI$$
propanone

This reaction is readily followed using a colorimeter. The yellow colour of the iodine fades as the reaction progresses.

Table 12.9 shows data obtained at $20\,^{\circ}C$ from four separate experiments to measure the initial rates of reaction.

The data are from real experiments so we must bear in mind experimental errors. Note that in each experiment the initial concentration of just one reagent has been changed from that in experiment 1.

Compare experiments 1 and 2. You will see that the concentration of $H^+(aq)$ in experiment 2 is half the value of that in experiment 1. The initial rate has also been approximately halved. From this information we can deduce that the reaction is first order with respect to the acid catalyst.

Now compare experiments 1 and 3. The propanone concentration in experiment 3 is half that in experiment 1. Again the initial rate has been halved. We deduce that the reaction is first order with respect to propanone.

Finally, compare experiments 1 and 4. The iodine concentration has been halved but the initial rate stays approximately the same. We deduce that the reaction is zero order with respect to iodine.

SAQ 12.8

a Write the rate equation for the acid-catalysed reaction of iodine with propanone using the above deductions.

b Calculate the rate constant for this reaction.

c Deduce the units of the rate constant.

Rate constants and temperature changes

An increase in the temperature of a reaction mixture by $10\,^{\circ}C$ approximately doubles the rate of reaction. How can this increase in rate be explained by the rate equation? A general form of the rate equation for reaction of A and B to form products is

$$\text{rate of reaction} = k[A]^m[B]^n$$

As temperature will not change the concentrations of A or B, the rate constant, k, must change if the reaction rate is to increase. We can predict that an increase in temperature will increase the value of k. An example of the rate constants for a reaction over a range of temperatures confirms our prediction.

Table 12.10 (overleaf) shows the rate constants for the reaction of hydrogen and iodine at different temperatures. The equation for this reaction is

$$H_2(g) + I_2(g) \rightarrow 2HI(g)$$

The rate equation is:

$$\text{rate of reaction} = k[H_2(g)][I_2(g)]$$

From the above examples we can make some important deductions about the kinetics of chemical processes. As we stressed in Chemistry 1, chapter 14, the first step in a kinetic investigation is to establish the stoichiometry of the reaction, so we must analyse all the reaction

Exp.	[HCl] (mol dm⁻³)	[propane] (mol dm⁻³)	[iodine] (10⁻³ mol dm⁻³)	Initial rate (10⁻⁶ mol dm⁻³ s⁻¹)
1	1.25	0.5	1.25	10.9
2	0.625	0.5	1.25	4.7
3	1.25	0.25	1.25	5.1
4	1.25	0.5	0.625	10.7

● Table 12.9 Experimental results for the reaction of propanone with iodine at varying aqueous concentrations.

Temperature (K)	Rate constant ($dm^3\,mol^{-1}\,s^{-1}$)
500	4.3×10^{-7}
600	4.4×10^{-4}
700	6.3×10^{-2}
800	2.6

● **Table 12.10** Rate constants for the reaction of hydrogen and iodine over a range of temperatures.

products. The stoichiometry for a reaction shows the mole ratio of reactants and products in the balanced equation for the reaction. However, there is no correspondence between the stoichiometric equation for the reaction and the rate equation. We certainly cannot predict one from the other.

Rate equations – the pay-off

Chemists are particularly interested in the mechanisms of chemical reactions – which chemical bonds are broken, which are made and in what order. Such an understanding helps chemists to design the synthesis of new compounds (see *figure 12.12*). For example, an understanding of the mechanism of stereoregular polymerisation (see chapter 7) has led to new catalysts for the polymerisation of ethene or propene. The polymers produced by the new catalysts (called metallocenes) are stronger and more tear-resistant than other polymers. They can be used for food packaging as they are very impermeable to air and moisture.

By using the rate equation, sometimes along with other items of information, we can deduce something about the separate bond-making and bond-breaking processes that go to make up the overall reaction.

Some reactions may consist of a single step. For example, when aqueous sodium hydroxide is mixed with dilute hydrochloric acid, the reaction is simply one in which hydrogen ions pair up with hydroxide ions to form water. The other ions do not participate in the reaction – they are called spectator ions and just get left alongside each other in solution:

$$Na^+(aq) + OH^-(aq) + H^+(aq) + Cl^-(aq)$$
$$\rightarrow H_2O(l) + Na^+(aq) + Cl^-(aq)$$

Very frequently, a reaction is made up of a number of sequential steps. Each step will have a rate associated with it, but to find the overall rate of reaction, all we need to know is the rate of the *slowest* step (also called the **rate-determining step**). This is the case when all other steps are much faster. Fast steps, like selecting items off shelves in a supermarket, become insignificant when compared to the slow step, like queuing at the checkout.

We use the following principle, by which we can use the rate equation to construct the reaction mechanism: *If the concentration of a reactant appears in the rate equation, then that reactant or something derived from it takes part in the slow step of the reaction. If it does not appear in the rate equation, then neither the reactant nor anything derived from it participates in the slow step.*

This is the key to the interpretation of rate equations in terms of mechanisms of reactions. We can now consider some of the reactions we have looked at above, in terms of what their kinetic character, and other data, may tell us of their mechanism.

● **Figure 12.12** A very thin film of polymer produced using a metallocene catalyst. The strength and puncture resistance are being tested using a ball point pen.

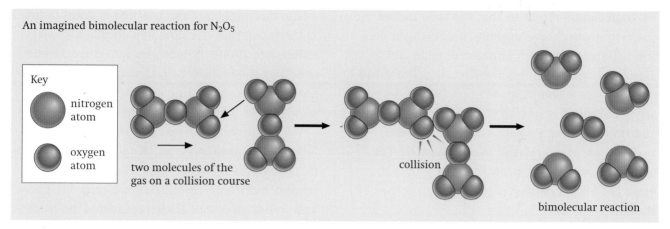

An imagined bimolecular reaction for N_2O_5

Key
nitrogen atom
oxygen atom

two molecules of the gas on a collision course

collision

bimolecular reaction

● **Figure 12.13** The equation for the decomposition of dinitrogen pentoxide suggests that a reaction between two molecules occurs (a bimolecular reaction). The rate equation tells us otherwise.

Reaction mechanisms

We look again at the reaction for the decomposition of dinitrogen pentoxide:

$$2N_2O_5(g) \rightarrow 4NO_2(g) + O_2(g)$$

You may have been surprised that this did not turn out to be a second-order reaction. The stoichiometry is bimolecular – we need two molecules of dinitrogen pentoxide to balance the equation. So we can imagine that the reaction might start by two N_2O_5 molecules colliding and breaking up as suggested in the equation shown in *figure 12.13*.

But the rate equation tells us something different.

rate of reaction = $k[N_2O_5]$

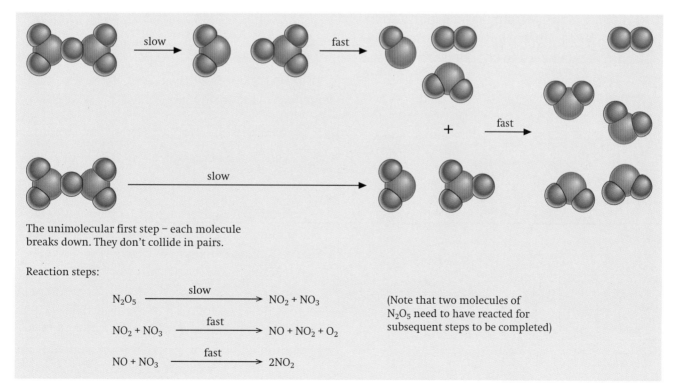

slow

fast

fast

slow

The unimolecular first step – each molecule breaks down. They don't collide in pairs.

Reaction steps:

$$N_2O_5 \xrightarrow{\text{slow}} NO_2 + NO_3$$

$$NO_2 + NO_3 \xrightarrow{\text{fast}} NO + NO_2 + O_2$$

$$NO + NO_3 \xrightarrow{\text{fast}} 2NO_2$$

(Note that two molecules of N_2O_5 need to have reacted for subsequent steps to be completed)

● **Figure 12.14** The rate equation tells us that the decomposition of individual molecules of dinitrogen pentoxide is the rate-determining step. The subsequent reactions are much faster by comparison, and do not have much influence on the overall rate. Try to match the equations with the illustrations to get a picture of what is happening.

The rate equation tells us that the slow step of the reaction involves *one* molecule of dinitrogen pentoxide decomposing (to nitrogen dioxide and nitrogen trioxide). This is the first step. The subsequent steps are comparatively fast. (*Fast* and *slow* are not absolute terms, so when we speak of fast and slow steps within the context of a given reaction, we mean relative to one another.) The actual mechanism of this reaction is shown in *figure 12.14*. The first step of the reaction is the slow step.

Now let's look at the acid-catalysed reaction of propanone with iodine:

$$CH_3COCH_3(aq) + I_2(aq) \xrightarrow{\ H^+(aq)\ } CH_3COCH_2I(aq) + HI(aq)$$

It appears that hydrogen ions from the acid are not directly involved. Either they are not used up or they are regenerated with the products, at the same rate as they are used up. In either case the hydrogen ions behave as a catalyst.

The rate equation sheds some light on this (also see page 113). It is

rate of reaction = $k[CH_3COCH_3]^1[H^+]^1[I_2]^0$

Therefore, the rate-determining step must involve propanone and hydrogen ions. The concentration of iodine does not need to be included in the rate equation as iodine does not participate in the rate determining step – the reaction is zero order with respect to iodine, which means that the reaction proceeds until all the iodine is used up.

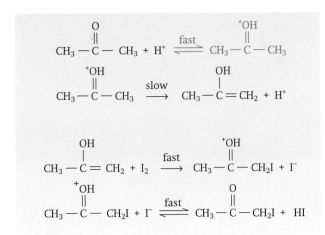

● **Figure 12.15** The slow step involves the reaction of hydrogen ions with propanone molecules. The protonated propanone intermediate forms rapidly and then slowly breaks down to give the products.

The mechanism of the reaction is given in *figure 12.15*. Notice that the slow step does not involve either propanone or hydrogen ions directly, but *something more rapidly derived from them both*, protonated propanone. Iodine intrudes later in the sequence, in what must be a subsequent fast step.

We can picture the reaction sequence as follows. The propanone exists in equilibrium with its protonated form (we shall discuss something more of acid–base equilibria in chapter 14). Every now and then one of these protonated molecules decomposes to lose H^+, not from the oxygen atom but from carbon, to yield the intermediate

$$CH_3 - \overset{\overset{\displaystyle OH}{|}}{C} = CH_2$$

We could not have deduced this reaction scheme precisely from the rate equation, but it does fit in with that equation. Confirmatory evidence is given by the fact that if we carry out the reaction not with iodine, but with heavy water, D_2O, a deuterium atom, D (a hydrogen atom with a neutron as well as a proton in the nucleus) is taken up by the methyl group of the propanone at exactly the same rate as iodine is in the first reaction. The two reactions have the same rate-determining steps.

A reaction revisited

The rate equation for the reaction between methanol and hydrochloric acid:

$$CH_3OH(aq) + HCl(aq) \longrightarrow CH_3Cl(aq) + H_2O(l)$$

as established by experiment is

rate of reaction = $k[CH_3OH][HCl]$

Extra information can help us to formulate a reaction mechanism. The rate equation suggests that a simple readjustment of bonds in a single-step reaction is involved (*figure 12.16*).

However, experiments show that the rate can be increased by the addition of a strong acid, H^+ ions, to the reaction mixture as well as by the addition of sodium chloride or a similar source of chloride ions, Cl^-. It is clear that the rate equation does not cater for the separate effects of varying concentrations of hydrogen ions and chloride ions. The new rate equation that is correct for hydrochloric acid, but also accounts for the separate effects of

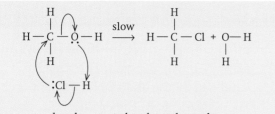

bonds seem to break...and remake

● **Figure 12.16** An apparent mechanism for the reaction between methanol and hydrochloric acid.

hydrogen ions and chloride ions, is

$$\text{rate} = k[CH_3OH][H^+][Cl^-]$$

Now let us re-examine the proposed mechanism for this reaction in the light of the more general rate equation. The first stage consists of a protonation equilibrium:

$$H_3C-OH + H^+ \rightleftharpoons H_3C-\overset{+}{\underset{H}{O}}\overset{H}{{}}$$

This is followed by an attack by the chloride ion.

SAQ 12.9

Write the second stage of the reaction between methanol and hydrochloric acid so that it fits the rate equation based upon the supplementary facts we know about the reaction.

SUMMARY

◆ The rate of reaction is a measure of the rate of use of reactants and the rate of production of products. It is measured in units of concentration per unit time ($\text{mol dm}^{-3}\text{s}^{-1}$).

◆ The rate of reaction is related to the concentrations of the reactants by the rate equation, which (for two reactants A and B) is of the form:
rate of reaction = $k[A]^m[B]^n$

where k is the rate constant, [A] and [B] are the concentrations of the reactants, m is the order of reaction with respect to A and n is the order of reaction with respect to B.

◆ The rate equation cannot be predicted from the stoichiometric equation.

◆ The overall order of reaction is the sum of the individual orders of the reactants. For the example above:
overall order = $m + n$

◆ The order of reaction may be determined by the initial-rates method, in which the initial rate is measured for several experiments using different concentrations of reactants. One concentration is changed whilst the others are fixed, so that a clear and systematic set of results is obtained.

◆ The order of reaction may also be determined from a single experiment, in which a concentration–time graph is recorded over a period of time. Tangents taken from several points on the graph give a measure of how the reaction rate changes with time. The rate of reaction at a particular point is the gradient of the graph at that point.

◆ The half-life of a first-order reaction is the time taken for the initial concentration of a reactant to halve, and it is independent of the concentration(s) of reactant(s).

◆ The increase in rate of a reaction with increasing temperature is accompanied by an increase in the value of the rate constant, k, for the reaction.

◆ The order of reaction with respect to a particular reactant indicates how many molecules of that reactant participate in the slow step (rate-determining step) of a reaction mechanism. This slow step determines the overall rate of reaction.

◆ Determination of the slow step provides evidence for the mechanism of a reaction.

◆ The rate equation for a reaction may be deduced given its slowest step.

Questions

1 Nitrogen(II) oxide is formed at high temperature in car engines which run on petrol. When this gas is released from the car exhaust into the atmosphere it oxidises to nitrogen(IV) oxide. The following equation shows one reaction in which NO is oxidised to NO_2 in air.

$$2NO(g) + O_2(g) \rightarrow 2NO_2(g)$$

The following table shows data obtained from four experiments to investigate the effect of changing concentrations of NO and NO_2 on the rate of this reaction at a temperature of 20 °C.

Experiment	Initial [NO] $(10^{-2}\,mol\,dm^{-3})$	Initial [O$_2$] $(10^{-2}\,mol\,dm^{-3})$	Initial rate of formation of NO$_2$ $(10^{-4}\,mol\,dm^{-3}\,s^{-1})$
1	1.0	1.0	0.7
2	2.0	1.0	2.8
3	1.0	2.0	1.4
4	3.0	2.0	18.9

a (i) Using the results for experiments 1 to 3, deduce the order of reaction with respect to each of NO and O_2. Explain your reasoning.

(ii) Use the orders of reaction that you have deduced in part (i) to explain the numerical value of the rate of reaction in experiment 4.

b (i) Write the expression for the rate equation for this reaction.

(ii) Use the results for experiment 2 together with your rate equation to calculate the rate constant for this reaction. Give the units of this rate constant.

(iii) The overall order for this reaction is unusual. State the overall order and suggest a reason why this order of reaction is unusual.

2 Ethyl ethanoate, $CH_3COOCH_2CH_3$, hydrolyses very slowly in water. The reaction is catalysed by the addition of an acid such as sulphuric acid. The equation for this hydrolysis reaction is:

$$CH_3COOCH_2CH_3(l) + H_2O(l)$$
$$\rightleftharpoons CH_3COOH(l) + CH_3CH_2OH(l)$$

Data obtained for this reaction at a temperature of 50 °C is shown in the table below.

[CH$_3$COOCH$_2$CH$_3$] (mol dm^{-3})	0.50	0.39	0.31	0.17	0.13	0.09
time (10^4 s)	0.00	0.20	0.40	0.90	1.10	1.40

a Using these results, deduce the order of this reaction with respect to ethyl ethanoate. Explain your reasoning.

b Outline further experiments you would need to carry out in order to establish the rate equation for the reaction.

3 A student investigated the rate of the reaction of methanoic acid, HCOOH, with aqueous bromine and obtained the results shown in the table. She used a large excess of methanoic acid and maintained the reaction mixture at a constant temperature whilst making her measurements. The equation for the reaction is shown below.

$$HCOOH(aq) + Br_2(aq)$$
$$\rightarrow CO_2(g) + 2H^+(aq) + 2Br^-(aq)$$

[Br$_2$] (10^{-3} mol dm^{-3})	Rate (10^{-5} mol dm^{-3} s^{-1})
10.0	–
9.2	3.2
8.4	2.9
7.0	2.4
5.0	1.7
2.5	0.9
1.2	0.4

a (i) Explain why she used a large excess of HCOOH.

(ii) Suggest two methods the student might have chosen to follow this reaction.

b (i) Describe how she would have obtained the rate figure from a graph that she plotted of concentration of bromine against time.

(ii) Using the data in the table and an appropriate graph, deduce the order of reaction with respect to bromine.

(iii) Using your answer to **b**(ii), state the rate equation under these conditions.

(iv) Calculate a value of the rate constant when $[Br_2] = 7.0 \times 10^{-3}\,mol\,dm^{-3}$.

4 A good example of the effect of a catalyst is the decomposition of hydrogen peroxide to oxygen:

$$2H_2O_2(aq) \rightarrow 2H_2O(l) + O_2(g)$$

This occurs slowly at room temperatures. The reaction is accelerated by the addition of a small amount of water-soluble iodide. The reaction mechanism is as follows:

$$H_2O_2(aq) + I^-(aq) \rightarrow IO^-(aq) + H_2O(l) \quad (slow)$$
$$H_2O_2(aq) + IO^-(aq) \rightarrow H_2O(l) + O_2(g) + I^-(aq) \quad (fast)$$

Deduce the rate equation from this reaction mechanism.

5 The rate equation for the hydrolysis of 2-bromo-2-methylpropane by water is

rate of reaction
$= k[\text{2-bromo-2-methylpropane}]$.

Suggest a mechanism for this hydrolysis.

CHAPTER 13

How far?

By the end of this chapter you should be able to:

1 understand and use the terms *concentration*, *mole fraction* and *partial pressure*;

2 calculate a concentration or partial pressure present at *equilibrium*, given appropriate data;

3 deduce, for *homogeneous reactions*, expressions for the *equilibrium constants* K_c, in terms of concentrations, and K_p, in terms of partial pressures;

4 calculate the values of the equilibrium constants K_c or K_p, including determination of units, given appropriate data;

5 recall that, for an equilibrium system, changes in concentration and pressure have no effect on the magnitude of the equilibrium constant and an increase in temperature decreases the value of K_c or K_p for an exothermic reaction and increases the value of K_c or K_p for an endothermic reaction;

6 understand that a large value of K_c or K_p indicates a high *theoretical yield* of products, and vice versa;

7 appreciate that most organic reactions are in equilibrium.

This chapter picks up the chemical ideas that you met in *Chemistry 1*, chapter 15, on chemical equilibria and introduces a more quantitative approach. You will find out how the concentrations (or pressures) of reactants and products from the stoichiometric equation can be combined in the form of a constant known as the equilibrium constant. This constant may be used to predict the effect of changing concentration, pressure or temperature on the position of equilibrium. In *Chemistry 1*, chapter 15 Le Chatelier's principle was used for this purpose. However, by using the equilibrium constant, equilibrium concentrations or pressures may also be calculated.

Crocodiles, blood and carbon dioxide

An equilibrium reaction that you studied in *Chemistry 1* is the one that exists in a can of fizzy drink. You will be very familiar with the observation of bubbles of carbon dioxide being released

when the drink is poured into a glass. The equilibrium involved is represented by the following equation:

$$CO_2(g) \rightleftharpoons CO_2(aq)$$

Remember the $\rightleftharpoons$ sign indicates that the reaction is reversible. In the can, carbon dioxide gas dissolves in the drink under pressure. An equilibrium exists between undissolved carbon dioxide gas and the carbon dioxide dissolved in the drink. Within the sealed can, the rate at which the carbon dioxide is dissolving equals the rate at which the gas is escaping from the drink. We describe the equilibrium as a dynamic equilibrium.

Provided that the temperature is constant and the can is not opened, the equilibrium concentration of the carbon dioxide in the drink is constant. Equilibria are only reached in closed systems such as in the sealed can or where all reactants and products are in the same aqueous solution. A further characteristic of a dynamic

Box 13A Dynamic equilibrium

When we view a system at equilibrium, we are not aware that constant change is taking place at the microscopic level of molecules and ions. Properties we can see or measure easily remain constant. We call these macroscopic properties. Once dynamic equilibrium is achieved, the macroscopic properties such as concentration, pressure, temperature, mass or volume remain constant.

equilibrium is the constancy of macroscopic properties such as concentration (see *box 13A*).

In summary, the characteristic features of a dynamic equilibrium are that

- it is dynamic at the molecular or ionic level;
- the position of equilibrium can be approached from either side of the chemical equation;
- both forward and reverse processes occur at equal rates;
- a closed system is required;
- macroscopic properties remain constant.

So where do crocodiles and blood fit into all this? Crocodiles kill their prey by diving under water once their prey is firmly between their powerful jaws (*figure 13.1*). Crocodiles can survive under water for much longer than their prey, which dies from drowning long before the crocodile needs to surface for air.

As carbon dioxide builds up in body tissues it is converted to hydrogencarbonate ions, $HCO_3^-(aq)$, as shown in the following equilibrium equation (another that you met in *Chemistry 1*).

$$CO_2(aq) + H_2O(l) \rightleftharpoons H^+(aq) + HCO_3^-(aq) \qquad (13.1)$$

● **Figure 13.1** A crocodile drowns its prey under water. Why does the crocodile not drown like its prey?

Haemoglobin (Hb) and oxygen are also in equilibrium in the blood. This equilibrium can be represented by an equilibrium equation:

$$Hb(aq) + O_2(aq) \rightleftharpoons HbO_2(aq) \qquad (13.2)$$

The secret of a crocodile's ability to stay under water whilst its prey drowns lies in a difference in its haemoglobin. This difference allows an increase in $[HCO_3^-(aq)]$, resulting from the increase in $[CO_2(aq)]$, to release more of the oxygen carried by the crocodile haemoglobin, enabling the crocodile to survive. Meanwhile, the prey's haemoglobin is incapable of a similar response, so the prey dies.

SAQ 13.1

a Explain, in terms of the equilibrium shown in *reaction 13.1*, why $[HCO_3^-]$ increases as the crocodile drowns its prey.

b (i) Describe and explain the changes in equilibrium concentrations which take place in *reaction 13.2* in the crocodile's blood as the crocodile drowns its prey.

   (ii) In which direction does the position of equilibrium change?

Scientists in the UK and USA are applying knowledge and understanding of the behavior of haemoglobin from several animal sources and of the basic structure-function relationships to the development of recombinant human haemoglobin. Recombinant human haemoglobin, produced by genetically modified bacteria, may one day significantly reduce the need for blood donors for blood transfusion. *Figure 13.2* shows a chromatography column loaded with recombinant human haemoglobin.

The genetic coding responsible for the behaviour of both crocodile haemoglobin and that of certain fish has now been identified and introduced into the bacterium used to make artificial human haemoglobin. Artificial haemoglobin which behaves as crocodile or fish haemoglobin might allow humans to stay under water for longer periods. Such haemoglobin could be useful to divers. More importantly, it might also be helpful to those people with diseases which cause breathing difficulties.

Many other reactions in living organisms involve chemical equilibia. A study of chemical equilibria leads us to a better understanding of

● **Figure 13.2** Recombinant human haemoglobin being purified from bacteria at Baxter Haemoglobin Therapeutics, USA.

such processes. You can learn more about the structure of haemoglobin (including the role of the iron) in the optional *Biochemistry* modular text.

Equilibria in organic reactions

Like many biochemical reactions, many of the organic reactions that you met in *Chemistry 1* and in chapters 1–8 of this book also involve equilibria.

One example of an organic equilibrium reaction that you met earlier (chapter 4 of this book) is the hydrolysis of the ester ethyl ethanoate, $CH_3COOCH_2CH_3$. This ester hydrolyses slowly, forming ethanoic acid and ethanol when mixed with water and an acid catalyst such as sulphuric or hydrochloric acid. The equation for the reaction is as follows.

$$CH_3COOCH_2CH_3(l) + H_2O(l)$$
$$\rightleftharpoons CH_3COOH(l) + CH_3CH_2OH(l)$$

Table 13.1 shows the initial and equilibrium concentrations for four experiments. The mixtures were prepared by mixing together known masses of ester and water. The mixtures were placed in stoppered flasks and $1.0\ cm^3$ of concentrated sulphuric acid was added to each flask. The flasks were then left undisturbed for one week at room temperature. One week is necessary for the mixtures to reach equilibrium, even though a catalyst is used! After one week, the flasks were opened and the contents analysed by titration with standardised sodium hydroxide. A separate titration was also carried out to determine the volume of sodium hydroxide required to neutralise the sulphuric acid. The data in *table 13.1* were calculated from these titration results and the initial weighings. The last column of the table contains the symbol K_c, which is known as the equilibrium constant. The small subscript 'c' refers to concentration. You will see that the values of K_c for the data in experiments 2 and 3 are in close agreement. How is this constant calculated from the data? First of all we write the equation for the reaction:

$$CH_3COOCH_2CH_3(l) + H_2O(l)$$
$$\rightleftharpoons CH_3COOH(l) + CH_3CH_2OH(l)$$

Now we can write the equilibrium constant, K_c, as the ratio of the product concentrations (multiplied together) divided by the reactant concentrations (multiplied together), as follows:

$$K_c = \frac{[CH_3COOH][CH_3CH_2OH]}{[CH_3COOCH_2CH_3][H_2O]}$$

SAQ 13.2

Try substituting the data for experiment 2 in the above expression for K_c. Check your answer with the value in *table 13.1*.

Calculate the missing values of K_c. Remember the results are experimental, so not all values of K_c will be as close as those for experiments 2 and 3.

Finding the balance

Iodine gas is purple. The more there is, the deeper the shade of purple. A colorimeter can be used to measure this intensity, and hence the concentration of iodine in a reaction vessel.

Experiment	Concentration (mol dm^{-3})				K_c
	CH$_3$COOCH$_2$CH$_3$	H$_2$O	CH$_3$COOH	CH$_3$CH$_2$OH	
1	7.22	2.47	2.03	2.03	
2	6.38	3.69	2.56	2.56	0.278
3	4.69	8.16	3.28	3.28	0.281
4	2.81	16.6	3.56	3.56	

● **Table 13.1** Data for the hydrolysis of ethyl ethanoate.

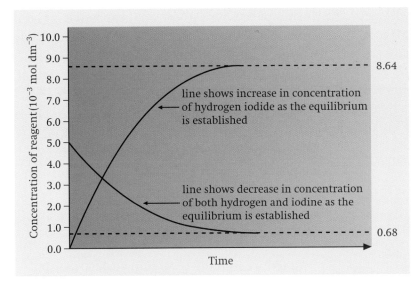

- **Figure 13.3** The changes in the concentrations of reagents as 5.00 moles of each of hydrogen and iodine react to form an equilibrium with hydrogen iodide in a vessel of volume 1 m³.

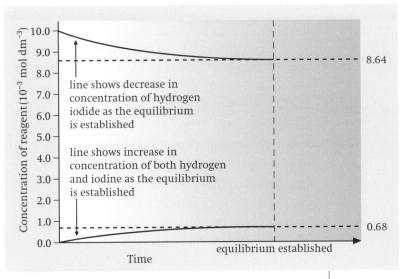

- **Figure 13.4** The changes in the concentrations of reagents as 10 moles of hydrogen iodide react to form an equilibrium with hydrogen and iodine gases in a vessel of 1 m³.

The equilibrium

$$H_2(g) + I_2(g) \rightleftharpoons 2HI(g)$$

can be approached from either side:

- by using a mixture of hydrogen gas and iodine gas (purple), which reacts to form colourless hydrogen iodide, or
- by using pure hydrogen iodide, which dissociates to form hydrogen and iodine.

The equation for the reaction is

$$H_2(g) + I_2(g) \rightleftharpoons 2HI(g)$$

Figure 13.3 illustrates what happens when 5.00 moles of each of hydrogen molecules and iodine molecules react at 500 K. As time passes, the purple colour of the iodine fades until a steady state is reached. Analysis shows that the final amount of the iodine is 0.68 moles. There must also be 0.68 moles of hydrogen left, as the equation shows. The remaining 4.32 moles of each gas have been converted to 8.64 moles of hydrogen iodide molecules.

SAQ 13.3

The same equilibrium can be achieved starting with 10 moles of hydrogen iodide molecules (*figure 13.4*). Describe what happens and satisfy yourself that, if 0.68 moles of iodine molecules are found to be in the final mixture, then there must be 8.64 moles of hydrogen iodide molecules present.

We can find the concentrations of the three components in any equilibrium by analysing the amount of iodine present in the equilibrium mixture, knowing the amount of hydrogen and iodine we had to start with. *Table 13.2* shows some values obtained. The fourth column shows the value of $[HI]^2/[H_2][I_2]$, which, as you can see, is constant (allowing for experimental error). It is called the equilibrium constant, K_c, for the reaction, and in this case it is given by the square

$[H_2]$(mol dm⁻³)	$[I_2]$(mol dm⁻³)	$[HI]$(mol dm⁻³)	$\dfrac{[HI]^2}{[H_2][I_2]}$
0.68×10^{-3}	0.68×10^{-3}	8.64×10^{-3}	161
0.50×10^{-3}	0.50×10^{-3}	6.30×10^{-3}	159
1.10×10^{-3}	1.10×10^{-3}	13.9×10^{-3}	160
1.10×10^{-3}	2.00×10^{-3}	18.8×10^{-3}	161
2.50×10^{-3}	0.65×10^{-3}	16.1×10^{-3}	160

- **Table 13.2** Equilibrium concentrations of hydrogen, $H_2(g)$, iodine, $I_2(g)$, and hydrogen iodide, $HI(g)$, at 500 K.

of the equilibrium concentration of the hydrogen iodide, divided by the product of the equilibrium concentrations of the hydrogen and the iodine.

From *table 13.2*, K_c can be found:

$$K_c = \frac{[HI][HI]}{[H_2][I_2]}$$

$$= \frac{[HI]^2}{[H_2][I_2]}$$

Notice that the 2HI in the reaction equation becomes $[HI]^2$ in the equilibrium constant expression. As a general rule, each concentration is raised to the number of moles of the relevant reactant in the balanced equation.

The units of the HI equilibrium K_c can also be found:

$$= \frac{(\cancel{mol\,dm^{-3}})^2}{(\cancel{mol\,dm^{-3}}) \times (\cancel{mol\,dm^{-3}})}$$

As the units in this expression cancel, this K_c has no units. However, each equilibrium constant must be considered individually. K_c will not have units whenever the equilibrium is homogeneous and the total number of molecules on each side of the balanced equation is the same.

Consider the equilibrium for the Contact process for the manufacture of sulphuric acid. In this process, a key stage involves the oxidation of sulphur dioxide to sulphur trioxide by oxygen. The equation and equilibrium constant for this reaction are:

$$2SO_2(g) + O_2(g) \rightleftharpoons 2SO_3(g)$$

$$K_c = \frac{[SO_3]^2}{[SO_2]^2 \times [O_2]}$$

$$\text{units of } K_c = \frac{(\cancel{mol\,dm^{-3}})^2}{(\cancel{mol\,dm^{-3}})^2 \times (mol\,dm^{-3})}$$

$$= \frac{1}{(mol\,dm^{-3})} = dm^3\,mol^{-1}$$

SAQ 13.4

Write the formula for K_c for each of the following reactions, and work out the units for K_c assuming the concentrations of the gases are measured in $mol\,dm^{-3}$.

a $2NO_2(g) \rightleftharpoons N_2O_4(g)$
b $2NO(g) + O_2(g) \rightleftharpoons 2NO_2(g)$
c $N_2(g) + 3H_2(g) \rightleftharpoons 2NH_3(g)$

Use of the equilibrium constant expression has an additional advantage in that, if we can determine one equilibrium concentration and we know the initial concentrations of other compounds present, we can determine the equilibrium concentrations of the other chemical species present. From this information, we can calculate a value for K_c.

For example, propanone reacts with hydrogen cyanide as follows (see chapter 3, page 24).

$$H_3C-\overset{\overset{\displaystyle O}{\|}}{C}-CH_3 + HCN \rightleftharpoons H_3C-\underset{\underset{\displaystyle CN}{|}}{\overset{\overset{\displaystyle OH}{|}}{C}}-CH_3$$

A mixture initially containing $0.0500\,mol\,dm^{-3}$ propanone and $0.0500\,mol\,dm^{-3}$ hydrogen cyanide in ethanol is left to reach equilibrium at room temperature. At equilibrium the concentration of the product is $0.0233\,mol\,dm^{-3}$. Calculate the equilibrium constant for this reaction under these conditions.

A helpful approach is shown below.

Step 1 Write out the equation with the initial data underneath. Notice how the chemical formulae for the compounds enable the information to be tabulated.

Step 2 The equilibrium concentration of the only product is $0.0233\,mol\,dm^{-3}$. As 1 mole of each reactant produces 1 mole of product, the concentration of each of the reactants decreases by $0.0233\,mol\,dm^{-3}$. Hence the equilibrium concentration of each reactant is now $0.0500 - 0.0233\,mol\,dm^{-3} = 0.0267\,mol\,dm^{-3}$.

$$H_3C-\overset{\overset{\displaystyle O}{\|}}{C}-CH_3 + HCN \rightleftharpoons H_3C-\underset{\underset{\displaystyle CN}{|}}{\overset{\overset{\displaystyle OH}{|}}{C}}-CH_3$$

Initial concentrations ($mol\,dm^{-3}$)	0.0500	0.0500	0
Equilibrium concentrations ($mol\,dm^{-3}$)	0.0500 − 0.0233 = 0.0267	0.0500 − 0.0233 = 0.0267	0.0233

Step 3 Write the equilibrium constant for this reaction in terms of concentrations.

$$K_c = \frac{[product]}{[propanone][hydrogen\ cyanide]}\ dm^3\,mol^{-1}$$

Note that the units are

$$\frac{\cancel{mol\,dm^{-3}}}{\cancel{mol\,dm^{-3}} \times mol\,dm^{-3}} = \frac{1}{mol\,dm^{-3}} = dm^3\,mol^{-1}$$

Step 4 The equilibrium concentrations can now be used to calculate K_c.

$$K_c = \frac{0.0223}{0.0267 \times 0.0267} \, dm^3 \, mol^{-1}$$

$$= 31.3 \, dm^3 \, mol^{-1}$$

SAQ 13.5

Calculate the equilibrium constant for the following reaction.

$$H_2(g) + CO_2(g) \rightleftharpoons CO(g) + H_2O(g)$$

The initial concentration of hydrogen is $10.00 \, mol \, dm^{-3}$ and of carbon dioxide is $90.00 \, mol \, dm^{-3}$. At equilibrium $9.47 \, mol \, dm^{-3}$ of carbon monoxide are formed.

K_c and Le Chatelier's principle

In *Chemistry 1*, chapter 15, you saw how Le Chatelier's principle (see *box 13B*) can be used to predict the effects of changes in concentration, pressure or temperature on the position of an equilibrium. For example, increasing the concentration of a reactant will lead to an increase in the concentrations of the products at a new position of equilibrium.

Predictions using Le Chatelier's principle of the effects of temperature changes are summarised, with examples, in *table 13.3*.

Box 13B

Le Chatelier's principle, expressed in modern language, states that
when any of the conditions affecting the position of a dynamic equilibrium are changed, then the position of that equilibrium will shift to minimise that change.

Example	Endothermic reaction, $2HI(g) \rightleftharpoons H_2(g) + I_2(g)$	Exothermic reaction, $2SO_2(g) + O_2(g) \rightleftharpoons 2SO_3(g)$
temperature increase	equilibrium position shifts towards products: more hydrogen and iodine form	equilibrium position shifts towards reactants: more sulphur dioxide and oxygen form
temperature decrease	equilibrium position shifts towards reactant: more hydrogen iodide forms	equilibrium position shifts towards product: more sulphur trioxide forms

● **Table 13.3** The effect of temperature change on equilibria.

Reaction	Temperature (K)	K_c
$2HI(g) \rightleftharpoons H_2(g) + I_2(g)$	300	1.26×10^{-3}
	500	6.25×10^{-3}
	1000	18.5×10^{-3}

● **Table 13.4** Equilibrium constants and their variation at different temperatures for the decomposition of hydrogen iodide.

K_c and temperature changes

A consequence of the effects shown in *table 13.3* of changing the temperature of a reaction is that the equilibrium constant K_c must also change. We can now understand why we must carry out experiments to determine values of K_c at a constant temperature.

For example, the information in *table 13.3* states that an increase in temperature for an endothermic reaction, such as the decomposition of hydrogen iodide, causes more hydrogen and iodine to form. For this reaction:

$$K_c = \frac{[H_2][I_2]}{[HI]^2}$$

We can see that, if the concentrations of products increase, the concentration of HI must fall and K_c must increase. *Table 13.4* shows some values for the equilibrium constant for the decomposition of hydrogen iodide at different temperatures.

SAQ 13.6

Deduce the effect of an increase in temperature on K_c for the oxidation of SO_2, shown in *table 13.3*.

For the oxidation of SO_2 shown in *table 13.3*, an increase in temperature produces less of the product, SO_3. The concentrations of the reactants will rise and K_c will decrease. This reaction is the key stage in the manufacture of concentrated sulphuric acid in which temperatures of 700 to 800 K are used. Despite these temperatures, a very high percentage conversion (over 99.5%) is achieved by passing the reactants through a total of four beds of the catalyst, vanadium(v) oxide (V_2O_5).

	Endothermic reaction, ΔH positive	Exothermic reaction, ΔH negative
temperature increase	equilibrium constant increases	equilibrium constant decreases
temperature decrease	equilibrium constant decreases	equilibrium constant increases

● **Table 13.5** The effect of temperature changes on equilibrium constants.

The effects of temperature changes on K_c are summarised in *table 13.5*.

The equilibrium constant expression can be also be used to predict the outcome of changes in concentration or pressure. However, unlike temperature changes, concentration or pressure changes do not affect the magnitude of K_c.

K_c and concentration changes

Consider again the decomposition of hydrogen iodide:

$$2HI(g) \rightleftharpoons H_2(g) + I_2(g)$$

The equilibrium constant, at 500 K, is:

$$K_c = \frac{[H_2][I_2]}{[HI]^2} = 6.25 \times 10^{-3}$$

Suppose more hydrogen iodide is introduced into the equilibrium mixture, whilst maintaining a constant volume and a temperature of 500 K. [HI] will increase and the mixture will no longer be in a state of equilibrium. To restore equilibrium, both [H$_2$] and [I$_2$] must increase whilst [HI] decreases. Equilibrium will be restored when the values of these concentrations, when entered in the equilibrium constant expression, once again equal the value of K_c at 500 K (6.25×10^{-3}).

Equilibrium constants and pressure changes

So far we have expressed equilibrium constants in terms of K_c, where the small subscript 'c' indicates concentration. Where gases are involved in the reactions, chemists prefer to use pressures rather than concentrations. The equilibrium constant in terms of pressures has the symbol K_p, where the subscript 'p' indicates pressure.

For the decomposition of hydrogen iodide, the equilibrium constant in terms of partial pressures is:

$$K_p = \frac{p(H_2) \times p(I_2)}{p(HI)^2}$$

The term $p(H_2)$ indicates the equilibrium partial pressure of hydrogen in a closed system containing the equilibrium mixture at a constant temperature.

In a closed container, the partial pressure of a gas in a mixture of gases is the pressure exerted by that gas *alone* whilst disregarding the presence of the other gases. In the Haber process to form ammonia from hydrogen and nitrogen, the partial pressures of hydrogen, nitrogen and ammonia are required. The total pressure of these gases in any mixture is the sum of the partial pressures (*figure 13.5*).

Calculating partial pressures

We can calculate the partial pressure of each gas present if we know both the total pressure and the number of moles of each gas present.

For example, a sample of air at 500 kPa pressure contains 1 mole of oxygen and 4 moles of nitrogen. Calculate the partial pressure of each.

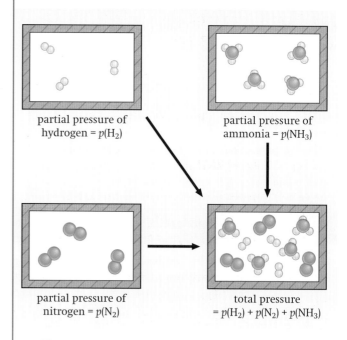

partial pressure of hydrogen = $p(H_2)$

partial pressure of ammonia = $p(NH_3)$

partial pressure of nitrogen = $p(N_2)$

total pressure = $p(H_2) + p(N_2) + p(NH_3)$

● **Figure 13.5** Each gas (hydrogen, nitrogen and ammonia) contributes its partial pressure to the total pressure.

Step 1 Calculate the **mole fraction** of each gas. In total there is 1 mole of oxygen plus 4 moles of nitrogen, so the total number of moles is 5.

mole fraction of oxygen = $\frac{1}{5}$ = 0.200

mole fraction of nitrogen = $\frac{4}{5}$ = 0.800

Check: the sum of the mole fractions should add up to 1.00.

Step 2 The next step is to calculate the partial pressure of each gas by multipling the mole fraction by the total pressure.

partial pressure oxygen = $p(O_2)$ = 0.200 × 500 kPa
= 100 kPa;
partial pressure nitrogen = $p(N_2)$
= 0.800 × 500 kPa
= 400 kPa.

Step 3 Make a final check – does the sum of the partial pressures equal the total pressure?

100 + 400 = 500 kPa, so we can have confidence in our calculation.

The Haber process and calculating K_p

We return to the Haber process for the production of ammonia from nitrogen and hydrogen. You studied the Haber process in *Chemistry 1* chapter 15. The conditions used for this process are a compromise between a sufficiently fast rate without too much reduction in yield. The reaction is exothermic so increasing the temperature decreases the yield of ammonia whilst increasing the reaction rate.

The equation for the Haber process reaction is as follows:

$$N_2(g) + 3H_2(g) \rightleftharpoons 2NH_3(g)$$

The conditions used in a modern plant are as follows:

- a pressure between 2.5 and 15 MPa;
  1 MPa = 1 × 10^6 Pa
- a temperature of between about 670 and 770 K.

In terms of the partial pressures of nitrogen, hydrogen and ammonia, the equilibrium constant expression is:

$$K_p = \frac{p(NH_3)^2}{p(N_2) \times p(H_3)^3}$$

SAQ 13.7
Write down the expression and units for K_p in the following equilibria:

a $N_2(g) + O_2(g) \rightleftharpoons 2NO(g)$
b $C_2H_4(g) + H_2O(g) \rightleftharpoons C_2H_5OH(g)$

SAQ 13.8
At a temperature of 670 K and 5 MPa pressure, an equilibrium mixture in the Haber process was found to contain 0.925 mol nitrogen, 2.775 mol hydrogen and 0.150 mol ammonia.

a (i) Use the above data to calculate the mole fraction of each of the gases in the mixture.
(ii) Hence calculate the partial pressure of each gas.
b (i) Use the equilibrium constant expression above, together with your answer from a(ii), to calculate a value for the equilibrium constant, K_p, for the Haber process reaction.
(ii) Determine the units for your value of K_p.

Using K_c and K_p

You should try to develop a 'feel' for values of K_c and K_p, so that when you look at an equilibrium and the values for the equilibrium constants you can begin to imagine the extent of the formation of product from reactant. High values of K_c or K_p indicate a high percentage of products compared to reactants.

Another way is to tackle problems involving equilibrium constants – something expected of you in A-level examinations. Some examples are given below.

Question
Write the equation for the equilibrium established in the reaction between nitrogen and oxygen to produce nitrogen monoxide, NO. Write the expression for the equilibrium constant K_p for this reaction. What are the units for K_p?

Answer
Equation is

$$N_2(g) + O_2(g) \rightleftharpoons 2NO(g)$$

$$K_p = \frac{p(NO)^2}{p(N_2)\, p(O_2)} \quad \text{units:} \quad \frac{(Pa)^2}{Pa \times Pa}$$

The units all cancel, i.e. K_p is a number – it has no units.

Question

The value of the equilibrium constant for the above reaction at 293 K and 100 kPa pressure is 4.0×10^{-31}. What does this value tell you about the equilibrium?

Answer

The extremely low value indicates that at 293 K and 100 kPa the equilibrium is very much to the left-hand side, i.e. the reaction hardly occurs at all. (This is just as well – we live in a nitrogen/oxygen atmosphere, which would fuel this reaction!)

Question

$\Delta H^{\ominus}$ is positive for the above equilibrium between nitrogen and oxygen. How would you expect K_p to change with temperature?

Answer

If ΔH is positive, the reaction is endothermic, i.e. heat is required to move the equilibrium to the right. If the temperature of the reaction is raised, the system would have to absorb more energy. Le Chatelier's principle predicts that the equilibrium would respond to minimise this effect. The additional energy could be used to create more nitrogen oxide, i.e. move the equilibrium to the right. (See *box 13C*.)

You have now been introduced to the quantitative approaches that chemists use for a chemical equilibrium. In the next chapter, we will apply this quantitative approach to understand how acids, bases and buffers work.

Box 13C Pollution and the equilibrium $N_2(g) + O_2(g) \rightleftharpoons 2NO(g)$

At 1100K the value of K_c increases to 4×10^{-8}, still very small. However, calculations show that in 1cm^3 of air at this temperature there would be around 2×10^{15} molecules of nitrogen oxide in an equilibrium – a small fraction of the total but enough to pose a pollution threat. Vehicle engines are a significant source of nitrogen oxide molecules. They contribute to a complex series of reactions with other molecules such as carbon monoxide, sulphur dioxide and hydrocarbons. Light energy plays its part, and the result can be a 'photochemical smog' of the form experienced in cities (*figure 13.6*). The irritating chemicals produced include low-level ozone, O_3, and peroxyacetyl nitrates (PAN: $RCO \cdot O_2 \cdot NO_2$), which make your eyes water. Both of these are implicated in triggering asthma attacks.

In *Chemistry 1*, chapter 14, you found out how the work of chemists contributed to the development of catalytic converters for use in cars. However, whilst these converters remove NO, CO and unburnt hydrocarbons, they are only really a stopgap solution. Vehicles that burn hydrocarbons contribute large quantities of CO_2 to the atmosphere. This CO_2 is now accepted as making a major contribution to global warming by the greenhouse effect. Also, the metals in the catalytic converters, such as platinum, are gradually lost from catalytic converters. Measurable quantities of platinum have been found in road dust. This loss is a problem as these metals are very expensive and many people have an adverse reaction to platinum and its compounds. The supplies of fossil fuels such as oil are limited and scientists are seeking alternatives. However, even these alternatives may have environmental consequences. A car burning hydrogen as a fuel will produce NO if the combustion temperature is high.

In view of such problems we should be questioning our reliance on individual motorised transport and seeking major improvements in public transport in order to reduce the number of sources of pollutants.

Some photochemical smog occurs naturally. The haze of the Smoky Mountains in the USA seems to be caused by the reactions between oils from the pine forests and citrus groves with naturally occurring ozone. Atmospheric chemistry is both fascinating and complex: there will always be a need for research in this area. You may learn more about this subject in *Environmental Chemistry*.

● **Figure 13.6** Photochemical smog caused by light reacting with pollutant molecules.

SUMMARY

◆ The mole fraction of one gas in a mixture of gases is the number of moles of the particular gas divided by the total number of moles of all the gases present in a given volume.

◆ The partial pressure of a gas in a mixture of gases is the mole fraction × the total pressure.

◆ An equilibrium constant, K_c (for concentrations) may be written using a balanced chemical equation for the reaction. For example, in the reaction
$N_2(g) + 3H_2(g) \rightleftharpoons 2NH_3(g)$
$K_c = \dfrac{[NH_3]^2}{[N_2][H_2]^3} \, dm^6 \, mol^{-2}$
The concentration (in square brackets) is raised to the power of the number of moles shown in the equation. Units must be worked out for each equilibrium constant. This may be done by placing them in the equation and cancelling out, as appropriate.

◆ For gas-phase reactions an alternative equilibrium constant, K_p (for partial pressures), is often used. For the reaction above to produce ammonia
$K_p = \dfrac{p(NH_3)^2}{p(N_2) \times p(H_2)^3} \, MPa^{-2}$

◆ For an equilibrium system, changes in pressure or concentration have no effect on the value of the equilibrium constant. However, an **increase** in **temperature** for an **exo**thermic reaction **decreases** the value of the equilibrium constant and for an **endo**thermic reaction **increases** the value of the equilibrium constant.

◆ Large values for equilibrium constants indicate high theoretical yields of product (and vice versa). Most organic reactions achieve an equilibrium with appreciable amounts of both reactants and products present.

Question

1 The key step in the Contact process for the manufacture of sulphuric acid involves the oxidation of sulphur dioxide to sulphur trioxide over a vanadium(V) oxide catalyst. The equation for this oxidation is shown below.
$2SO_2(g) + O_2(g) \rightleftharpoons 2SO_3(g) \; \Delta H^\circ = -197 \, kJ \, mol^{-1}$
The industrial conditions chosen for this reaction are a temperature of 700 K and a pressure of 5×10^5 Pa.

  a Suggest reasons for this choice of temperature and pressure.

  b Under the above conditions of temperature and pressure, 20.0 mol of sulphur dioxide and 10.0 mol of oxygen produced an equilibrium mixture in which 90% of the sulphur dioxide had been oxidised.

    (i) Determine the amount in moles of sulphur dioxide present at equilibrium.

    (ii) Hence calculate the amounts of oxygen and sulphur trioxide at equilibrium.

    (iii) Calculate the mole fraction of each gas at equilibrium when the total pressure is 5×10^5 Pa.

    (iv) Hence calculate the partial pressure of each gas at equilibrium.

  (c) (i) Write the equilibrium constant expression for this reaction in terms of partial pressures.

    (ii) Using your data from part **b**, calculate a value for this equilibrium constant and state the units.

CHAPTER 14

Acids, bases and buffers

By the end of this chapter you should be able to:

1 describe and use the *Brønsted–Lowry theory* of acids and bases, to include conjugate acid–base pairs;

2 define the terms pH, K_w, K_a and pK_a;

3 calculate pH from $[H^+(aq)]$ and $[H^+(aq)]$ from pH for strong monobasic acids and bases and for weak monobasic acids;

4 using acid–base titration *pH curves* for strong and weak acids and bases, recognise their shapes, deduce suitable *indicators*, from supplied pH ranges and explain why phenolphthalein is unsuitable for titrations involving weak bases and why methyl orange is unsuitable for titrations involving weak acids;

5 explain the choice of suitable indicators for acid–base titrations, given the pH range of the indicator;

6 explain what is meant by a *buffer solution* (as a system that minimises pH changes on addition of an acid or a base);

7 explain the role of each component in a buffer solution in the control of pH;

8 calculate the pH of a buffer solution, for example from the K_a value of a weak acid and the equilibrium concentrations of the conjugate acid–base pair;

9 state the importance of buffer solutions for controlling pH in blood and shampoos.

Definitions of acids and bases

In 1923, the Danish chemist J. N. Brønsted and the English chemist T. M. Lowry made the suggestion that an acid may be defined as a proton donor, and a base as a proton acceptor. A proton is a positive hydrogen ion, H⁺. This is a long way from the first definitions you may have used for acids and bases (see *box 14A*).

Modern definitions are more precise than those which define an acid as something with a sour taste that turns blue litmus red, and a base as something that tastes bitter, feels soapy and turns red litmus blue (*figure 14.1*). Such statements have some validity, but are limited and arbitrary. Health and safety legislation prevents us using taste to identify acids or bases in the laboratory.

● **Figure 14.1**

a The sour taste of lemons is due to citric acid and that of vinegar is due to ethanoic (acetic) acid.

b A solution of washing soda feels soapy. Washing soda is used to soften water prior to washing clothes.

Box 14A Acids and bases

Here are some definitions of acids and bases. (An alkali is a water-soluble base.)
Chemists tend to use the Brønsted–Lowry definition, as we will in this book.

Definition of acid	Definition of base	Advantage of definition
Tastes sharp or sour, like lemon	Tastes bitter, feels soapy or greasy	Is there any?
Turns purple cabbage juice red	Turns purple cabbage juice green or yellow	You can make your own indicator to test liquids
Turns blue litmus red	Turns red litmus blue	You can use test papers
Turns universal indicator red, orange or yellow	Turns universal indicator green, blue or purple	You can compare strengths of various acids and alkalis
Produces an excess of hydrogen ions, $H^+(aq)$, in aqueous solution (Arrhenius 1884)	Produces an excess of hydroxide ions, $OH^-(aq)$, in aqueous solution (Arrhenius 1884)	Enables acid–base reactions, e.g. neutralisation, to be explained as a reaction: $H^+(aq) + OH^-(aq) \rightarrow H_2O(l)$
Donates protons during a chemical reaction (Brønsted and Lowry 1923)	Accepts protons during a chemical reaction (Brønsted and Lowry 1923)	Explains the role of water and why (for example) HCl(aq) is acidic but dry HCl(g) is not

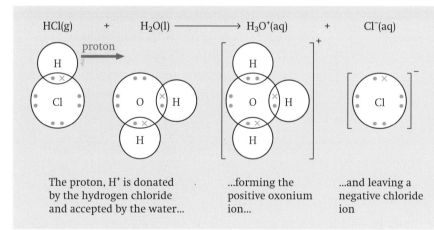

The proton, H^+ is donated by the hydrogen chloride and accepted by the water...

...forming the positive oxonium ion...

...and leaving a negative chloride ion

● **Figure 14.2** An acid is a proton donor. Hydrogen chloride is the acid in this reaction. A base is a proton acceptor. Water is the base in this reaction. Remember that a proton is a hydrogen ion, H^+.

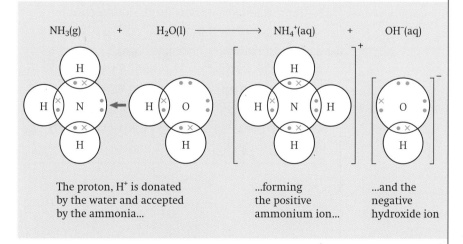

The proton, H^+ is donated by the water and accepted by the ammonia...

...forming the positive ammonium ion...

...and the negative hydroxide ion

● **Figure 14.3** Water is the proton donor (it is the acid); ammonia is the proton acceptor (it is the base).

Nor do such statements help to explain what is going on when acids and bases take part in chemical reactions.

The Brønsted–Lowry definition is particularly appropriate when considering the chemistry of aqueous solutions. We will start with the formation of one of the most familiar acids of all – hydrochloric acid. It is made when hydrogen chloride, a gas, dissolves and reacts in water.

In aqueous solution, hydrogen chloride donates a proton to water to form the oxonium ion, $H_3O^+(aq)$, as shown in *figure 14.2*.

In contrast, a base will accept a proton to give the hydroxide ion, $OH^-(aq)$, as shown for ammonia in *figure 14.3*. Note that water behaves as a base in the hydrogen chloride solution, and as an acid in the ammonia solution. Substances which can act as an acid or a base are described as **amphoteric**. Aluminium oxide, Al_2O_3, is another example of an amphoteric compound.

In both cases we have omitted an important fact: the reactions should, strictly speaking, be written as equilibria. So for the first case we write

$$HCl(g) + H_2O(l) \rightleftharpoons H_3O^+(aq) + Cl^-(aq)$$

When we think about the forward reaction, $HCl(g)$ is an acid because it donates a proton, H^+. Water is a base because it receives this proton. In *Chemistry 1*, chapter 15, hydrochloric acid was described as a strong acid. Strong acids are fully dissociated into ions, so this equilibrium lies well to the right of the above reaction equation.

Now consider the reverse reaction:

$$H_3O^+(aq) + Cl^-(aq) \rightleftharpoons HCl(g) + H_2O(l)$$

The proton is donated to the chloride ion to form hydrogen chloride. (The oxonium ion, H_3O^+, a proton donor, is an acid.) At the same time the chloride ion, $Cl^-(aq)$, accepts a proton to become hydrogen chloride. The chloride ion, a proton acceptor, is therefore a base. This can be summarised as shown:

conjugate pair

$$HCl(g) + H_2O(l) \rightleftharpoons H_3O^+(aq) + Cl^-(aq)$$

B–L acid   B–L base   B–L acid   B–L base

conjugate pair

Look at the relationship between the species. The chlorine-containing species, $HCl(g)$ and $Cl^-(aq)$, form a pair. They are acid and base respectively, with the acid the richer in protons. We call this couple a **conjugate pair** (B–L is Brønsted–Lowry).

Consider the equilibrium between ammonia and water. The conjugate pairs of acids and bases are shown in the following equation.

conjugate pair

$$NH_3(aq) + H_2O(l) \rightleftharpoons NH_4^+(aq) + OH^-(aq)$$

B–L base   B–L acid   B–L acid   B–L base

conjugate pair

An ammonia molecule accepts a proton from water. Ammonia is thus behaving as a Brønsted–Lowry base in forming an ammonium ion, its conjugate pair acid. Water, meanwhile, has donated a proton to an ammonia molecule. Water is behaving as a Brønsted–Lowry acid in forming a hydroxide ion, its conjugate pair base.

How to spot an acid or a base

Know these definitions:

- A Brønsted–Lowry acid is a proton (or H^+) donor.
- A Brønsted–Lowry base is a proton acceptor.

The Brønsted–Lowry definition applies to chemical changes in which protons, H^+, are transferred. Examine the change, and find the donors and acceptors.

We shall now look at the following example. Which are the conjugate pairs of acid and base in this reaction?

$$NH_4^+(aq) + CO_3^{2-}(aq) \rightleftharpoons HCO_3^-(aq) + NH_3(aq)$$

We can see that the ammonium ion donates a proton to the carbonate ion, and forms ammonia. Thus the ammonium ion is an acid, and the ammonia is its conjugate base. The carbonate ion accepts a proton, forming a hydrogencarbonate ion. Thus the carbonate ion is a base, and the hydrogencarbonate ion is its conjugate acid. In both cases the conjugate acids are richer in protons than their conjugate bases. The equation can therefore be annotated as shown below:

conjugate pair

$$NH_4^+(aq) + CO_3^{2-}(aq) \rightleftharpoons HCO_3^-(aq) + NH_3(g)$$

B–L acid   B–L base   B–L acid   B–L base

conjugate pair

SAQ 14.1

Use the Brønsted–Lowry definition of acid and base to identify the acids and bases in these equilibria and their conjugate bases and acids. Note that one of the reactions is not occurring in aqueous solution, a situation that could not be covered by earlier definitions of acid and base.

a $H_2SO_4(l) + H_2O(l) \rightleftharpoons H_3O^+(aq) + HSO_4^-(aq)$

b $CH_3COOH(aq) + H_2O(l) \rightleftharpoons CH_3COO^-(aq) + H_3O^+(aq)$

c $CH_3NH_2(aq) + H_2O(l) \rightleftharpoons CH_3NH_3^+(aq) + OH^-(aq)$

d $NH_3(g) + HCl(g) \rightleftharpoons NH_4^+Cl^-(s)$

The role of water

Water seems a familiar, almost benign substance, not one to be involved when acids react with bases, e.g. in the formation of common salt from sodium hydroxide and hydrochloric acid. It seems to sit on the sidelines:

$$NaOH(aq) + HCl(aq) \rightleftharpoons NaCl(aq) + H_2O(l)$$

Don't be misled. Water is not an innocent by-stander in acid–base reactions. Water plays a crucial part. It helps to understand this if you know more about pure water itself.

Water: facts and models

It is a fact that pure water conducts electricity, even if ever so slightly. It is quite unlike liquid helium, for example, or cyclohexane, which do not conduct electricity at all. Unlike these two substances, water contains ions that can carry charge – indeed pure water can be electrolysed by a direct current. The conductivity of pure water is very low.

SAQ 14.2

What does the low conductivity of water tell you about the number of ions available for carrying a direct current?

We can imagine a model for the formation of ions from water molecules, in terms of proton transfer. Suppose every now and then one water molecule could react with another to form ions. It could be as shown in *figure 14.4*. Protons leave one molecule of water for another, ions are formed, and these ions can transfer electrons during electrolysis.

This reaction can be summarised as

$$2H_2O(l) \rightleftharpoons H_3O^+(aq) + OH^-(aq)$$

or more simply as

$$H_2O(l) \rightleftharpoons H^+(aq) + OH^-(aq)$$

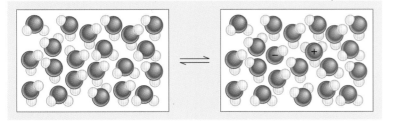

● **Figure 14.4** A proton is transferred from one water molecule to another, so that a positive ion, H_3O^+, is formed and a negative ion, OH^-, is left behind.

SAQ 14.3

Experimental evidence tells us that the equilibrium constant for this reaction is very, very small. At 298 K it is 1×10^{-14} mol^2 dm^{-6}. What does this tell you about the relative proportions of water molecules, protons and hydroxide ions? Does this fit in with your knowledge of the electrical conductivity of pure water?

Base behaviour and neutralisation

Acids react with bases and are said to neutralise each other. It is interesting to look at what neutralises what. Consider what is present in two separate solutions of hydrochloric acid and sodium hydroxide.

■ In the acid $H^+(aq)$, $Cl^-(aq)$ and $H_2O(l)$
■ In the base $Na^+(aq)$, $OH^-(aq)$ and $H_2O(l)$

When this soup of ions is mixed, the protons and hydroxide ions meet and react as follows:

$$H^+(aq) + OH^-(aq) \rightleftharpoons H_2O(l);$$
$$\Delta H^\ominus = -57 \, kJ \, mol^{-1}$$

As we saw above, the reaction favours the formation of water molecules – the equilibrium is well to the right. Hardly any of the protons and hydroxide ions remain. The vast majority neutralise each other to form water. This is what neutralisation is – the formation of water by the exothermic forward reaction shown above. The ions remaining, Na^+ and Cl^-, stay dissolved in that water – and would form salt crystals if the water was allowed to evaporate.

All reactions between acids and alkalis are like this. However, not all reagents release their protons and hydroxide ions in large numbers as do the so-called strong acids hydrochloric acid and the strong bases such as sodium hydroxide. We need to consider the relative strengths of acids and bases, and what this means for neutralisation.

Acids and bases of varying strength

Strong acids and bases are those which are totally ionised when dissolved in water. The strong acids include hydrogen halides and strong bases include the

Group I metal hydroxides. Consider what happens when examples of these dissolve in water and then react.

For every mole of these solutes, a mole of each positive and negative ion is produced in solution:

$$LiOH(s) \xrightarrow{\text{water}} Li^+(aq) + OH^-(aq)$$

$$HCl(g) \xrightarrow{\text{water}} H^+(aq) + Cl^-(aq)$$

If a mole of protons mixes with a mole of hydroxide ions they combine to form a mole of water molecules.

Weak acids and weak bases do not ionise totally when they dissolve in water; in fact, they may hardly ionise at all. When it comes to donating protons, weak acids are very limited. Ethanoic acid is a good example. Hardly any protons are liberated when it reacts in water, so that the concentration of protons is low. In the reaction shown below, the equilibrium is very much to the left:

$$CH_3COOH(l) \rightleftharpoons H^+(aq) + CH_3COO^-(aq)$$

Organic acids such as ethanoic acid (the sharp-tasting liquid in vinegar), and citric acid (the mouth-watering stuff of lemons) are typical weak acids. As proton donors go, they are pretty feeble. Weak bases are similarly feeble when it comes to accepting protons. They include the conjugate bases of strong acids, such as chloride and sulphate ions.

Table 14.1 shows some examples of conjugate acid-base pairs, together with their relative strengths.

As you will see, the relative strengths of acids and bases need to be known in order to monitor reactions between them. You need to understand the arithmetic behind measuring their relative strengths.

Introducing K_W, the ionic product of water

As shown already, pure water dissociates according to this equation:

$$H_2O(l) \rightleftharpoons H^+(aq) + OH^-(aq); \qquad \Delta H^\ominus = -57 \, kJ \, mol^{-1}$$

The equilibrium constant expression is:

$$K_c = \frac{[H^+][OH^-]}{[H_2O]}$$

As $[H_2O]$ is effectively constant, we can write:

$$K_w = [H^+][OH^-]$$

The product, $[H^+][OH^-]$, is called the **ionic product of water**, K_w. At 298 K, $K_w = 1.00 \times 10^{-14} \, mol^2 \, dm^{-6}$.

From the equation

$$H_2O(l) \rightleftharpoons H^+(aq) + OH^-(aq)$$

we can see that the concentration of protons equals the concentration of hydroxide ions.

We have defined K_w:

$$K_w = [H^+][OH^-] = 1 \times 10^{-14} \, mol^2 \, dm^{-6} \text{ (at 298 K)}$$

This means that the concentration of each species, $[H^+]$ and $[OH^-]$, is $1 \times 10^{-7} \, mol \, dm^{-3}$ ($1 \times 10^{-7} \times 1 \times 10^{-7} = 1 \times 10^{-14}$).

Introducing pH

The concentration of protons and hydroxide ions in pure water is clearly very small. Because it is awkward to fiddle about with tiny amounts like 1.0×10^{-7} (0.000 000 1, a tenth of a millionth), chemists revert to using logarithmic scales. They do the same for large numbers too – see *box 14B*.

	Acid				Base	
strongest acid	hydrochloric	HCl	$\rightleftharpoons$	$H^+ + Cl^-$	chloride	weakest base
	benzoic	C_6H_5COOH	$\rightleftharpoons$	$H^+ + C_6H_5COO^-$	benzoate	
	ethanoic	CH_3COOH	$\rightleftharpoons$	$H^+ + CH_3COO^-$	ethanoate	
	ammonium	NH_4^+	$\rightleftharpoons$	$H^+ + NH_3$	ammonia	
	phenol	C_6H_5OH	$\rightleftharpoons$	$H^+ + C_6H_5O^-$	phenoxide	
	hydrogen-carbonate	HCO_3^-	$\rightleftharpoons$	$H^+ + CO_3^{2-}$	carbonate	strongest base
weakest acid	water	H_2O	$\rightleftharpoons$	$H^+ + OH^-$	hydroxide	

Increasing acid strength (upward) / Increasing base strength (downward)

● **Table 14.1** Relative acid and base strength of some conjugate acid–base pairs.

Chemists define pH as $-\log[H^+]$, i.e. the negative logarithm to the base ten of the concentration of the hydrogen ion. (The negative part helps us to cope with very small numbers, actually negative powers of ten.) Now you can appreciate why a neutral aqueous solution has a pH of 7:

$$pH = -\log_{10}[H^+]$$

With a scientific calculator you need to learn how to use the log button. For some calculators, the calculation is as follows:

- *Step 1*: Enter the concentration

  10^{-7} or 0.0000001
- *Step 2*: Press the log button   Ans: −7
- *Step 3*: Change the sign from − to +   Ans: +7

Be careful to use the $\log_{10}$ (or $\lg_{10}$) button and *not* the ln button (which is $\log_e$)!

- You should ensure that you know how to carry out this calculation on *your* scientific calculator.

SAQ 14.4

Use the same process to calculate the pH of these solutions:

a An aqueous solution with $[H^+] = 3 \times 10^{-4}\,mol\,dm^{-3}$ (e.g. a cola drink).

b An aqueous solution with $[H^+] = 1 \times 10^{-2}\,mol\,dm^{-3}$ (stomach contents!).

c An aqueous solution with $[H^+] = 4 \times 10^{-8}\,mol\,dm^{-3}$ (blood).

You can use the reverse process to calculate the concentration of protons, $[H^+(aq)]$. For example, calculate the concentration of protons in an aqueous solution with pH = 3.2.

- *Step 1* Enter the pH value   3.2
- *Step 2* Change the sign   −3.2
- *Step 3* Press the inverse log button or press the 10^x button   0.00063 or 6.3×10^{-4}
- *Step 4* Remember the units:

  $$[H^+(aq)] = 6.3 \times 10^{-4}\,mol\,dm^{-3}$$

The pH values of some aqueous solutions with which you might be familiar are shown in *table 14.3*.

Box 14B Little numbers, large numbers and logs

Chemists deal with little and large. Miniscule molecules of water in enormous numbers are found in a sip of lemonade. To cope with this number range, we use powers of ten, as shown below:

Number of molecules of water in a sip of lemonade	300 000 000 000 000 000 000 000	3×10^{23}
Distance between the atoms in a molecule of water	0.000 000 000 111 metres	1.11×10^{-10} m

Other numbers that chemists might come across include the mass of the Earth (5.97×10^{24} kg) and the mass of a hydrogen atom (1.67×10^{-27} kg).

Ten to the power of 3 (10^3 or 1000) is ten times bigger than ten to the power of 2 (10^2 or 100). Powers of ten represent tenfold jumps in size and are called logarithms. Because we count in tens (unlike computers, which count in twos), we call these powers 'logarithms to the base ten', and write them as $\log_{10}$. In general, when we write 'number' = 1×10^x, the value of x is $\log_{10}$ ('number').

Table 14.2 shows how $\log_{10}$ is used to represent the range of numbers we might use.

Example	Number		$\log_{10}$
Molecules of ozone in 1 cm^3 of air on a good day	100 000 000 000 000	= 10^{14}	14.0
Speed of light ($m\,s^{-1}$)	300 000 000	= 3×10^8	8.5
Solubility of $Ca(OH)_2$ ($mol\,dm^{-3}$)	0.015 3	= 1.53×10^{-2}	−1.8
Concentration of protons in pure water at 298 K ($mol\,dm^{-3}$)	0.000 000 1	= 1×10^{-7}	−7.0
Concentration of protons in 0.1 $mol\,dm^{-3}$ NaOH(aq) ($mol\,dm^{-3}$)	0.000 000 000 000 1	= 1×10^{-13}	−13.0

- **Table 14.2** You will come across the term 'negative log' or '$-\log_{10}$'. This is not to complicate matters. It is simply a way of getting rid of the minus sign of the log of a small number. If $\log_{10}$('number') = −3, then $-\log10$ ('number') = $-1 \times -3 = 3$.

Calculating the pH of strong acids and strong bases

Strong acids dissociate completely. This means that we know, from the initial concentration of the strong acid, just how many protons are present in a solution. If one mole of a monobasic acid, which has one replaceable proton, such as hydrochloric acid is present in a decimetre cube of solution, then the concentration of protons is $1 \, mol \, dm^{-3}$. You can see this from the equation:

$$\overset{\text{water}}{HCl(g) \rightleftharpoons H^+(aq) + Cl^-(aq)}$$
$$\text{1mol} \qquad \text{1mol} \qquad \text{1mol}$$

The pH of a $1 \, mol \, dm^{-3}$ solution of hydrochloric acid is therefore $-\log_{10}[H^+] = -\log_{10}(1.0)$, i.e. zero.

Strong bases also contain stoichiometric amounts of protons in solution, although it is much less obvious. We tend to think of strong bases as producers of hydroxide ions, but of course there are protons present too – only in very small quantities. Follow the calculation below, for the pH of a $0.05 \, mol \, dm^{-3}$ solution of sodium hydroxide.

Sodium hydroxide ionises completely:

$$\overset{\text{water}}{NaOH(s) \longrightarrow Na^+(aq) + OH^-(aq)}$$
$$\text{1mol} \qquad \text{1mol} \qquad \text{1mol}$$
$$\text{0.05mol} \qquad \text{0.05mol} \qquad \text{0.05mol}$$

The concentration of hydroxide ions in a $0.05 \, mol \, dm^{-3}$ NaOH solution is clearly $0.05 \, mol \, dm^{-3}$. Now the ionic product of water, K_w, is constant and (at 298 K) equals $1 \times 10^{-14} \, mol^2 \, dm^{-6}$. This means we can write

$$K_w = [H^+][OH^-] = 1 \times 10^{-14} \, mol^2 \, dm^{-6}$$

so

$$[H^+] = \frac{1 \times 10^{-14} \, mol^2 \, dm^{-6}}{[OH^-] \, mol \, dm^{-3}} = \frac{1 \times 10^{-14}}{0.05} \, mol \, dm^{-3}$$
$$= 2 \times 10^{-13} \, mol \, dm^{-3}$$

so

$$pH = -\log_{10}[H^+] = -\log_{10}(2 \times 10^{-13}) = 12.7$$

There is a quicker way of getting the same answer: find $-\log_{10}[OH^-]$ and subtract it from 14. (This works because $-\log_{10}[H^+] - \log_{10}[OH^-] = 14$.)

SAQ 14.5

Find the pH of the following strong acids and strong bases given that $K_w = 1.0 \times 10^{-14} \, mol^2 \, dm^{-6}$ at 298 K.

a $1 \, mol \, dm^{-3}$ nitric acid, $HNO_3(aq)$.

b $0.5 \, mol \, dm^{-3}$ nitric acid, $HNO_3(aq)$.

c An aqueous solution containing 3 g of hydrogen chloride, HCl, per dm^3.

d A $0.001 \, mol \, dm^{-3}$ potassium hydroxide solution, KOH(aq).

e An aqueous solution containing 0.2 g of sodium hydroxide, NaOH, per dm^3.

Solution	pH
hydrochloric acid ($1 \, mol \, dm^{-3}$)	0.0
hydrochloric acid ($0.1 \, mol \, dm^{-3}$)	1.0
hydrochloric acid ($0.01 \, mol \, dm^{-3}$)	2.0
stomach 'juices' (contain HCl(aq))	1.0–2.0
lemon juice	2.3
vinegar	3
coffee	around 5
rain-water (normal)	5.7
saliva	6.3–6.8
urine	6.0–7.4
fresh milk	around 6.5
pure water	7.0
blood	7.4
pancreatic juices	7.1–8.2
sea-water	around 8.5
baking soda in water	around 9
milk of magnesia	10
soapy water (cheap soap!)	11
bench sodium hydroxide ($0.1 \, mol \, dm^{-3}$)	13
bench sodium hydroxide ($1 \, mol \, dm^{-3}$)	14

● **Table 14.3** pH values of some familiar aqueous solutions.

Ionic equilibria: the definition of K_a and pK_a

The following single equation summarises all strong acid–strong base neutralisations:

$$H^+(aq) + OH^-(aq) \rightleftharpoons H_2O(l); \qquad \Delta H^\ominus = -57 \, kJ \, mol^{-1}$$

In keeping with this, the same enthalpy change of reaction is observed whatever strong acid–strong base combination is involved (provided the solution is sufficiently dilute that the other ions do not interact), so that the reaction above goes to completion.

Most acids are weak. They do not react completely with water. A good example is ethanoic acid, of which vinegar is a dilute solution. Here the ethanoic acid will donate a proton to water, so it is indeed an acid, but the backward reaction, the acceptance of a proton by the ethanoate anion, must also be taken into account. When the two reactions are proceeding at the same rate, an equilibrium is set up:

$$CH_3COOH(aq) \rightleftharpoons H^+(aq) + CH_3COO^-(aq)$$

The equilibrium constant K_a can now be written:

$$K_a = \frac{[H^+][CH_3COO^-]}{[CH_3COOH]} \text{mol dm}^{-3}$$

This constant, K_a, is called the **acid dissociation constant**, and at 298 K for ethanoic acid its value is 1.7×10^{-5} mol dm^{-3}. Its value gives us a feel for the strength of the acid, and of course the extent to which it ionises in water. Chemists often write the general formula HA for a monobasic acid. Using this formula, the balanced equation for the ionisation of a weak acid becomes:

$$HA(aq) \rightleftharpoons H^+(aq) + A^-(aq)$$

so

$$K_a = \frac{[H^+][A^-]}{[HA]} \text{mol dm}^{-3}$$

If the acid dissociates to a large extent, $[H^+]$ and $[A^-]$ are relatively large, and $[HA]$ is smaller. Both effects would make K_a comparatively big. You can see this in *table 14.4*. Yet again we can be dealing with a large range of values, some of them very small. Just as pH was invented for hydrogen ion concentration, pK_a has been invented to deal with the dissociation of acids.

$$pK_a = -\log_{10}[K_a]$$

SAQ 14.6

Look at *table 14.4*. Work out which species are Brønsted–Lowry acids, and which are conjugate bases.

Calculating the pH of a weak acid

The pH of a weak acid may be calculated from the acid dissociation constant, K_a, the equilibrium constant expression and the concentration of the acid solution.

Acid or ion	Equilibrium in aqueous solution	K_a (mol dm^{-3})	pK_a
nitric	$HNO_3 \rightleftharpoons H^+ + NO_3^-$	About 40	21.4
sulphurous	$H_2SO_3 \rightleftharpoons H^+ + HSO_3^-$	1.5×10^{-2}	1.8
hydrated Fe^{3+} ion	$[Fe(H_2O)_6]^{3+} \rightleftharpoons H^+ + [Fe(H_2O)_5(OH)]^{2+}$	6.0×10^{-3}	2.2
hydrofluoric	$HF \rightleftharpoons H^+ + F^-$	5.6×10^{-4}	3.3
nitrous	$HNO_2 \rightleftharpoons H^+ + NO_2^-$	4.7×10^{-4}	3.3
methanoic	$HCOOH \rightleftharpoons H^+ + HCOO^-$	1.6×10^{-4}	3.8
benzoic	$C_6H_5COOH \rightleftharpoons H^+ + C_6H_5COO^-$	6.3×10^{-5}	4.2
ethanoic	$CH_3COOH \rightleftharpoons H^+ + CH_3COO^-$	1.7×10^{-5}	4.8
propanoic	$CH_3CH_2COOH \rightleftharpoons H^+ + CH_3CH_2COO^-$	1.3×10^{-5}	4.9
hydrated Al^{3+} ion	$[Al(H_2O)_6]^{3+} \rightleftharpoons H^+ + [Al(H_2O)_5(OH)]^{2+}$	1.0×10^{-5}	5.0
carbonic	$CO_2 + H_2O \rightleftharpoons H^+ + HCO_3^-$	4.5×10^{-7}	6.35
silicic	$SiO_2 + H_2O \rightleftharpoons H^+ + HSiO_3^-$	1.3×10^{-10}	9.9
hydrogencarbonate ion	$HCO_3^- \rightleftharpoons H^+ + CO_3^{2-}$	4.8×10^{-11}	10.3
hydrogensilicate ion	$HSiO_3^- \rightleftharpoons H^+ + SiO_3^{2-}$	1.3×10^{-12}	11.9
water	$H_2O \rightleftharpoons H^+ + OH^-$	1.0×10^{-14}	14.0

● **Table 14.4** Acid dissociation constants, K_a, for a range of acids, for aqueous solutions in the region of 0.0–0.01 mol dm^{-3}.

Unless we wish to determine pH to more than two decimal places, we make two assumptions to simplify the calculation.

- We assume that $[H^+] = [A^-]$.
- $[HA]$ is approximately equal to the concentration of the acid, making the assumption that none has dissociated.

The first of these assumptions may not seem to be an approximation until we remember that some water will have dissociated to form hydrogen ions. As very few water molecules will have dissociated in this way, this approximation will not affect a pH calculated to two decimal places. Using this assumption, the expression for K_a simplifies to

$$K_a = \frac{[H^+][A^-]}{[HA]} = \frac{[H^+]^2}{[HA]} \ mol \, dm^{-3}$$

The second assumption relies on the fact that we are dealing with a weak acid. Clearly, some molecules will dissociate but the proportion is such that the pH value calculated will not be significantly affected until we reach the third decimal place.

Having accepted that, for our puposes, these assumptions are sound, we can proceed to do a calculation. Suppose we wish to calculate the pH of $0.100 \, mol \, dm^{-3}$ ethanoic acid ($K_a = 1.7 \times 10^{-5} \, mol \, dm^{-3}$).

Ethanoic acid dissociates as shown:

$$CH_3COOH(aq) \rightleftharpoons H^+(aq) + CH_3COO^-(aq)$$

Using our simplified expression for K_a

$$[HA] = [CH_3COOH(aq)]$$
$$[H^+] = [H^+(aq)] \text{ and}$$
$$[A^-] = [CH_3COO^-(aq)]$$

So we can write

$$K_a = \frac{[H^+]^2}{[HA]} \ mol \, dm^{-3}$$

Putting numbers in we have

$$1.7 \times 10^{-5} = \frac{[H^+]^2}{0.100} \ mol \, dm^{-3}$$

Rearranging this equation

$$[H^+]^2 = 1.7 \times 10^{-5} \times 0.100 = 1.7 \times 10^{-6}$$

Taking square roots

$$[H^+] = 1.304 \times 10^{-3} \, mol \, dm^{-3}$$

Now we can calculate pH.

$$pH = -\log_{10}(1.304 \times 10^{-3}) = 2.9$$

Check that you arrive at the same value by keying the data into your calculator. Use the square root key to find the square root of 1.7×10^{-6}; remember to use $\log_{10}$ and to enter the powers of ten using the 'exp' key (remembering the minus sign for this as well as the minus in front of the $\log_{10}$).

SAQ 14.7

Using the data from *table 14.4* work out

a the pH of a solution containing $0.02 \, mol \, dm^{-3}$ of benzoic acid in water;

b the pH of an aqueous solution containing $0.01 \, mol \, dm^{-3}$ of aluminium ions;

c the pH of a solution of $0.1 \, mol \, dm^{-3}$ methanoic acid in water.

Measuring pH

Many dyes are susceptible to acids and alkalis. Their molecular structure can be modified by changes in pH so that they change colour (*figure 14.5*).

pH affects the colour of some dyes in quite dramatic ways. The dyes are used in the laboratory, sometimes as mixtures, to monitor the pH of chemical changes; when used in this way, they are called indicators. They usually change over a pH range of between 1 and 2 'units', with a recognised end-point somewhere in the middle. The end-point is the point where the indicator is most clearly seen to be between the two extremes of its colour.

For example, bromothymol blue is yellow in acidic solutions and blue in alkaline solutions. The colour change takes place from pH 6.0 to pH 7.6 and the end-point occurs when the pH is 7.0. The colours, ranges and end-points of indicators vary considerably, as can be seen in *table 14.5*. For example, phenolphthalein is colourless in solutions with pH less than 8.2 and does not reach its final red colour until the pH is 10. Hydrogen or hydroxide ions have a considerable effect on the molecular structure, as shown in *figure 14.6*.

Universal indicator is actually a choice mixture of dyes whose combined colours can create a range of hues, each corresponding to a pH unit –

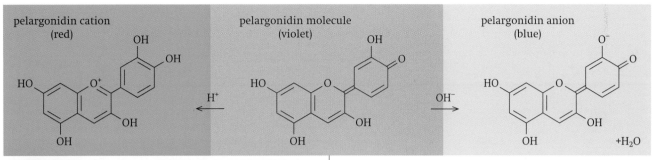

Figure 14.5 The red petals of geraniums contain the dye pelargonidin. Hydrogen or hydroxide ions can tweak its molecular structure to produce different colours.

or even fraction of a unit. Indicators can be designed to incorporate a wide pH range, e.g. 1–11, or for specific tasks a smaller range, e.g. pH 4–6 in intervals of 0.2 of a pH 'unit'.

Any measurement made using dyes must be subjective and far from accurate. There can also be problems with coloured solutions such as beer (where pH measurement is routine). For the accurate measurements required for research, particularly in biological and biochemical areas, pH measurement is done electrically. Great accuracy can be achieved with modern pH meters.

Acids with alkalis: monitoring change

Measuring the concentration of acid and alkaline solutions is a routine task. A traditional method involves titration,

i.e. measuring just how much of a reagent of known concentration is needed to react with all of another. *Figure 14.7* shows a familiar example, the titration of a strong acid against a strong base. Bear in mind that neutralisation means the reaction between equal amounts of hydrogen and hydroxide ions to form water (page 133).

Strong acids with strong bases

Figure 14.7 shows a strong acid being titrated 'against' a strong base. The acid is delivered slowly from the burette into the alkali in the flask, with constant stirring. The pH of the mixture is monitored using a pH meter, and values recorded manually or by a data logger. The graph shows how the pH changes as drop after drop is added. Note the sharp fall in the graph. In this region, tiny additional amounts of hydrogen ions from the acid have a drastic effect on pH. The midpoint of this steep slope corresponds to a pH of 7. An indicator such as bromothymol blue, which changes from blue to yellow over the range 6.0–7.6, would register this change. Note, however,

Name of dye	Colour at low pH	pH range	End-point	Colour at higher pH
Methyl violet	yellow	0.0–1.6	0.8	blue
Methyl yellow	red	2.9–4.0	3.5	yellow
Methyl orange	red	3.2–4.4	3.7	yellow
Bromophenol blue	yellow	2.8–4.6	4.0	blue
Bromocresol green	yellow	3.8–5.4	4.7	blue
Methyl red	red	4.2–6.3	5.1	yellow
Bromothymol blue	yellow	6.0–7.6	7.0	blue
Phenolphthalein	colourless	8.2–10.0	9.3	pink/violet
Alizarin yellow	yellow	10.1–13.0	12.5	orange/red

Table 14.5 Some of the chemical indicators used to monitor pH, with their pH ranges of use and pH of end-point.

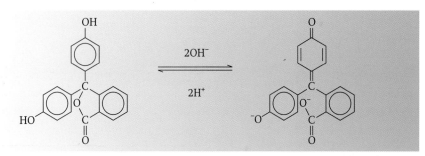

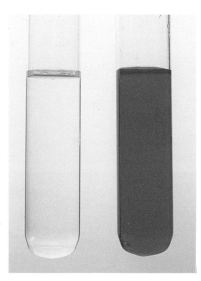

● **Figure 14.6** Colour change in phenolphthalein. At a pH of less than 8.2, the molecular structure isolates three benzene rings, each with its own delocalised electrons in a different plane from the other two. In more alkaline solutions, the structure changes: a planar ion is formed (a flat ion!) and delocalised electrons extend over virtually the entire structure. This extended electron system absorbs most, but not all, of the light in the visible spectrum, so that the solution is pink.

that the slope is steep over the range pH = 3.5 to pH = 10.5. Other indicators would also mark this sudden change. Phenolphthalein, effective in the pH range 8.2 to 10.0, could also be used (*figure 14.8*), although it can be difficult to judge when a colour just disappears.

SAQ 14.8 _____

Use *table 14.5* to identify those indicators which could used for a strong acid–strong base titration like this, and those which could not.

Strong acids with weak bases

A strong acid such as $0.1 \, mol \, dm^{-3}$ nitric acid reacts with a weak base like ammonium hydroxide as shown in *figure 14.9*. Which part of the graph corresponds to the graph in *figure 14.8*? Methyl orange would be a suitable indicator, as the sudden decrease of pH occurs in the range in which methyl orange changes colour, i.e. 3.2–4.4.

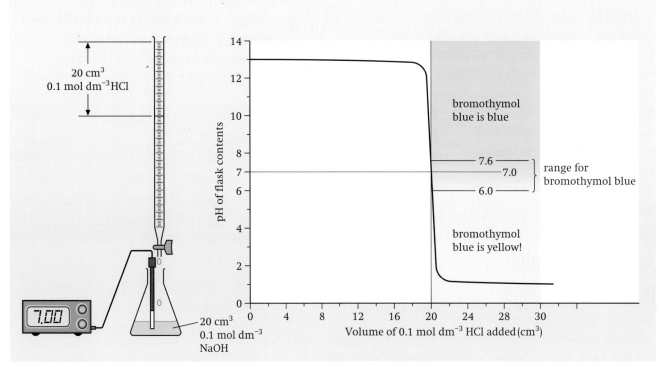

● **Figure 14.7** A strong acid–strong base titration produces a characteristic graph.

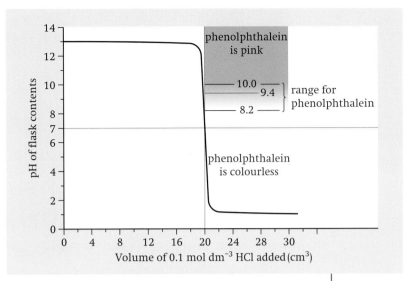

• **Figure 14.8** A strong acid–strong base titration with phenolphthalein as the indicator.

SAQ 14.9

Use *table 14.5* to find those indicators which could be used for a strong acid–weak base titration, and those which could not.

Weak acids with strong bases

The change in pH for the reaction of a weak acid such as benzoic acid with a strong base such as potassium hydroxide is shown in *figure 14.10*.

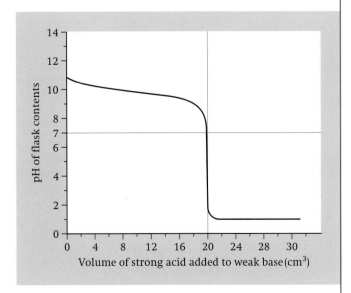

• **Figure 14.9** A typical strong acid–weak base titration.

SAQ 14.10

Compare *figure 14.10* to *figures 14.8* and *14.9*, noticing similarities and differences. Phenolphthalein, with its colour change at 9.3, is a suitable indicator for the end-point in *figure 14.10*. Why would methyl orange be unsuitable?

Weak acids with weak bases

As *figure 14.11* shows, there is no significant pH range in which the addition of a small amount of one reagent produces a sharp change. In circumstances like this, none of the indicators in *table 14.5* would be effective. In the example shown, bromothymol blue would start to change colour when $19.5\,cm^3$ of acid had been added, and would finish changing after another $1\,cm^3$ had been added. Such a large range is unacceptable in situations when an accuracy of $0.05\,cm^3$ is desirable.

SAQ 14.11

Suggest a suitable indicator to find the end-points of the reactions between:

a $0.05\,mol\,dm^{-3}$ nitric acid and $0.05\,mol\,dm^{-3}$ aqueous ammonia;

b $2\,mol\,dm^{-3}$ sodium hydroxide solution and $1\,mol\,dm^{-3}$ sulphuric acid;

c $0.005\,mol\,dm^{-3}$ potassium hydroxide and aspirin (2-ethanoyloxybenzoic acid), which has a K_a of $3 \times 10^{-4}\,mol\,dm^{-3}$.

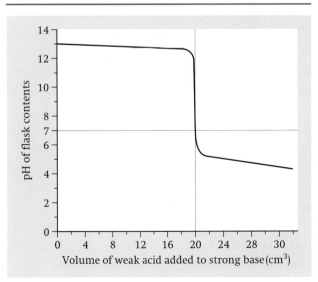

• **Figure 14.10** A typical weak acid–strong base titration.

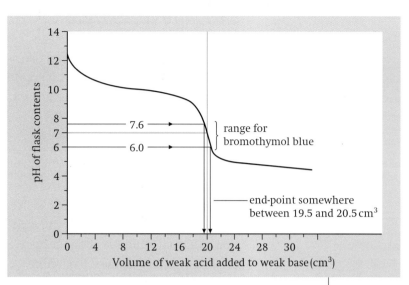

- **Figure 14.11** A typical weak acid–weak base titration.

Buffer solutions

In *table 14.3* the pH values of a number of commonly occurring solutions were given. Often it does not matter if these pH values vary slightly, but for biological solutions (stomach contents and saliva, for example), and for many industrial processes, it is important to maintain a steady pH value. It can be vital. If your blood pH increases or decreases by 0.5, you will lose consciousness and drift into a coma. Your blood has to have some sort of control system to cope with increases in hydrogen or hydroxide ion concentration. It has to have a buffer – something to soak up any increase in the hydrogen or hydroxide ion concentrations.

A **buffer solution** is one that minimises changes in pH, even when moderate amounts of acid or base are added to it. However, no buffer solution can cope with an excessive supply of acid or alkali.

A solution of sodium ethanoate in ethanoic acid is just such a solution. It operates because the equilibria involved respond to increases in hydrogen or hydroxide ion concentration in such a way as to minimise the increase – another practical application of Le Chatelier's principle.

Note that ethanoic acid and sodium ethanoate must both be present for the buffer solution to be effective. The sodium ethanoate dissociates completely to produce ethanoate ions:

$$CH_3COONa(aq) \rightarrow Na^+(aq) + CH_3COO^-(aq)$$

This complete dissociation influences the dissociation of ethanoic acid, which reaches an equilibrium:

$$CH_3COOH(aq) \rightleftharpoons H^+(aq) + CH_3COO^-(aq)$$

The result is that there are large reservoirs of the acid, CH_3COOH, and its conjugate base, CH_3COO^-.

An increase in hydrogen ion concentration would rapidly lower the pH of water. However, in this buffer solution it shifts the following equilibrium to the right.

$$CH_3COO^-(aq) + H^+(aq) \rightleftharpoons CH_3COOH(aq)$$
(mainly from sodium ethanoate)

Hydrogen ions are transferred to the ethanoate ions (of which there are plenty) so that ethanoic acid is formed. A moderate input of hydrogen ions therefore has a marginal effect on the overall pH.

The effect of an alkali, which in water would rapidly increase the pH, is minimised in a similar way. The following equilibrium shifts to the right as hydroxide ions remove protons from ethanoic acid molecules to form ethanoate ions and water.

$$CH_3COOH(aq) + OH^-(aq) \rightleftharpoons CH_3COO^-(aq) + H_2O(l)$$

In general, a buffer solution can be made from a conjugate acid and its base where either the acid or the base is weak. An example of a buffer solution involving a weak base is a solution containing both ammonia and ammonium chloride.

SAQ 14.12

Ammonia dissociates in water as follows
$$NH_3(aq) + H_2O(l) \rightleftharpoons NH_4^+(aq) + OH^-(aq)$$
whilst the ammonium chloride is fully ionised
$$NH_4Cl(aq) \rightarrow NH_4^+(aq) + Cl^-(aq)$$
a Using the above equations, identify the conjugate acid–base pair in a buffer solution containing ammonia and ammonium chloride.
b Explain how the ammonia/ammonium chloride buffer solution minimises changes in pH on adding dilute aqueous solutions of
 (i) hydrochloric acid
 (ii) sodium hydroxide

There is an alternative explanation for the way in which this buffer solution copes with an increase of hydroxide ions. The explanation suggests that the hydroxide ions first neutralise any hydrogen ions present, which are then replaced by the dissociation of more ethanoic acid. The fact is that we don't know which mechanism actually operates – so keep it simple. Remember the two components – the weak acid, which counters the addition of hydroxide ions, and the salt of the weak acid, which counters the addition of hydrogen ions.

'Bicarb' and pH control

On page 121 you were introduced to the reason why crocodiles survive longer than their prey under water. This is because more of the oxygen carried by the haemoglobin in the blood of the crocodile can be utilised than from the blood of its prey.

Oxygen from the air diffuses into your bloodstream in the lungs, and reacts with haemoglobin, Hb. This 'organo-metallic' compound, the first protein ever to be obtained as a crystalline solid, contains iron – hence its red colour. It reacts with oxygen as shown:

$$Hb + O_2 \rightleftharpoons HbO_2$$

This reaction is easily reversed in tissues all over the body, releasing oxygen for the energy-generating process called aerobic respiration. For example, glucose oxidises in an exothermic reaction, producing water, carbon dioxide and heat. The equation below is a gross over-simplification of the many reactions that it summarises.

$$C_6H_{12}O_6(aq) + 6O_2(g) \rightarrow 6CO_2(aq) + 6H_2O(aq);$$
$$\Delta H^\ominus = -2802\,kJ\,mol^{-1}$$

Your blood is now left with a waste-disposal problem, which is potentially poisonous. The problem, and part of the solution, lies in the equation below. The rates of both the forward and backward reactions in the equilibrium are rapid, thanks to the enzyme carbonic anhydrase.

$$H_2O(aq) + CO_2(aq) \underset{\text{anhydrase}}{\overset{\text{carbonic}}{\rightleftharpoons}} H^+(aq) + HCO_3^-(aq)$$

The generation of hydrogen ions, if unchecked, would lead to a lowering of blood pH and you would slip into a coma. Your blood needs a buffer.

In fact, it has at least *three*, the most important by far being the buffering action of hydrogencarbonate ion, $HCO_3^-(aq)$. Haemoglobin and plasma, both proteins, also act as buffers, but play much smaller parts.

Hydrogen ions in the blood are mopped up by hydrogencarbonate ions, the equation being the one above in which the equilibrium is well to the left. The carbon dioxide produced is carried to the lungs and breathed out. Lung infections that inhibit breathing can hinder this extraction process, leading to acidosis – i.e. decrease in blood pH.

The chemistry of pH control in the body is more complex than this section suggests, involving many other ions, particularly when acidosis is severe. The kidneys also play a crucial part. Understanding pH control is vital when treating certain diseases, e.g. coronary thrombosis. Anaesthetists constantly monitor blood pH in long operations that involve heart–lung machines, and may inject controlled amounts of sodium hydrogencarbonate – 'bicarb' – to cater for a pH fall.

Calculating the pH of a buffer solution

We can calculate the pH of a buffer solution given the following data:
- K_a of the weak acid;
- the equilibrium concentrations of the conjugate acid–base pair.

For example, a buffer solution could be made containing $0.600\,mol\,dm^{-3}$ propanoic acid and $0.800\,mol\,dm^{-3}$ sodium propanoate. The equilibrium constant, K_a, for propanoic acid is $1.3 \times 10^{-5}\,mol\,dm^{-3}$.

The equation for the equilibrium reaction is

$$C_2H_5COOH(aq) \rightleftharpoons H^+(aq) + C_2H_5COO^-(aq)$$

from which we can write the equilibrium constant expression

$$K_a = \frac{[H^+][C_2H_5COO^-]}{[C_2H_5COOH]}$$

Rearranging this equation gives

$$[H^+] = K_a \times \frac{[C_2H_5COOH]}{[C_2H_5COO^-]}\,mol\,dm^{-3}$$

Substituting the data given produces

$$[H^+] = 1.3 \times 10^{-5} \times \frac{0.600}{0.800} \, mol \, dm^{-3}$$

$$= 9.75 \times 10^{-6} \, mol \, dm^{-3}$$

so

$$pH = -\log_{10}(9.75 \times 10^{-6})$$
$$= -(-5.01) = 5.01$$

SAQ 14.13

Practise this calculation by doing the calculations below. Use *table 14.4* on page 137 for the values of K_a.

Calculate the pH of a solution containing
a 0.0500 mol dm^{-3} methanoic acid and
0.100 mol dm^{-3} sodium methanoate
b 0.0100 mol dm^{-3} benzoic acid and
0.0400 mol dm^{-3} sodium benzoate.

Of course, there is a limit to the efficiency of buffers, as we have indicated above. Rain-water has a pH of 5.7 in unpolluted regions, because it dissolves carbon dioxide, which in solution forms a dilute solution of the weak acid carbonic acid, $H_2CO_3(aq)$, with a pK_a of 6.4. This buffer solution will accommodate small additions of acid and alkali. But in highly polluted industrial regions, or in rural areas that lie down-wind of such contamination, the pH of rain-water is around 4, so-called 'acid rain'. Here the atmospheric pollutant gases are sulphur dioxide and sulphur trioxide, arising from the combustion of fossil fuels containing sulphur, and nitrogen monoxide and nitrogen dioxide, due mainly to nitrogen oxidation in internal combustion engines. These gases dissolve in rain-water and overwhelm the buffering effect.

Determining pK_a from a pH titration curve

This is a neat way of finding pK_a.
Consider the addition of 0.500 mol dm^{-3} sodium hydroxide to 20.0 cm^3 of 0.500 mol dm^{-3} ethanoic acid (*figure 14.12*). The pH of the solution rises steeply at first but then less steeply as the concentration of ethanoate ions increases. The pH rises less steeply as the mixture of the conjugate acid–base pair (ethanoic acid and ethanoate ion) is a buffer solution. As the end-point is neared, the

pH rises more steeply producing the stepped shape of a pH titration curve.
The equation for the ionisation of ethanoic acid is

$$CH_3COOH(aq) \rightleftharpoons H^+(aq) + CH_3COO^-(aq)$$

The acid dissociation constant is

$$K_a = \frac{[H^+][HCOO^-]}{[HCOOH]}$$

Rearranging this equation

$$[H^+] = K_a \times \frac{[HCOOH]}{[HCOO^-]} \, mol \, dm^{-3}$$

At the mid-point between the start of the titration and the end point

$$[CH_3COOH] = [CH_3COO^-]$$

(This mid-point can be called 'the point of half-neutralisation'.)
These equal values enable the equation above to be simplified as follows:

$$[H^+] = K_a \times \frac{[\cancel{HCOOH}]}{[\cancel{HCOO^-}]} \, mol \, dm^{-3}$$

so

$$[H^+] = K_a \, mol \, dm^{-3}$$

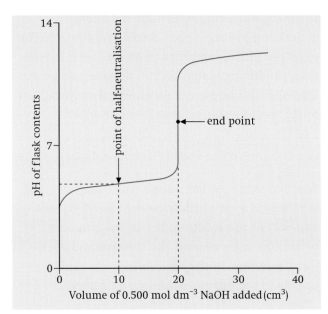

● **Figure 14.12** Determination of pK_a for a weak acid. Sodium hydroxide (0.500 mol dm^{-3}) is added from a burette to a 20.0 cm^3 sample of 0.500 mol dm^{-3} ethanoic acid. At the point of half-neutralisation pH = pK_a.

or

$$pH = pK_a$$

We can simply read off the pH from the graph and we have determined pK_a.

SAQ 14.14 _____

An acid is found to have $pK_a = 6.35$

a Calculate K_a for this acid.

b Refer to *table 14.4* on page 137 to identify the acid.

c Write the formula of the conjugate base of this weak acid.

Buffers in the bathroom and beyond

Tucked away on bathroom shelves and cabinets are all sorts of products whose acidity or alkalinity has to be controlled. From antacids and eye-drops to skin creams and baby lotion, buffers are used to maintain an appropriate pH. Safety is most important – the pH control system must be harmless. Non-toxic buffers have to be used.

Citric acid is a weak acid found in many products for the consumer, from fizzy lemonade to shampoos. The structure of citric acid is shown below.

$$\begin{array}{c} CH_2COOH \\ | \\ HO-C-COOH \\ | \\ CH_2COOH \end{array}$$

citric acid

Note the presence of three carboxylic acid groups. For most purposes, we can assume that only one of these groups ionises in aqueous solution. We can thus represent the ionisation of citric acid as shown.

$$HA(aq) \rightleftharpoons H^+(aq) + A^-(aq)$$

Citric acid is added to shampoos as a 'pH adjuster' Sodium hydroxide is also added. This will partly neutralise the citric acid to produce the citrate ion, $A^-(aq)$. The resulting buffer solution will counteract the alkalinity of the soaps and detergents present in the shampoo. With no citric acid present, the alkaline shampoo may irritate skin and eyes. The pH may be adjusted to be close to that of skin, which is about pH 5.5.

Baby lotion is buffered – 'pH balanced' as the adverts claim – to minimise nappy rash (*figure 14.13*). This skin irritation is caused by ammonia. Dirty nappies contain just the right ingredients for making ammonia – urine and faeces. The latter contains a bacterium, *Bacillus ammoniagenes*, which lives in the baby's colon. Urine contains water and urea. An enzyme from the bacterium reacts with water and urea, forming ammonia in reactions summarised by this equation:

$$\underset{\text{urea}}{CO(NH_2)_2(aq)} + H_2O(l) \rightarrow \underset{\text{ammonia}}{2NH_3(aq)} + CO_2(aq)$$

These bacteria multiply well in the pH range 7–9, but not at all at pH 6. Consequently, baby lotion is buffered to keep the pH about 6 – around the pH of the skin itself. The offending bacteria do not multiply and ammonia production is limited. Nappies should be washed well to kill these bacteria. A hot water wash at 60 °C does this.

Washing powders include buffers. Without them the high alkalinity of the detergent present would damage skin – they would not be kind to your hands! Buffers are also used in washing powders containing enzymes, to let them operate at the optimum conditions. For example, protease, an enzyme that breaks down proteins, operates best at pH from 9 to 10. Interestingly, this enzyme is produced by the bacterium *Bacillus licheniformis*, which would itself be digested by protease at this

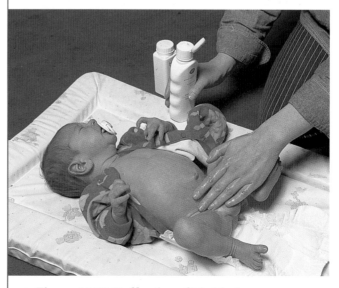

● **Figure 14.13** Buffers benefit babies!

pH. The biotechnologists who produce this enzyme use buffers to keep their fermenters at pH 7 to stop this.

Drugs must be manufactured with an eye to pH control. Most drugs are a mixture of substances, and some ingredients could affect the optimum pH without the use of buffers.

SUMMARY

- The Brønsted–Lowry definition of an acid is a proton donor; a base is a proton acceptor.

- Weak acids are only partially ionised in solution; strong acids are almost fully dissociated in solution.

- K_w is the ionic product of water:
  At 298 K, $K_w = [H^+][OH^-] = 1.0 \times 10^{-14} \ mol^2 \ dm^{-6}$

- pH is a measure of $[H^+(aq)]$, it is defined as:
  $pH = -\log_{10}[H^+]$

- K_a is the dissociation constant for an acid. It is the equilibrium constant for the dissociation of a weak acid, HA:
  $HA(aq) \rightleftharpoons H^+(aq) + A^-(aq)$
  $$K_a = \frac{[H^+][A^-]}{[HA]} \ mol \ dm^{-3}$$
  Chemists often use a more convenient scale for comparing acid strengths by using pK_a, defined as:
  $pK_a = -\log_{10}K_a$

- pH titration curves enable end-points for acid–base titrations to be found. The end-point of a titration is when the quantity of acid is sufficient to exactly neutralise the base present. The curves may also be used to suggest appropriate indicators for a particular acid–base titration. At the point of half-neutralisation pH = pK_a

- A buffer solution minimises pH changes on addition of an acid or a base. A buffer solution consists of a conjugate acid and its base where one of the pair is weak.

- Buffer solutions are important in controlling the pH of many fluids in living organisms, for example in blood. Commercial products may also contain buffer solutions to control pH, for example in shampoos.

Question

1 Shampoos frequently contain citric acid as a 'pH adjuster'. Some sodium hydroxide may also be added. The sodium hydroxide would neutralise some of the citric acid to produce sodium citrate. The presence of both citric acid and sodium citrate controls the pH of the shampoo by acting as a buffer solution. The structure of citric acid is shown below.

CH₂COOH
|
HO — C — COOH
|
CH₂COOH

citric acid

a Write a balanced equation to show the neutralisation of 1 mole of citric acid by 1 mole of sodium hydroxide. (You may assume that only the –COOH on the second carbon atom is neutralised.)

b (i) Define pH.
  (ii) Citric acid and a citrate ion are a **conjugate acid–base pair**. Explain what is meant by this term.
  (iii) Citric acid is a weak acid. Explain what is meant by the term **weak acid**.

(iv) Describe how an aqueous solution of a weak acid and its salt acts as a buffer solution.

c (i) Write an expression for the K_a of citric acid. You may represent citric acid as HA.

(ii) Calculate the pH of a solution containing $0.200\,mol\,dm^{-3}$ of citric acid and $0.100\,mol\,dm^{-3}$ sodium citrate. For citric acid $K_a = 7.24 \times 10^{-4}\,mol\,dm^{-3}$.

d Suggest a reason for the presence of a buffer solution containing citric acid in a shampoo.

Appendix: Periodic Table of the elements

s-Block

p-Block

Group

Period	I	II														III	IV	V	VI	VII	0
1	1.0 H Hydrogen 1																				4.0 He Helium 2
2	6.9 Li Lithium 3	9.0 Be Beryllium 4														10.8 B Boron 5	12.0 C Carbon 6	14.0 N Nitrogen 7	16.0 O Oxygen 8	19.0 F Fluorine 9	20.2 Ne Neon 10
3	23.0 Na Sodium 11	24.3 Mg Magnesium 12														27.0 Al Aluminium 13	28.1 Si Silicon 14	31.0 P Phosphorus 15	32.1 S Sulphur 16	35.5 Cl Chlorine 17	39.9 Ar Argon 18
4	39.1 K Potassium 19	40.1 Ca Calcium 20	45.0 Sc Scandium 21	47.9 Ti Titanium 22	50.9 V Vanadium 23	52.0 Cr Chromium 24	54.9 Mn Manganese 25	55.9 Fe Iron 26	58.9 Co Cobalt 27	58.7 Ni Nickel 28	63.5 Cu Copper 29	65.4 Zn Zinc 30				69.7 Ga Gallium 31	72.6 Ge Germanium 32	74.9 As Arsenic 33	79.0 Se Selenium 34	79.9 Br Bromine 35	83.8 Kr Krypton 36
5	85.5 Rb Rubidium 37	87.6 Sr Strontium 38	88.9 Y Yttrium 39	91.2 Zr Zirconium 40	92.9 Nb Niobium 41	95.9 Mo Molybdenum 42	– Tc Technetium 43	101 Ru Ruthenium 44	103 Rh Rhodium 45	106 Pd Palladium 46	108 Ag Silver 47	112 Cd Cadmium 48				115 In Indium 49	119 Sn Tin 50	122 Sb Antimony 51	128 Te Tellurium 52	127 I Iodine 53	131 Xe Xenon 54
6	133 Cs Caesium 55	137 Ba Barium 56	La to Lu	178 Hf Hafnium 72	181 Ta Tantalum 73	184 W Tungsten 74	186 Re Rhenium 75	190 Os Osmium 76	192 Ir Iridium 77	195 Pt Platinum 78	197 Au Gold 79	201 Hg Mercury 80				204 Tl Thallium 81	207 Pb Lead 82	209 Bi Bismuth 83	– Po Polonium 84	At Astatine 85	– Rn Radon 86
7	– Fr Francium 87	– Ra Radium 88	Ac to Lr	– Rf Rutherfordium 104	– Db Dubnium 105	– Sg Seaborgium 106	– Bh Bohrium 107	– Hs Hassium 108	– Mt Meitnerium 109	– Unn Ununnilium 110	– Uuu Unununium 111	– Uub Ununbium 112				– Uuu Ununtrium 113	– Uuq Ununquadium 114		– Uuh Ununhexium 116		– Uuo Ununoctium 118

a = relative atomic mass
X = symbol
b = proton number

a
X
Name
b

d-Block

f-Block

139 La Lanthanum 57	140 Ce Cerium 58	141 Pr Praseodymium 59	144 Nd Neodymium 60	– Pm Promethium 61	150 Sm Samarium 62	152 Eu Europium 63	157 Gd Gadolinium 64	159 Tb Terbium 65	163 Dy Dysprosium 66	165 Ho Holmium 67	167 Er Erbium 68	169 Tm Thulium 69	173 Yb Ytterbium 70	175 Lu Lutetium 71
Ac Actinium 89	Th Thorium 90	Pa Protactinium 91	U Uranium 92	Np Neptunium 93	Pu Plutonium 94	Am Americium 95	Cm Curium 96	Bk Berkelium 97	Cf Californium 98	Es Einsteinium 99	Fm Fermium 100	Md Mendelevium 101	No Nobelium 102	Lr Lawrencium 103

Answers to self-assessment questions

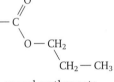
• Answer for SAQ 1.3

• Answer for SAQ 1.4

• Answer for SAQ 1.5a

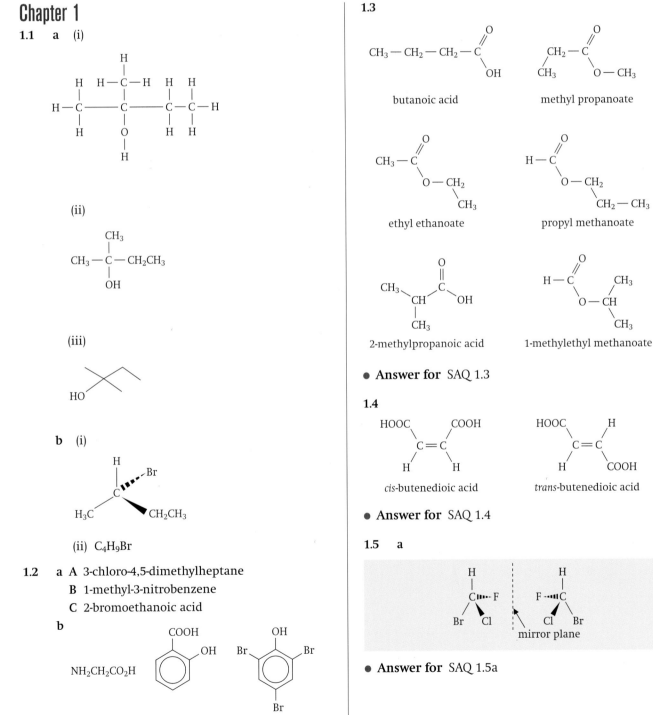

Chapter 1

1.1 a (i)

(ii)

CH₃ — C — CH₂CH₃
(CH₃ above C, OH below C)

(iii)

b (i)

(ii) C₄H₉Br

1.2 a A 3-chloro-4,5-dimethylheptane
B 1-methyl-3-nitrobenzene
C 2-bromoethanoic acid

b

NH₂CH₂CO₂H   COOH / OH   OH / Br / Br / Br

    D   **E**   **F**

1.3

CH₃ — CH₂ — CH₂ — C (=O) OH
butanoic acid

CH₂ — C (=O) O — CH₃ (CH₃ below CH₂)
methyl propanoate

CH₃ — C (=O) O — CH₂ CH₃
ethyl ethanoate

H — C (=O) O — CH₂ CH₂ — CH₃
propyl methanoate

CH₃ CH — C (=O) OH (CH₃ below CH)
2-methylpropanoic acid

H — C (=O) O — CH — CH₃ (CH₃)
1-methylethyl methanoate

1.4

HOOC / COOH C=C H / H
cis-butenedioic acid

HOOC / H C=C H / COOH
trans-butenedioic acid

1.5 a

b

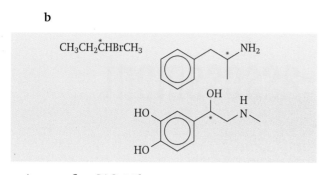

● **Answer for** SAQ 1.5b

1.6 **a** Homolytic fission is when a covalent bond is broken to form two free radicals.

b The two propagation steps constitute a chain reaction. In these steps chlorine free radicals, Cl·(g), are consumed and regenerated. As long as there is a sufficient supply of chlorine, Cl_2, and ethane, the reaction will continue.

c The chlorine free radicals are used up. OR chlorine is present in the product.

1.7 Two moles of bromine, Br_2.

1.8 **a** An electrophile is a reagent which attacks an electron-rich centre, leading to the formation of a new covalent bond.

b The $CH_2BrCH_2^+$ carbocation reacts with a water molecule (or an OH^- ion from water) to form 2-bromoethanol.

1.9 **a** A nucleophile is a reagent with a lone pair of electrons which attacks a centre (such as a carbon atom) which has a partial positive charge, δ+. The attack results in the formation of a new covalent bond.

b (i)

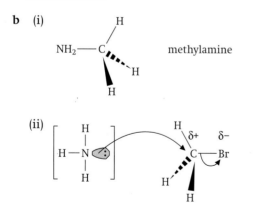

methylamine

(ii)

Chapter 2

2.1 **a**

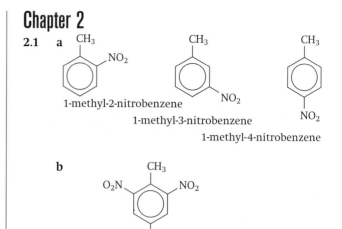

1-methyl-2-nitrobenzene

1-methyl-3-nitrobenzene

1-methyl-4-nitrobenzene

b

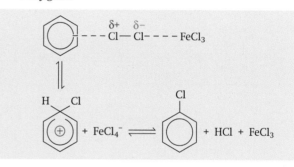

1-methyl-2,4,6-trinitrobenzene (TNT)

2.2 See *figure.*

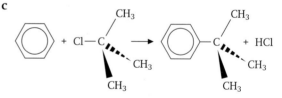

● **Answer for** SAQ 2.2

2.3 **a** anhydrous iron(III) chloride or anhydrous aluminium chloride .

b 2-chloro-2-methylpropane and benzene.

c

2.4 **a** The attacking species involved in the addition to benzene is a free radical.

b The attacking species involved in the addition of chlorine to an alkene is an electrophile.

2.5 See *figure.*

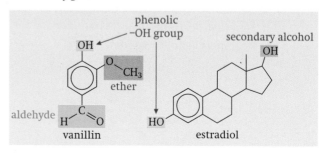

● **Answer for** SAQ 2.5

2.6 The bromine molecule is polarised by the delocalised π electrons on phenol. (The enhanced reactivity of the benzene ring, caused by the –OH group, is also required. Aqueous bromine will not react with benzene.)

Chapter 3

3.1 See *figure*.

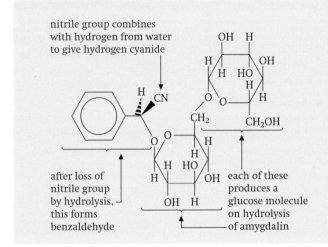

● **Answer for** SAQ 3.1

3.2 a See *figure*.

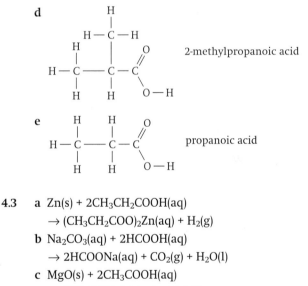

● **Answer for** SAQ 3.2a

b Hydrolysis involves the breaking of a covalent bond by reaction with water.

3.3 The hydrocarbon part of the molecules is only attracted to other molecules by weak, instantaneous dipole–induced dipole forces. The carbonyl group has a permanent dipole and will hydrogen bond to water molecules. Aldehydes and ketones with less than four carbon atoms are miscible (they mix freely) with water because the intermolecular forces in the mixture are similar in strength to those in the separate liquids. As the length of the carbon chain is increased, the intermolecular forces in the organic compounds decrease and become too weak for the hydrogen bonding between water molecules to be disrupted.

3.4 a

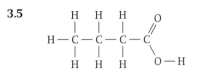

b $H_3C — CH_2 — CH_2 — CH_2OH$

3.5

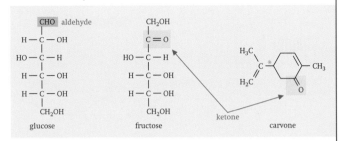

Chapter 4

4.1 a Ester.

b Carboxylic acid.

c Ester.

4.2 a ∿∿∿∿COOH

b ∿∿∿∿∿COOH

c Octadeca-*cis*-9-*cis*-12-dienoic acid.

d

2-methylpropanoic acid

e

propanoic acid

4.3 a $Zn(s) + 2CH_3CH_2COOH(aq)$
$\rightarrow (CH_3CH_2COO)_2Zn(aq) + H_2(g)$

b $Na_2CO_3(aq) + 2HCOOH(aq)$
$\rightarrow 2HCOONa(aq) + CO_2(g) + H_2O(l)$

c $MgO(s) + 2CH_3COOH(aq)$
$\rightarrow (CH_3COO)_2Mg(aq) + H_2O(l)$

d
COOH(s) + NaOH(aq) ⟶ COONa(aq) + H₂O(l)

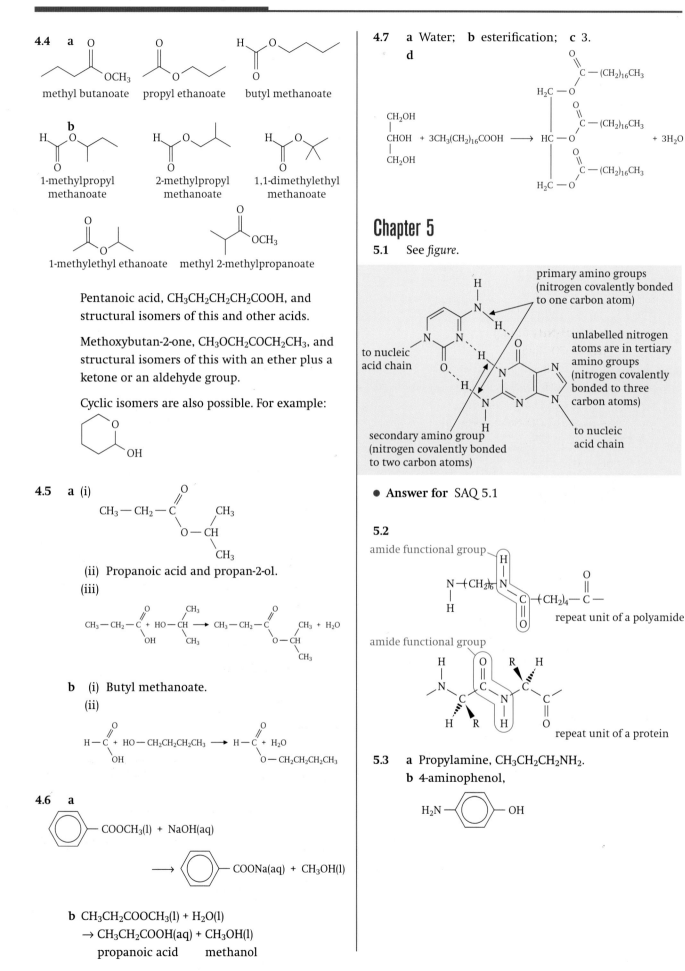

4.4 a O

methyl butanoate   propyl ethanoate   butyl methanoate

b

1-methylpropyl methanoate   2-methylpropyl methanoate   1,1-dimethylethyl methanoate

1-methylethyl ethanoate   methyl 2-methylpropanoate

Pentanoic acid, $CH_3CH_2CH_2CH_2COOH$, and structural isomers of this and other acids.

Methoxybutan-2-one, $CH_3OCH_2COCH_2CH_3$, and structural isomers of this with an ether plus a ketone or an aldehyde group.

Cyclic isomers are also possible. For example:

4.5 a (i)

$CH_3 - CH_2 - C$ ... $O - CH$ ... CH_3 ... CH_3

(ii) Propanoic acid and propan-2-ol.

(iii)

$CH_3 - CH_2 - C + HO - CH \longrightarrow CH_3 - CH_2 - C + H_2O$

b (i) Butyl methanoate.

(ii)

$H - C + HO - CH_2CH_2CH_2CH_3 \longrightarrow H - C + H_2O$

4.6 a

$COOCH_3(l) + NaOH(aq)$

$\longrightarrow COONa(aq) + CH_3OH(l)$

b $CH_3CH_2COOCH_3(l) + H_2O(l)$

$\rightarrow CH_3CH_2COOH(aq) + CH_3OH(l)$

propanoic acid   methanol

4.7 a Water; **b** esterification; **c** 3.

d

CH_2OH
$CHOH + 3CH_3(CH_2)_{16}COOH \longrightarrow$
CH_2OH

$H_2C - O$ ... $C - (CH_2)_{16}CH_3$
$HC - O$ ... $C - (CH_2)_{16}CH_3$
$H_2C - O$ ... $C - (CH_2)_{16}CH_3$
$+ 3H_2O$

Chapter 5

5.1 See *figure*.

primary amino groups (nitrogen covalently bonded to one carbon atom)

to nucleic acid chain

unlabelled nitrogen atoms are in tertiary amino groups (nitrogen covalently bonded to three carbon atoms)

secondary amino group (nitrogen covalently bonded to two carbon atoms)

to nucleic acid chain

● **Answer for SAQ 5.1**

5.2

amide functional group

$N - (CH_2)_6 - N$ ... $C - (CH_2)_4 - C -$

repeat unit of a polyamide

amide functional group

repeat unit of a protein

5.3 a Propylamine, $CH_3CH_2CH_2NH_2$.
b 4-aminophenol,

$H_2N - \bigcirc - OH$

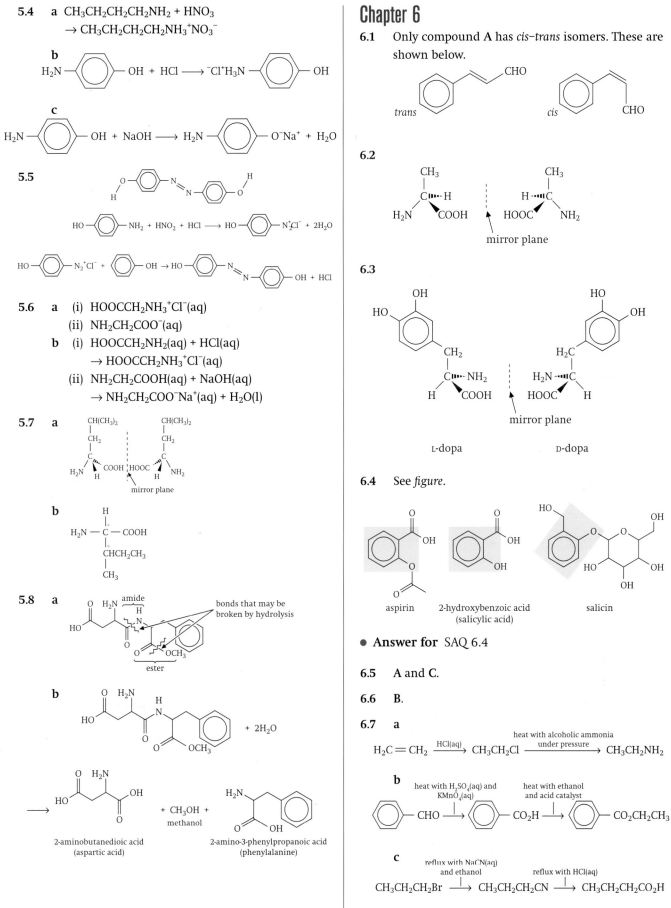

5.4   **a** $CH_3CH_2CH_2CH_2NH_2 + HNO_3$
$\rightarrow CH_3CH_2CH_2CH_2NH_3^+NO_3^-$

b

H_2N—⬡—$OH + HCl \longrightarrow$ $^-Cl^+H_3N$—⬡—OH

c

H_2N—⬡—$OH + NaOH \longrightarrow$ H_2N—⬡—$O^-Na^+ + H_2O$

5.5

HO—⬡—$NH_2 + HNO_2 + HCl \longrightarrow HO$—⬡—$N_2^+Cl^- + 2H_2O$

HO—⬡—$N_2^+Cl^- +$ ⬡—$OH \rightarrow HO$—⬡—$N{=}N$—⬡—$OH + HCl$

5.6   **a**   (i) $HOOCCH_2NH_3^+Cl^-(aq)$
(ii) $NH_2CH_2COO^-(aq)$
b   (i) $HOOCCH_2NH_2(aq) + HCl(aq)$
$\rightarrow HOOCCH_2NH_3^+Cl^-(aq)$
(ii) $NH_2CH_2COOH(aq) + NaOH(aq)$
$\rightarrow NH_2CH_2COO^-Na^+(aq) + H_2O(l)$

5.7   **a**

b

5.8   **a**

b

2-aminobutanedioic acid
(aspartic acid)

2-amino-3-phenylpropanoic acid
(phenylalanine)

Chapter 6

6.1   Only compound A has *cis–trans* isomers. These are shown below.

trans   *cis*

6.2

mirror plane

6.3

L-dopa   D-dopa

6.4   See *figure.*

aspirin   2-hydroxybenzoic acid   salicin
(salicylic acid)

● **Answer for** SAQ 6.4

6.5   A and C.

6.6   B.

6.7   **a**

$H_2C{=}CH_2 \xrightarrow{HCl(aq)} CH_3CH_2Cl \xrightarrow[\text{under pressure}]{\text{heat with alcoholic ammonia}} CH_3CH_2NH_2$

b

⬡—$CHO \xrightarrow[\text{KMnO}_4\text{(aq)}]{\text{heat with H}_2\text{SO}_4\text{(aq) and}}$ ⬡—$CO_2H \xrightarrow[\text{and acid catalyst}]{\text{heat with ethanol}}$ ⬡—$CO_2CH_2CH_3$

c

$CH_3CH_2CH_2Br \xrightarrow[\text{and ethanol}]{\text{reflux with NaCN(aq)}} CH_3CH_2CH_2CN \xrightarrow{\text{reflux with HCl(aq)}} CH_3CH_2CH_2CO_2H$

d

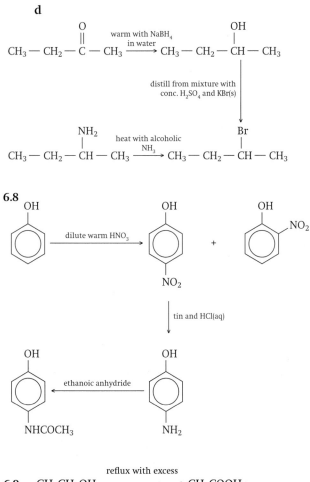

6.8

6.9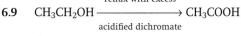

$$CH_3COOH + CH_3CH_2OH \rightarrow CH_3COOCH_2CH_3 + H_2O$$

heat, acid catalyst

For the investigation:

1 Effect of temperature: try equal amounts of ethanol and ethanoic acid **a** with reflux and **b** without reflux.

2 Effect of a catalyst: repeat experiment **1** for each of the following acid catalysts (five drops of the catalyst are sufficient):
a H_2SO_4, **b** H_3PO_4 and **c** HCl.

3 Repeat experiments **1** and **2** to check the results.

4 Effect of changing concentration: repeat the experiment that gave the best yield, but this time use excess ethanol. Repeat again with excess ethanoic acid. Repeat this step to check the results.

6.10 $CH_3CH_2OH + HBr \rightarrow CH_3CH_2Br + H_2O$

M_r for ethanol is 46; for hydrogen bromide it is 81. Hence 2.0 g of hydrogen bromide require:

$$\frac{46}{81} \times 2.0 = 1.14\,g \text{ of ethanol.}$$

6.11 a Optical isomerism.

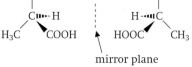

mirror plane

b (i) The mechanism is as follows.

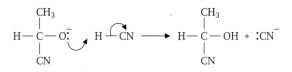

(ii) The reaction is catalysed by the presence of a base. Hydrogen cyanide is a very weak acid and the presence of a base increases the concentration of cyanide ions.

(iii) The nucleophilic attack can occur from either side of the ethanal molecule, resulting in equimolar amounts of the two isomers.

Chapter 7

7.1 a

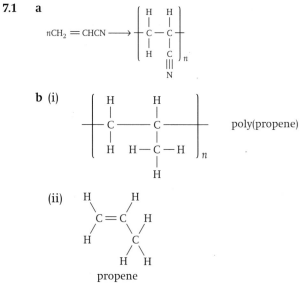

b (i)

poly(propene)

(ii)

propene

7.2 a

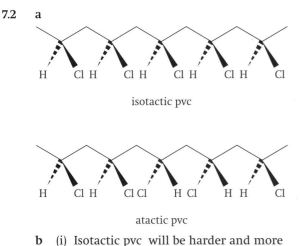

isotactic pvc

atactic pvc

b (i) Isotactic pvc will be harder and more rigid, atactic pvc will be softer and more flexible.

(ii) Isotactic pvc will be more heat resistant, atactic pvc will have less heat resistance and melt easily.

c The regular structure of isotactic pvc allows the molecular chains to pack more closely (greater crystallinity) than the irregular structure in atactic pvc allows. The dipole-dipole forces of attraction in pvc will thus be greater in isotactic pvc. Hardness, rigidity and heat resistance all increase with increasing intermolecular forces.

7.3 Ethene, propene and other alkenes together with some longer chain alkanes might be formed on pyrolysis of poly(ethene). The alkenes could be used to make poly(alkene)s or other useful products (such as ethane-1,2-diol from ethene). The alkanes could be used to make petrol or diesel fuel.

7.4

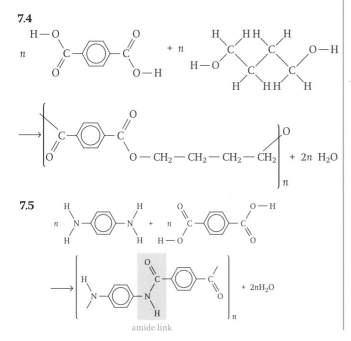

7.5

amide link

Chapter 8

8.1 −COOH is a carboxylic acid group, −COOCH$_3$ contains an ester group.

8.2

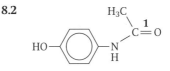

8.3 M_r (hydrocarbon) = 190

8.4

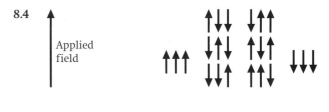

Applied field

| number of arrangements | 1 | 3 | 3 | 1 |

8.5 a

Chemical shift, δ (ppm)	Relative number of protons	Splitting pattern
1.2	3	triplet
1.9	3	singlet
4.0	2	quartet

● **Answer for** SAQ 8.5a

b From the splitting patterns given, the following can be deduced.

■ To produce a triplet, the three protons at chemical shift 1.2 must be adjacent to a −CH$_2$− group.

■ To produce a quartet the two protons at chemical shift 4.0 must be adjacent to a −CH$_3$ group.

■ To produce a singlet the three protons at chemical shift 1.9 must have no protons on the adjacent carbon atom.

c The types of protons are as follows

Chemical shift, δ (ppm)	Type of proton
1.2	CH$_3$−R
1.9	$\overset{\displaystyle O}{\underset{\displaystyle \parallel}{}}$ −C−CH$_3$
4.0	−O−CH$_2$−R

● **Answer for** SAQ 8.5c

The presence of the >C=O group is supported by the infrared data as 1750 cm^{-1} is the absorption frequency for this bond.

d The structure of the compound is

$$CH_3 - C \overset{O}{\underset{O - CH_2 - CH_3}{\big\Vert}}$$

8.6 Methyl propanoate has the following structure

$$CH_3 - CH_2 - C \overset{O}{\underset{O - CH_3}{\big\Vert}}$$

The chemical shifts and splitting patterns are as follows

Type of proton	Chemical shift, δ (ppm)	Relative number of protons	Splitting pattern
CH_3–O	3.3–4.3	3	singlet
CH_3–R	0.7–1.6	3	triplet
$\overset{O}{\underset{}{\big\Vert}}$ —C—CH_2-R	2.0–2.9	2	quartet

● **Answer for** SAQ 8.6

Chapter 9

9.1 **a** The energy change associated with a chemical reaction.

b A chemical change in which energy is released to the surroundings; $\Delta H^{\ominus}$ is negative.

c A chemical change in which energy is taken in from the surroundings; $\Delta H^{\ominus}$ is positive.

9.2 The total enthalpy change for a chemical reaction is independent of the route by which the reaction takes place, provided initial and final conditions are the same.

9.3 **a** $\frac{1}{2}O_2(g) \rightarrow O(g)$

b $Cs(g) \rightarrow Cs^+(g) + e^-$

c $K(s) + \frac{1}{2}Cl_2(g) \rightarrow KCl(s)$

d $I(g) + e^- \rightarrow I^-(g)$

e $Ba(s) \rightarrow Ba(g)$

9.4 **a**

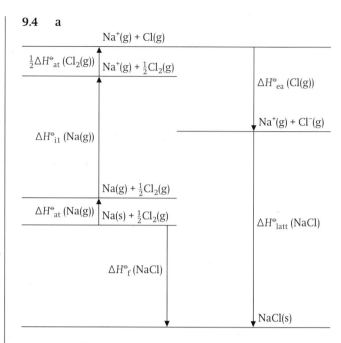

● **Answer for** SAQ 9.4

b $-787\,kJ\,mol^{-1}$

9.5 **a**

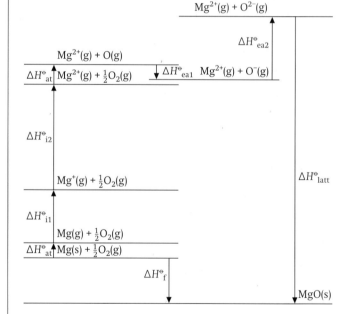

● **Answer for** SAQ 9.5a

b

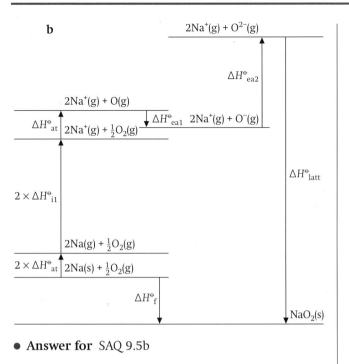

● **Answer for** SAQ 9.5b

9.6 **a** CaO **b** K$_2$O **c** SrI$_2$

9.7 LiF, Li$_2$O, MgO.

LiF is composed of singly charged ions so has the least attraction between ions, Li$_2$O has one doubly charged ion and MgO has two doubly charged ions so has the most attraction between ions.

9.8 Mg^{2+} has a greater charge density than Ca^{2+} because it is smaller, therefore it polarises the anion to a greater extent which aids decomposition.

Chapter 10

10.1 Burns with a red flame; white solid produced.

Ca(s) + $\frac{1}{2}$O$_2$(g) → CaO(s)

10.2 2S(s) + 3O$_2$(g) → 2SO$_3$(g)

10.3 **a** Giant ionic lattice
b Simple molecular
c Giant ionic lattice

10.4 **a** MgO(s) + H$_2$O(l) → Mg(OH)$_2$(aq); pH 9–11
b SO$_2$(g) + H$_2$O(l) → H$_2$SO$_3$(aq); pH 1–2

10.5 Ca(s) + Cl$_2$(g) → CaCl$_2$(s)

10.6 A colourless liquid, PCl$_3$, would be formed.

10.7 pH 7, neutral

10.8 **a** hydrolysis reaction
b SiCl$_4$(l) + 2H$_2$O(l) → SiO$_2$(s) + 4HCl(g)
or SiCl$_4$(l) + 4H$_2$O(l) → Si(OH)$_4$(aq) + 4HCl(g)
c White fumes given off, exothermic, white solid produced.

10.9 **a** Mg(s) + H$_2$O(g) → MgO(s) + H$_2$(g)
b Mg(s) + 2H$_2$O(l) → Mg(OH)$_2$(aq) + H$_2$(g)

Chapter 11

11.1 **a** [Ar]3d^{5}4s^1
b [Ar]3d^3
c [Ar]3d^{10}4s^1
d [Ar]3d^9
e [Ar]3d^{5}4s^2
f [Ar]3d^5

11.2 **a** +6 **b** +3

11.3 **a**

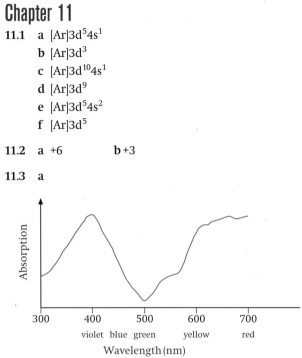

● **Answer for** SAQ 11.3

b green
c Ni^{2+}

11.4 **a** Ni^{2+} (aq) + 2OH$^-$ (aq) → Ni(OH)$_2$ (s)
b Ti^{3+} (aq) + 3OH$^-$ (aq) → Ti(OH)$_3$ (s)

11.5 **a** [Fe(Cl)$_4$]$^-$
b [Ti(H$_2$O)$_6$]$^{3+}$

11.6 **a** octahedral
b octahedral
c tetrahedral

11.7 The colour changes as the NH$_3$ ligands substitute H$_2$O ligands. (The complexes involved are [Ni(H$_2$O)$_6$]$^{2+}$, which is green, and [Ni(NH$_3$)$_6$]$^{2+}$ which is dark blue.

11.8 **a** a volumetric pipette
b a burette

11.9 1 Ni^{2+}:1 edta

11.10 6Fe^{2+} + Cr$_2$O$_7$$^{2-}$ + 14H$^+$ → 6Fe^{3+} + 2Cr^{3+} + 7H$_2$O

11.11 **a** 0.28g
b 67%

Chapter 12

12.1 a Infrared

b 2.00×10^{-13} s

12.2 Experimental evidence shows that the rate of reaction is directly proportional to the concentration of cyclopropane. If the concentration of cyclopropane is halved, the rate of reaction is halved.

12.4 The reaction is first order with respect to cyclopropane and first order overall.

12.5 By titrating small samples of the reaction mixture with standardised base, for example 1.0 mol dm^{-3} aqueous sodium hydroxide, you could find the concentration of hydrochloric acid as the reaction progressed. You could also monitor this concentration using either a pH meter or a conductivity meter. Both devices respond to changes in hydrogen ion concentration, which is itself an indication of the concentration of hydrochloric acid.

12.6 (Remember that the temperature of the reaction mixture must be constant throughout).

a (i) Both reactants are affecting the rate.

  (ii) Several approaches are possible. To provide a fair test, the experiment should be designed to study the effect of changing the concentration of only one reagent. One approach is to ensure a large excess of methanol. Relative to the concentration of HCl, the methanol concentration could then be assumed to be constant. This would allow the concentration of the acid to be monitored. The data obtained would enable the order with respect to the HCl to be deduced.

b Separate experiments need to be conducted. In each experiment, the concentration of just one reactant is allowed to change, with other reactants present in excess. The effect of changing the concentration of H$^+$(aq) can be investigated by the addition of a strong acid (such as sulphuric acid). Similarly, the effect of changing the concentration of Cl$^-$(aq) can be investigated by the addition of sodium chloride.

12.7 a The reaction rate = $k[N_2O_5]$, so the order of the reaction is 1.

b $k = 1.05 \times 10^{-5}$ s^{-1}

12.8 a Reaction rate = $k[H^+][CH_3COCH_3][I_2(aq)]^0$

b & c Substituting data from experiment 1 in the rate equation:

10.9×10^{-6} mol dm^{-3} s^{-1}

$= k \times 1.25$ mol dm$^{-3} \times 0.5$ mol dm^{-3}

$k = \dfrac{10.9 \times 10^{-6} \,\text{mol dm}^{-3}\,\text{s}^{-1}}{1.25\,\text{mol dm}^{-3} \times 0.5\,\text{mol dm}^{-3}}$

$= 1.74 \times 10^{-5}$ mol^{-1} dm^3 s^{-1}

12.9

Chapter 13

13.1 a As the [CO$_2$] builds up in the crocodile's blood, the position of equilibrium moves to the right and [HCO$_3^-$] increases.

b (i) As the [CO$_2$] builds up, more O$_2$ is released, so [Hb] increases and [HbO$_2$] decreases. [O$_2$] continues to fall as it is used for tissue respiration.

  (ii) The position of equilibrium moves to the left.

13.2 experiment 1, $K_c = 0.231$; experiment 4, $K_c = 0.272$.

13.3 The ten moles of hydrogen iodide begin to dissociate, forming hydrogen and iodine:

$2HI(g) \rightleftharpoons H_2(g) + I_2(g)$

For every molecule of iodine formed, two molecules of hydrogen iodide have to split up. To form 0.68 moles of iodine molecules, 2×0.68 moles of hydrogen iodide must dissociate. This means a total loss of 1.36 moles of hydrogen iodide, from 10 down to 8.64 moles.

13.4 a $K_c = \dfrac{[N_2O_4(g)]}{[NO_2(g)]^2}$ dm^3 mol^{-1}

b $K_c = \dfrac{[NO_2(g)]^2}{[NO(g)]^2[O_2(g)]}$ dm^3 mol^{-1}

c $K_c = \dfrac{[NH_3(g)]^2}{[N_2(g)]\,[H_2(g)]^3}$

The units for K_c are given by:

units $(K_c) = \dfrac{(\text{mol dm}^{-3})^2}{(\text{mol dm}^{-3})\,(\text{mol dm}^{-3})^3}$

$= \dfrac{\text{mol}^2\,\text{dm}^{-6}}{\text{mol dm}^{-3}\,\text{mol}^3\,\text{dm}^{-9}} = \dfrac{1}{\text{mol}^2\,\text{dm}^{-6}}$

$= \text{dm}^6\,\text{mol}^{-2}$

13.5

	$H_2(g)$	+	$CO_2(g)$	$\rightleftharpoons$	$CO(g)$	+	$H_2O(g)$
initial concentrations (mol dm^{-3})	10.00		90.00		0		0
equilibrium concentrations (mol dm^{-3})	10.00 − 9.47 = 0.53		90.00 − 9.47 = 80.53		9.47		9.47

$$K_c = \frac{[CO][H_2O]}{[H_2][CO_2]}$$

$$= \frac{9.47 \times 9.47}{0.53 \times 80.53}$$

$$= 2.10$$

(No units as in this homogeneous reaction total moles reactants = total moles products, so units cancel out.)

13.6 K_c decreases.

13.7 a $K_p = \dfrac{p(NO)^2}{p(N_2)\,p(O_2)}$ no units

b $K_p = \dfrac{p(C_2H_5OH)}{p(C_2H_4)\,p(H_2O)}$ Pa^{-1}

13.8 a

(i) Total moles gas = 0.925 + 2.775 + 0.150 = 3.850 mol

	$N_2(g)$	+	$3H_2(g)$	$\rightleftharpoons$	$2NH_3(g)$
mole fraction	$\frac{0.925}{3.850}$		$\frac{2.775}{3.850}$		$\frac{0.150}{3.850}$
	= 0.240		= 0.721		= 0.039

(ii) partial pressure (kPa)

0.240 × 5000	0.721 × 5000	0.039 × 5000
= 1200	= 3605	= 195

b (i) $K_p = \dfrac{(195)^2}{(1200) \times (3605)^3} = 6.76 \times 10^{-10}$

(ii) K_p units $= \dfrac{kPa^2}{kPa \times kPa^3} = kPa^{-2}$

Chapter 14

14.1 a $H_2SO_4(l) + H_2O(l) \rightleftharpoons H_3O^+(aq) + HSO_4^-(aq)$

B–L acid   B–L base   B–L acid   B–L base

b $CH_3COOH(aq) + H_2O(l) \rightleftharpoons CH_3COO^-(aq) + H_3O^+(aq)$

B–L acid   B–L base   B–L acid   B–L base

c $CH_3NH_2(aq) + H_2O(l) \rightarrow CH_3NH_3^+(aq) + OH^-(aq)$

B–L base   B–L acid   B–L base   B–L acid

d $NH_3(g) + HCl(g) \rightarrow NH_4^+(s) + Cl^-(s)$

B–L base   B–L acid   B–L acid   B–L base

14.2 Pure water is a poor conductor of electricity, which shows that it contains very few ions that can carry a direct current.

14.3 $K_c = \dfrac{[H^+][OH^-]}{[H_2O]}$

K_c is very small, so the concentrations of the products must be very much smaller then the concentration of water itself. This indicates that only a tiny proportion of pure water exists at any one time as protons and hydroxide ions, a deduction backed by the evidence that water is a poor conductor of electricity.

14.4 a 3.52

b 2.00

c 7.40

14.5 a 0.0

b 0.3

c The aqueous solution contains 3 g of hydrogen chloride, HCl, per dm^3. To find the pH we need the hydrogen ion concentration in mol dm^{-3}. The relative molecular mass of HCl = (1 + 35.5) = 36.5.

Thus the concentration of hydrogen chloride = 3/36.5 mol dm^{-3}

= 0.082 mol dm^{-3}

Because the hydrogen chloride dissociates completely to form hydrogen ions and chlorine ions, the concentration of hydrogen ions is 0.082 mol dm^{-3}. The pH of this acid = $-\log_{10}[H^+]$ = $-\log_{10}[0.082]$ = 1.1.

d Potassium hydroxide dissociates completely in solution:

$$KOH(s) \xrightarrow{H_2O} K^+(aq) + OH^-(aq)$$
0.001 mol   0.001 mol 0.001 mol

The concentration of hydroxide ions is the same as the concentration of the potassium hydroxide.

$K_w = [H^+][OH^-] = 1 \times 10^{-14}$ mol^2 dm^{-6}

so

$[H^+] = 1 \times 10^{-14}$ mol^2 dm^{-6}/[OH$^-$]

$= 1 \times 10^{-14}$ mol^2 dm^{-6}/0.001 mol dm^{-3}

$= 1 \times 10^{-11}$ mol dm^{-3}

The pH of this acid

$= -\log_{10}[H^+] = -\log_{10}[10^{-11}] = 11.0$

e Sodium hydroxide ionises completely in aqueous solution:

$$NaOH(s) \xrightarrow{H_2O} Na^+(aq) + OH^-(aq)$$

The relative molecular mass of NaOH = (23 + 16 + 1) = 40.

An aqueous solution containing 0.2 g of NaOH per dm^3 contains $(0.2/40)$ mol NaOH, i.e. 5×10^{-3} mol dm^{-3}. The concentration of hydroxide ions is therefore 5×10^{-3} mol dm^{-3}.

$$k_w = [H^+][OH^-] = 1 \times 10^{-14} \text{ mol}^2 \text{ dm}^{-6}$$

$$\therefore [H^+] \times 5 \times 10^{-3} = 1 \times 10^{-14}$$

$$[H^+] = \frac{1 \times 10^{-14}}{5 \times 10^{-3}} = 2 \times 10^{-12} \text{ mol dm}^{-3}$$

$$\therefore pH = -\log_{10}[H^+] = -\log_{10}(2 \times 10^{-12})$$
$$= 11.7$$

14.6 See *table*.

Acid	Base
HNO_3	NO_3^-
H_2SO_3	HSO_3^-
$[Fe(H_2O)_6]^{3+}$	$[Fe(H_2O)_5(OH)]^{2+}$
HF	F^-
HNO_2	NO_2^-
HCOOH	$HCOO^-$
C_6H_5COOH	$C_6H_5COO^-$
CH_3COOH	CH_3COO^-
C_2H_5COOH	$C_2H_5COO^-$
$[Al(H_2O)_6]^{3+}$	$[Al(H_2O)_5(OH)]^{2+}$
$CO_2 + H_2O$	HCO_3^-
$SiO_2 + H_2O$	$HSiO_3^-$
HCO_3^-	CO_3^{2-}
$HSiO_3^-$	SiO_3^{2-}
H_2O	OH_{-2}

14.7 **a** pH = 2.95

b pH = 3.5. Aqueous solutions of aluminium salts are surprisingly acidic. An accidental tipping of aluminium salts into a reservoir in Cornwall created tap-water acidic enough to dissolve copper from pipes and to worry large numbers of people about the possibility of being poisoned.

c pH = 2.4

14.8 Strong acid–strong base: the slope of the graph is steep over the range pH = 3.5 to pH = 10. Any indicator with a colour-change range within these limits is suitable: bromocresol green, methyl red, bromothymol blue or phenolphthalein. The others in the table are not suitable.

14.9 Strong acid–weak base: the slope is steep over the range 7.0–2.0. The indicators we could use are methyl yellow, methyl orange, bromophenol blue, bromocresol green or methyl red. We might get away with using bromothymol blue, but all the others in the table are unsuitable.

14.10 Weak acid–strong base: methyl orange starts changing colour when the pH is 3.2 and stops at pH 4.4. A large amount of strong base would have to be added to cover this range, so there would be no degree of accuracy.

14.11 **a** Strong acid–weak base: methyl orange or bromophenol blue.

b Strong acid–strong base: bromocresol green, methyl red, bromothymol blue or phenolphthalein.

c The equilibrium constant for aspirin is similar to that of methanoic acid, so aspirin is a weak acid. Potassium hydroxide is a strong base, so the sensitive region for the indicator would be in the range pH 7–11. Phenolphthalein would be the best choice of indicator.

14.12 **a** The conjugate acid is NH_4^+ and the conjugate base is NH_3.

b (i) When dilute hydrochloric acid is added, the additional hydrogen ions are accepted by the ammonia molecules.

(ii) When dilute sodium hydroxide is added, the equilibrium shifts to the left, trapping the $OH^-(aq)$ ions.

14.13 **a** The equation for the equilibrium reaction is
$$HCOOH(aq) \rightleftharpoons H^+(aq) + HCOO^-(aq)$$
from which we can write the equilibrium constant expression
$$K_a = \frac{[H^+][HCOO^-]}{[HCOOH]}$$
Rearranging this equation
$$[H^+] = K_a \times \frac{[HCOOH]}{[HCOO^-]} \text{ mol dm}^{-3}$$
Substituting the data given produces
$$[H^+] = 1.6 \times 10^{-4} \times \frac{0.0500}{0.100} \text{ mol dm}^{-3}$$
$$= 8.00 \times 10^{-5} \text{ mol dm}^{-3}$$
so
$$pH = -\log_{10}(8.00 \times 10^{-5})$$
$$= -(-4.096) = 4.10$$

b Using the method in part **a**, pH = 4.8

14.14 **a** $K_a = 4.0 \times 10^{-7}$ mol dm^{-3}

b Carbonic acid, H_2CO_3

c $HCO_3^-(aq)$

Glossary

acid a chemical species which can donate a proton, H^+. **Strong** acids dissociate fully into ions; **weak** acids only partially dissociate into ions.

Acid dissociation constant, K_a is the equilibrium constant for a weak acid HA:

$$K_a = \frac{[H^+][A^-]}{[HA]} \text{ mol dm}^{-3}$$

activation energy the energy barrier which must be surmounted before reaction can occur.

addition polymer a polymer formed by a repeated addition reaction.

addition reaction the joining of two molecules to form a single product molecule.

adsorption weak bonds forms between, for example, gaseous molecules and atoms at the surface of a solid catalyst.

aliphatic an organic compound that does not contain an arene rings.

alkali a soluble base.

alkylbenzene a compound that contains a benzene ring with an alkyl group attached to it.

amide group:

amine group: $-NH_2$.

amino acids are naturally occurring building blocks of protein molecules. The structure of an amino acid consists of a carboxylic acid group and an amino group attached to the same carbon atom.

aromatic compounds contain one or more arene rings.

atomic number the number of protons in the nucleus of each atom of an element.

atomic orbital a representation of the region of space where there is a high probability of finding an electron in an electron subshell. Orbitals in different subshells have different shapes; s-orbitals spherically surround the nucleus in the centre of the sphere, p-orbitals have two spherical lobes either side of the nucleus.

atomic radius half the distance between the nuclei of two covalently bonded atoms.

Avogadro's constant, L the number of atoms or molecules in one mole of a substance ($L = 6.01 \times 10^{23}$).

azo group:

$$-N{\diagdown} \atop {N-}$$

base a base reacts with an acid to form a salt.

Boltzmann distribution the distribution of molecular energies.

bond enthalpy the amount of energy need to break one mole of a bond in a gaseous molecule.

Born–Haber cycle is an enthalpy cycle for the formation of an ionic solid that includes the lattice enthalpy.

Brønsted–Lowry theory of acids and bases a Brønsted–Lowry acid is a proton (H^+) donor; a Bronsted-Lowry base is a proton (H^+) acceptor.

buffer solution is a solution that minimises changes in pH, even when moderate amounts of acid or base are added to it. It consists of a conjugate acid and its base, where one of the pair is weak.

carbocation a carbon atom in an organic molecule which has lost an atom or a group of atoms from a carbon atom creating a single positive charge.

catalyst a catalyst increases the rate of a reaction but is not itself used up during the reaction.

charge density is the amount of charge in a given volume, for example, a small ion has a larger charge density than a large ion of the same charge.

chemical shift is the δ/ppm value of a signal in an n.m.r. spectrum,.

chiral centre (or chiral carbon) is a carbon atom in a molecule attached to four different groups.

chiral molecules are molecules hat cannot be superimposed on each other, but are mirror images of each other.

cis-trans **isomerism** arises in alkenes that have two identical groups, one on each of the carbon atoms involved in the double bond. A *cis*-isomer has each set of identical groups on the same side of the double bond. A *trans*-isomer has each set of identical groups on opposite sides of the double bond. *cis-trans* isomerism occurs because a C=C cannot freely rotate.

closed system a closed system can only transfer energy to or from its surroundings. Substances cannot be exchanged.

colorimetry is an instrumental technique that records the wavelength of visible light passing through a coloured solution.

complex ion is an ion containing a central atom or ion to which other atoms, ions or molecules are bonded. In a transition metal complex the central atom or ion is a transition metal. The atoms, ions or molecules are bonded to it with dative covalent bonds and are called ligands.

condensation polymerisation is a polymerisation reaction in which the monomers are joined together by condensation reactions.

condensation reaction is a reaction in which two molecules join together to form a larger molecule, with elimination of a small molecule such as H_2O, HCl, NH_3 etc.

conjugate acid-base pairs. In an acid-base equilibrium there are two conjugate acid-base pairs:
- the acid in the forwards reaction and the base in the back reaction
- the base in the forwards reaction and the acid in the back reaction.

coupling reaction is the reaction between a diazonium salt and an arene to form a dye.

covalent bonding involves a pair of electrons between two atoms.

cracking the thermal decomposition of an alkane into a smaller alkane and an alkene.

curly arrows show the movement of a pairs of electrons in a reaction mechanism.

dative covalent bond (co-ordinate bond) a covalent bond where both electrons come from one atom.

decomposition temperature is the temperature at which a compound breaks up chemically into different substances.

delocalisation is where electron pairs are shared between three or more atoms as, for example, in benzene.

desorption weak bonds break between, for example, gaseous molecules and atoms at the surface of a solid catalyst.

diazotisation is the formation of a diazonium salt from a primary amine.

displacement reaction a reaction in which one element produces another from an aqueous solution of its ions.

displayed formula shows all the covalent bonds and all the atoms present.

dynamic equilibrium an equilibrium is dynamic at the molecular level; both forward and reverse processes occur at the same rate; a closed system is required and macroscopic properties remain constant.

electron affinity (first) is the enthalpy change when one electron is added to each gaseous atom in one mole, to form one mole of gaseous ions.

electron shielding the negative charge of filled inner shells of electrons repels electrons in the outer shells reducing the effect of the positive nuclear charge.

electronegativity describes the ability of an atom to attract the bonding electrons in a covalent bond.

electronic configuration is the arrangement of electrons in an atom or ion shown in sub-shells – for example; the electronic configuration of Na is $1s^2 2s^2 2p^6 3s^1$.

electron-pair repulsion theory enables predictions of the shapes and bond angles in a molecule to be made from the numbers of bonding pairs and lone pairs of electrons present.

electrophile an atom (or group of atoms) which is attracted to an electron-rich centre or atom, where it accepts a pair of electrons to form a new covalent bond.

elimination when a small molecule is removed from a larger molecule.

empirical formula the simplest whole number ratio of the elements present in a compound.

endothermic term used to describe a reaction in which heat energy is absorbed from the surroundings (enthalpy change is positive).

enthalpy cycle a diagram displaying alternative routes between reactants and products which allows the determination of one enthalpy change from other known enthalpy changes using Hess's law.

enthalpy profile a diagram for a reaction to show the difference in enthalpy of the reactants compared with that of the products.

enthalpy, *H* the term used by chemists for heat energy transferred during reactions.

equilibrium constant, K_c, in terms of concentrations for the formation of ammonia from nitrogen and hydrogen,
$N_2 + 3H_2 \rightarrow 2NH_3$ is given by
$$K_c = \frac{[NH_3]^2}{[N_2][H_2]^3} \text{ mol}^{-2}\text{dm}^6$$

equilibrium constant, K_p, in terms of partial pressures for the formation of ammonia from nitrogen and hydrogen,
$N_2 + 3H_2 \rightarrow 2NH_3$ is given by
$$K_p = \frac{p(NH_3)^2}{p(N_2) \times p(H_2)^3} \text{ kPa}^{-2}$$

esterification the acid-catalysed formation of an ester from a carboxylic acid and an alcohol.

exothermic term used to describe a reaction in which heat energy is transferred to the surroundings (enthalpy change is negative).

fatty acids are carboxylic acids obtained from oils or fats. Mono-unsaturated fatty acids contain one carbon-carbon double bond. Poly-unsaturated fatty acids contain more than one carbon-carbon double bond.

feedstock a primary source of substance for the production of other chemicals.

free radical an atom or group of atoms with an unpaired electron.

functional group an atom or group of atoms which gives rise to an homologous series. Compounds in the same homologous series show similar chemical properties.

general formula a formula which may be written for each homologous series (C_nH_{2n+2} for alkanes).

half-life, $t_{\frac{1}{2}}$ is the time taken for the concentration of a reactant to fall to half its original value.

halogen carriers are reagents which increase the rate of reaction of a halogen with an organic compound, for example iron(III) chloride in the reaction of chlorine with benzene to form chlorobenzene.

Hess's law the total enthalpy change for a chemical reaction is independent of the route by which the reaction takes place, provided initial and final conditions are the same.

heterogeneous catalysis a catalyst that is present in a different phase to the reactants; frequently reactants are in a gaseous phase with a solid catalyst.

heterolytic fission when a bond breaks to form a positive ion and a negative ion.

homogeneous catalysis the catalyst and reactants are in the same phase, which is most frequently the aqueous phase.

homologous series a series of organic molecules with the same functional group.

homolytic fission when a bond breaks to form two free radicals.

hydrogen bond a weak intermolecular bond formed between molecules containing hydrogen bonded to the most electronegative elements (N, O, F).

hydrolysis involves the breaking of a bond by reaction with water.

inductive effect is the tendency of a group to push or pull electrons. A group with a positive inductive effect has the tendency to push electrons towards a neighbouring atom. A group with a negative inductive effect has the tendency to pull electrons away from a neighbouring atom.

infrared spectroscopy is a technique used to identify the bonds within molecules by passing a beam of infrared radiation through them.

infrared spectrum is a chart from an infrared spectrometer showing peaks at different wavenumbers (cm^{-1}). The peaks represent the presence of various bonds in the molecules of the sample.

initial-rates method of determining the order of a reaction. The initial rate of reaction is measured with several different reactant concentrations in separate experiments.

initiation the first step in a free-radical substitution in which the free radicals are generated by heat or ultraviolet light.

intermolecular forces the weak forces of attraction between molecules based on instantaneous or permanent dipoles.

ion a positively or negatively charge atom or (covalently bonded) group of atoms.

ionic bonding the electrostatic attraction between oppositely charged ions.

ionic product of water, K_w = $[H^+][OH^-]$ = $1.0 \times 10^{-14}\, mol^2\, dm^{-6}$.

ionisation energy the first ionisation energy is the energy needed to remove one electron from each atom in one mole of gaseous atoms of an element. Successive ionisation energies are the sequence of first, second, third, fourth, etc ionisation energies needed to remove the first, second, third, fourth, etc electrons from each atom in one mole of gaseous atoms of an element.

isomerisation the conversion of a straight chain alkane to a branched-chain isomer.

isotopes are atoms of an element with the same number of protons but different numbers of neutrons.

isotopic abundance the abundance of each isotope present in a sample of an element.

lattice enthalpy is the enthalpy change when 1 mole of an ionic compound is formed from its gaseous atoms under standard conditions (298 K, 100 kPa).

Le Chatelier's principle when any of the conditions affecting the position of a dynamic equilibrium are changed, then the position of that equilibrium will shift to minimise that change.

ligand is the atom, ion or molecule which is bonded with dative covalent bonds to the central atom or ion in a complex.

ligand substitution is the replacement of one ligand by another in a complex.

mass number the total number of protons and neutrons in the nucleus of an atom.

molar mass the mass of one mole of a substance, calculated from its formula.

mole fraction of a gas in a mixture of gases is the number of moles of the gas divided by the total number of moles in the mixture.

mole the unit of amount of substance (abbreviation: mol). One mole of a substance is the mass that has the same number of particles (atoms, molecules, ions or electrons) as there are atoms in exactly 12 g of carbon-12.

molecular formula shows the total number of atoms present in a molecule of the compound.

molecular ion peak (M) in a mass spectrum, the peak which represents the unfragmented (whole) ionised molecule. Usually the peak with the highest m/e value is the (M+1) peak, and the next highest m/e value is the M peak.

molecule a covalently bonded group of atoms.

monomer the small molecule used to build a polymer molecule.

n.m.r. spectrum is a chart from an n.m.r. spectrometer showing signals at different chemical shifts. Each signal indicates a different type of H atom.

nitrating mixture is a mixture of concentrated nitric acid and concentrated sulphuric acid that produces nitration of an arene ring (substitution of a hydrogen atom by the $-NO_2$ group).

nitrile: the $-C{\equiv}N$ group.

nitro compound is an organic compound containing the $-NO_2$ group.

nomenclature the international system of naming compounds such as organic compounds.

nuclear magnetic resonance (n.m.r.) spectroscopy is a technique that provides information about the relative numbers and different environments of hydrogen atoms in an organic molecule.

nucleophile a chemical that can donate a pair of electrons with the subsequent formation of a covalent bond.

optical isomers are molecules that are non-superimposable mirror images of each other. They contain one or more chiral centres.

order of reaction is the power to which the concentration of a reactant is raised in the rate equation. *Zero-order* indicates the reactant concentration does not affect the rate, rate α $[A]^0$. *First-order* indicates that the reactant concentration is directly proportional to the rate, rate α $[A]^1$. *Second-order* indicates that the square of the reactant concentration is directly proportional to the rate, rate α $[A]^2$.

oxidation state (number) a number (with a positive or negative sign) assigned to the atoms of each element in an ion or compound. Oxidation states are determined using a set of rules devised by chemists.

oxidation the loss of electrons from an atom of an element.

partial pressure of a gas in a mixture of gases is its mole fraction multiplied by the total pressure of the gas.

peptide link is the amide link in polypeptides and proteins.

$pH = -\log_{10}[H^+]$

pH is the negative logarithm to the base ten of the concentration of the hydrogen ion.

pharmacophore is the part of a molecule that gives rise to its pharmacological activity.

phenols are aromatic alcohols. They contain a benzene ring with an $-OH$ group attached to it.

phenyl group is a C_6H_5- group forming part of another molecule.

pK_a is the negative logarithm to the base ten of the acid dissociation constant $pK_a = -\log_{10}[K_a]$

π-bond a molecular orbital formed from overlap of atomic p orbitals in the formation of a double bond.

polarising power is the ability of an ion to distort another ion next to it.

polymer the long molecular chain built up from monomer units.

polypeptide is a length of amino acids joined by condensation polymerisation. A polypeptide is shorter in length than a protein molecule.

principal quantum shell electron shells are numbered 1, 2, 3, 4, etc. Each quantum number corresponds to a principal quantum shell.

propagation is the second stage of a free-radical mechanism in which the products are formed and the radicals re-generated.

rate constant is the proportionality constant k in a rate equation (rate = $k[A]^x[B]^y$).

rate equation has the form rate = $k[A]^x[B]^y$ which shows how the rate of a chemical reaction depends on the concentration of reactants (A & B) and the rate constant k.

rate of reaction the amount in moles of a reactant which is used up in a given time.

rate-determining step is the slowest step in the reaction.

receptor molecules are molecules that medicines or other agents bind to in the body.

redox reactions which involve reduction and oxidation processes.

reduction the gain of electrons by an atom of an element.

reforming the conversion of alkanes to cycloalkanes or arenes.

relative atomic mass, A_r, of an element is the weighted average mass of an atom of the element relative to the mass of an atom of carbon-12, which has a mass of exactly 12.

relative formula mass the weighted average mass of the formula of a compound relative to an atom of carbon-12, which has a mass of exactly 12.

relative isotopic mass the mass of an isotope of an atom of an element relative to an atom of carbon-12, which has a mass of exactly 12.

relative molecular mass the weighted average mass of a molecule of a compound relative to an atom of carbon-12, which has a mass of exactly 12.

repeat unit is the smallest section of a polymer which, when reproduced, gives the polymer.

saturated hydrocarbon contains only C–C single bonds.

skeletal formula shows the carbon skeleton only, hydrogen atoms are omitted, other atoms are shown as in a structural formula. For example, the skeletal formula of propylcyclohexane is:

splitting pattern (in n.m.r. spectroscopy) signals in the spectrum can be split into two (doublets), three (triplets) etc. This splitting gives information on the neighbouring H atoms to the H atom(s) responsible for the peak.

standard conditions (enthalpy changes) a temperature of 298 K and a pressure of 100 kPa.

standard enthalpy change of atomisation is the enthalpy change when one mole of gaseous atoms are formed from an element in its standard state.

standard enthalpy change of combustion the enthalpy change when one mole of an element or compound reacts completely with oxygen under standard conditions.

standard enthalpy change of formation the enthalpy change when one mole of a compound is formed from its elements under standard conditions; both compound and elements are in their standard states.

standard enthalpy change of reaction the enthalpy change when amounts of reactants, as shown in the reaction equation, react together under standard conditions to give products in their standard states.

stereoisomers are molecules containing the same atoms with the same order of bonds but with different spatial arrangements of atoms.

stoichiometry the stoichiometry (or stoichiometric ratio) for a reaction shows the mole ratio of reactants and products in the balanced equation for the reaction.

strong acid is an acid fully dissociated into ions in aqueous solution.

structural formula shows how the atoms are joined together in a molecule.

structural isomerism structural isomers have the same molecular formula but different structural formulae.

substitution reaction an atom (or group of atoms) is substituted by a different atom (or group of atoms).

systematic name is the name of an organic compound, following internationally agreed rules.

termination is the last stage of a free-radical mechanism in which the radicals combine to end the reaction.

three-dimensional formula – the structural formula of an organic molecule using wedged lines and dotted lines for bonds (wedged lines = bond pointing forwards, dotted line = bond pointing backwards). A normal line indicates a bond in the plane of the paper. For example the three-dimensional formula of methane is:

Tollen's reagent – an aqueous solution of silver nitrate in excess ammonia. It produces a silver mirror with an aldehyde, but not with a ketone.

transition element (or transition metal) is an element that forms at least one ion with a partly-filled d orbital.

unsaturated hydrocarbon contains one or more C=C double bonds.

van der Waals' forces the weak forces of attraction between molecules based on instantaneous or permanent dipoles.

volatility a measure of the ease with which a solid or liquid evaporates to a gas. Volatility increases as boiling point decreases.

weak acid is an acid partly dissociated into ions in aqueous solution.

zwitterion is an 'internal' salt of an amino acid, in which the –COOH group donates a proton to the –NH_2 group:

$^-OOC–CHR–NH_2{}^+–$

Index

Terms shown in **bold** also appear in the glossary (see pages 161–6). Pages in *italics* refer to figures.